THE THREAD OF LIFE

SYMBOLISM OF MINIATURE ART FROM ECUADOR

JOHANNES WILBERT

Dumbarton Oaks   Trustees for Harvard University   Washington, D.C. 1974

Acknowledgments

I HAVE EXAMINED for the present study an esti-mated eight thousand spindle whorls from Ecuador. This examination was made possible through the co-operation of the Museum of Cultural History at U.C.L.A., the Los Angeles County Museum of Natural History, the National Museum at Bogotá, Colombia, the Ethnographical Museum of Göteborg, Sweden, the private collections of Becky Holmes and Franklin D. Murphy, and the holdings of several art dealers in the Los Angeles area and in Quito. I cannot overemphasize my appreciation for all the help I have received from these individuals and institutions.

In addition to the pieces that were actually at my disposal, I examined the illustrations of some five hundred Ecuadorian spindle whorls depicted in two previous publications. I am referring to the well-documented publications by James Warren Felter (1967) and María Antonieta Funes Sánchez (1970).

Special mention must be made of the great benefits I derived from the work of the late Víctor Emilio Estrada. Together with his colleagues from the United States, Clifford Evans and Betty J. Meggers, Estrada has laid the groundwork for modern archae-ology in Ecuador. The present study takes its leit-motiv from Estrada's elaboration of the prehistoric Ecuadorian "cult of fertility."

The spindle whorls were drawn by the artist Helga Adibi. No words can adequately express my admira-tion for her work. Ms. Adibi spent countless hours studying the whorls before she absorbed their subtle nuances thoroughly enough to reproduce them in freehand drawings. Her artistic feeling and astute perception coupled with her boundless patience pro-duced the illustrations of this book which, because of their fidelity, do honor and justice to the artists of about two thousand years ago.

The maps and illustrations other than spindle whorls were done by Trish Caldwell. Becky Holmes, William B. Lee, and Hans-Werner Wilbert helped me with the photographic work. Diego Delgado's suggestions concerning the identification of whorl designs were much appreciated.

I could not have wished for a better editor of my book. Dr. Peter T. Furst refined the style of the original manuscript, improved the rendering, and suggested the inclusion here and there of additional comparative information. Throughout the years of research, I have had countless conversations with him and his wife, Dee, about the spindle-whorl art and I acknowledge gratefully their substantial contribution to this study. I also wish to thank my colleagues, Dr. Christopher B. Donnan and Dr. José Ricasens, for their many suggestions.

Karin Simoneau assisted me with the rather ex-tensive library research and helped me place the spindle whorls in their ethnographic context. Never have I enjoyed more competent research assistance. Audry Zielonka had the patience and the competence to type the various drafts and the final version of this book.

Of the many friends and colleagues who responded to my multiple requests for help and material, I am especially thankful to Drs. Olaf Holm from Ecuador and Henry Wassén from Sweden.

To all the persons mentioned and to all the authors cited in the bibliography I extend my heartfelt feel-ings of gratitude and appreciation.

JOHANNES WILBERT

University of California
Los Angeles, California
September, 1972

Contents

Introduction   7
PART I
Prehistoric Coastal Ecuador   12

The Ethnographic Setting   13
    The Guangala Culture   13
    The Manteño Culture   16

Ecuador and Beyond   19
PART II
Spindle Whorls and Techniques of Spinning   24

The Thread of Life   29

Spindle Whorls and Their Decoration   33
    Birds and Bird Symbols   33
    Head Portrait of Death—the Owl   37
    The Pachota   43
    The Pelican   47
    The Bat   55
    The Jaguar   69
    The Monkey   79
    The Opossum   82
    Fishes   86
    Reptiles: Snake and Lizard   91
    Frogs, Toads, and Slugs   95
    The Hocker or "Splayed Creature"   98
    Geometrical Designs and Others   102

Bibliography   109

To Franklin D. Murphy

If we are to see things in their right perspective, we need to understand the past of man as well as his present. That is why an understanding of myths and symbols is of essential importance.

C. G. Jung

Fig. 1 Spindle whorl. Black, conical. Max. height: 13.9 mm. Max. width: 14.1 mm. Diameter of holes: 3.6 and 3.8 mm.

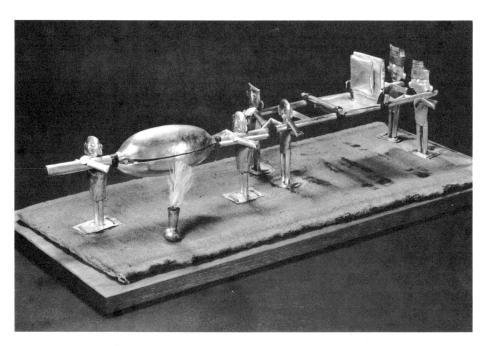

Fig. 2 A procession of small figures in silver found in a grave of the Inca period in the Chicama Valley, Peru. It is believed to represent a funeral procession; the container preceding the litter (which probably carried the body) would have held material belongings which were also interred. (Osborne 1968: 136. Photo courtesy American Museum of Natural History.)

Introduction

In one of his important papers on coastal Ecuador, the late Emilio Estrada (1957a: 46) suggested the existence of a so-called "cult of fertility" among the peoples that inhabited the coast of prehistoric Ecuador. Evidence for such a cult throughout much of the area, he said, includes ceremonial pottery, spindle whorls, stamps, dishes, figurines, and copper axes decorated with the same or related designs, which emphasized, among other things, human couples and such animals as monkeys, jaguars, anteaters, birds, fishes, and certain reptiles. Frequently a death's head was also depicted. All of these animal symbols may be observed on the spindle whorls. In the accompanying text I shall endeavor to call attention to and, where possible, interpret one or another aspect of these representations and their relationship to the problem of "fertility," or, to put it another way, the symbolic cycle of life and death—survival itself—of man and all life on earth.

At the outset I wish to emphasize that the body of spindle-whorl art in this book was not selected with life-and-death symbolism—or, indeed, symbolism of any kind—in mind. The author was originally attracted exclusively by the Ecuadorian spindle whorls as a remarkable example of ancient American miniature art, and especially by their strong aesthetic appeal and delicate quality of workmanship in a particularly difficult medium. As so often happens in the analysis of ancient art, it was only in the course of looking at several thousand examples in detail that I gradually came to realize that, contrary to first impression, the selection of subject matter for the designs was not haphazard. Rather, the ancient artists seemed to have selected only certain subjects from their natural environment for depiction. Instead of a representative cross section of the local fauna, certain animals appeared over and over in spindle-whorl art, to the apparent exclusion of many others that one would have thought were important either in the economy or the symbolic universe of coastal Ecuador. I say "apparent" because there was the possibility that the mass of spindle whorls available to me—several thousand in the collections of the University of California at Los Angeles alone—was not in fact completely representative of the totality of Ecuadorian spindle-whorl iconography. Accordingly, I began to look at new collections of spindle whorls for the purpose of finding additional subject matter, rather than, as earlier, only for several good examples of each kind of design for comparative purposes. In this way I hoped to establish a reasonably accurate cross section of most, if not all, of the iconography of spindle-whorl art.

In the course of this search I came across the remarkable whorl (Fig. 1) depicting what appeared to be birdmen, possibly representing owls, carrying a person on a litter. This started me on a wholly new train of thought. Litters, which in other parts of the world are used to transport living persons, especially nobles and dignitaries, occur in the New World only sporadically. From descriptions of Ecuadorian, Inca (Fig. 2), and Maya burials, however, we know that deceased chiefs were often borne to the grave on litters, and that grave-goods which accompanied them included, among other things, spindles and spindle whorls (Thompson 1966: 221). Together with other evidence discussed in these pages, these descriptions suggest rather forcefully that the person being carried by the birdmen attendants on the Ecuadorian spindle whorl was dead rather than alive. In other words, it seemed to me that we were dealing here, not with the pomp and circumstance of aristocratic life in prehistoric Ecuador, but with the subtleties pertaining to death.

Why was the symbolism of birds used in relation to death? Here, and, for that matter, for much of the symbolic interpretation in these pages, we can only turn to other cultures—especially those of Mexico, Central America, and South America—for relevant comparative data, for, unfortunately, there are no written records or other direct evidence to document the religious life, mythologies, and other sacred oral literatures of the coastal populations of pre-Conquest Ecuador. Birds as alter egos or spirit helpers of shamans or as messengers to the Otherworld are a widespread phenomenon in aboriginal belief and ritual. Also, there is a differentiation between those birds that soar into the sky and customarily fly high and those that dive, especially into the sea or other bodies of water, the latter species being frequently related to the concept of descent into the Underworld. Owls, too, as denizens of the night, are often associated with the Underworld and death. Accordingly, we might speculate that the birdmen-attendants depicted on the spindle whorl represent spirit companions facilitating the journey of the deceased to the land of the dead—wherever that might have been located in the particular cosmology of the prehistoric coastal Ecuadorians. There are additional dimensions to this particular scene, to which we shall return presently.

It need hardly be emphasized that the comparative method of analysis and interpretation of possible meanings of Ecuadorian spindle-whorl art, to which we are forced to resort for lack of direct historical evidence, has its limitations. As a general principle, it may be said that however close the thematic or formal analogies from other cultures may be, at best they can only be a crutch to assist in elucidating hidden meanings. In the case of Ecuador, fortunately, the validity of interpretation by analogy with other New World cultures finds support in an increasing body of evidence for pre-Hispanic contact and even a common archaic substratum between the Andes and Mesoamerica. Thus, quite apart from the possibility that the human psyche is itself responsible for producing basically similar symbols independently in different parts of the world, the diffusion of specific iconographic symbols related to spindle-whorl art is a distinct probability.

Of course, for the ethnologist or student of comparative religion seeking to understand symbolic systems by which men achieved balance between themselves and the visible and invisible universe, even a tentative reconstruction, however fragmentary and speculative, is better than none at all. The careful use of analogous data, therefore, can add a sense of discovery to sheer aesthetic appreciation, whatever one's initial purpose in collecting or analyzing this particular form of pre-Columbian miniature art.

Fig. 3 Ecuador on the west coast of South America.

Part I

Prehistoric Coastal Ecuador

LITTLE IS KNOWN of the first people who settled the Ecuadorian coast prior to 3000 B.C., beyond the fact that they lived in small bands and made their living as hunters, gatherers, and fishermen along this westernmost shoreline of South America (Fig. 3). Following this initial pre-ceramic period, the archaeological record for the Ecuadorian coast becomes considerably richer, so much so that the region can be conveniently divided into three major periods or stages (Fig. 4).

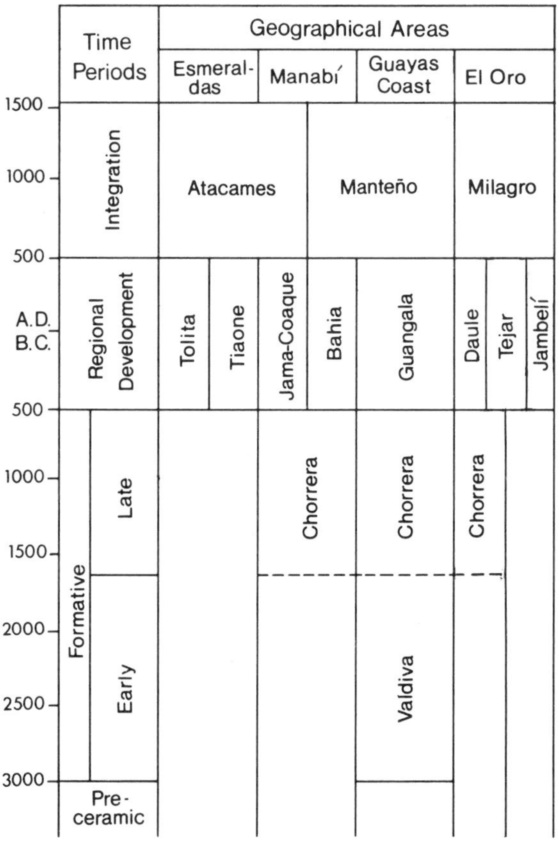

The first period, the *Formative*, opens with the introduction of pottery making, *ca.* 3000 B.C., and lasts until *ca.* 500 B.C. It, in turn, has been subdivided into two major stages, Valdivia and Chorrera. The people of the Valdivia Culture were strictly coastal, semi-sedentary, and pre-agricultural. During the Chorrera Phase which succeeded it, people began expanding inland. There are strong indications that they also practiced an incipient form of agriculture.

The second major period of coastal development, lasting from *ca.* 500 B.C. to *ca.* A.D. 500, has been appropriately named *Regional Development*. It is characterized by a series of distinct local coastal cultures, among them, from north to south, Tolita, Tiaone, Jama-Coaque, Bahía, Guangala, Daule, Tejar, and Jambelí.

The third period, that of *Integration*, saw the blending of the above regional complexes into two distinct coastal cultures, the Atacames and the Manteño, and a highland culture, the Milagro, whose southernmost part covered the El Oro coast just north of Peru. They lasted until the coming of the Spaniards and were—especially the Manteño and Milagro Cultures —characterized by an advanced socio-political organization, large urban centers, and a high level of artistic achievement as evidenced by stone carving and metallurgy (Meggers 1966).

Time Periods		Geographical Areas			
		Esmeraldas	Manabí	Guayas Coast	El Oro
Integration		Atacames		Manteño	Milagro
Regional Development		Tolita / Tiaone / Jama-Coaque	Bahia	Guangala	Daule / Tejar / Jambelí
Formative	Late		Chorrera	Chorrera	Chorrera
	Early			Valdiva	
Pre-ceramic					

Fig. 4 Culture history of coastal Ecuador. After Meggers 1966: 25.

The Ethnographic Setting

CHRONOLOGICALLY, the spindle whorls with zoomorphic and anthropomorphic designs (as opposed to the more general type with geometric motifs) are limited to the Guangala Culture of the Regional Development Period and to the Manteño Culture of the period of Integration. Geographically, they occur mainly in Manabí, on Puná Island, and on the Guayas coast. Instances of single, isolated finds elsewhere in all probability prove only the existence of trade connections. It seems that a number of whorls with zoomorphic designs found in the Guayaquil area in association with archaeologically recent cultures can be attributed to a late influx of coastal influence, immediately before the Conquest (Estrada 1957a: 40, 44). (See shaded areas on Figs. 5 and 6.)

THE GUANGALA CULTURE

THE GUANGALA CULTURE occupied the southern Manabí coast and a portion of the Guayas coast, the Santa Elena peninsula (Fig. 5). With the exception of the Cordillera de Colonche, this area is low-lying, with a fairly constant temperature throughout the year. Although there is a wet season and a dry season, the amount of annual rainfall is variable, so much so that in some years the Santa Elena peninsula receives no rain at all.

Guangala settlements are small and typically quite scattered. They are confined to the immediate coastal areas and along the major rivers. Of the house structures there are no remaining traces, although "clay

Fig. 5 Geographical distribution of the various archaeological phases of the Regional Development Period. After Meggers 1966: 71.

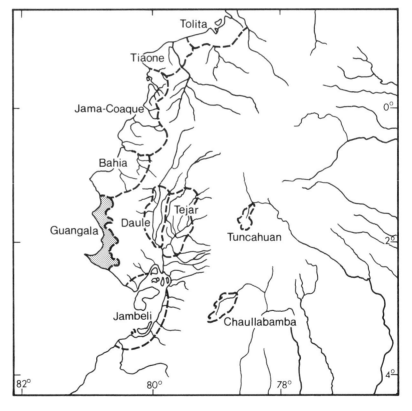

13

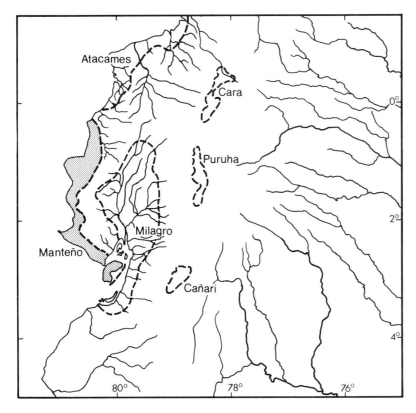

Fig. 6 Geographical distribution of the archaeological phases of the Integration Period. After Meggers 1966: 123.

with twig impressions indicates that houses were of wattle-and-daub construction, probably with thatched roofs" (Meggers 1966: 70). Information available about the Guangala Culture comes almost exclusively from excavated mounds, which are supposed to have been house sites.

Estrada (1958: 15–16) takes the dispersion of these mounds to indicate a semi-agrarian economy, although it seems that the drought during the season when the crops most need rain, and the frequent scarcity of rain during the wet season, would preclude a principally agricultural subsistence system. Bushnell (1951: 1, 3) notes: "The sources of water supply at the present time are shallow pits, dug in the alluvium in the dry river beds . . . and these are supplemented by water caught during the rainy season in ponds formed by damming certain lines of drainage. Few of these ponds retain any water from one rainy season to the next. . . ." Since the local rivers shrink

almost to the point of disappearing during the dry season, and no man-made wells have been found, one must conclude that the water supply of the Guangala Phase people was rather precarious.

The economy was probably based on fishing and shellfish gathering, supplemented by maize agriculture, as evidenced by a large number of *mano* and *metate* fragments. Possibly sweet manioc was used as well. Objects made from deer bones show that deer were also hunted.

The most characteristic features of Guangala pottery are a distinctive decorative technique of brilliant polychrome painting, and a type of five- or six-footed vessel decorated with a human face. There is an obvious distinction between utility jars, which tend to be large and relatively thick-walled, and small jars and vessels, which may have been mainly ceremonial, with thin walls and beautifully decorated and polished surfaces. The following kinds of pottery have been found in association with burials: open bowls, everted-lip bowls, vases, plates with annular feet, polypods, cooking pots, and jars. Also found, though thus far not in association with burials, are duck-shaped vessels, graters, and bottles (Bushnell 1951: 36–52). Other ceramic objects include: flutes with one end molded into a bird, fish, or human head; whistles in the form of birds or felines; and hollow anthropomorphic figurines, many of which are whistles. Some figurines represent a standing man, nude and carrying a child; others are in the form of a woman, kneeling with hands on thighs. There is also a type of highly simplified human figurine consisting of nothing more than a rectangular clay bar, with head and legs barely indicated. Ceramic animals, perforated for suspension, with three knoblike legs and decoration of dots and incised lines, may possibly represent stylized lizards, snails, or turtles (Bushnell 1951: 56). Also occurring among ceramic objects are earplugs, spoons, net weights, cylindrical or flat stamps (believed to have been used to decorate the body), textiles, and bead-shaped spindle whorls of hard red or brown ware, plain or with incised decoration. A spindle whorl of shell has also been found. Only two kinds of zoomorphic designs are specifically mentioned for Guangala spindle whorls: pelicans (Estrada 1957a: 45, fn.) and snakes (Bushnell 1951: 59).

Implements of stone and shell include celts (frequently used as wedges), chisels, drills, fishhooks and spear-thrower hooks, spoons, as well as a large number of very crude implements that may have been used as scrapers, gravers, etc. (Bushnell 1951: 66). According to Meggers (1966: 72) ". . . celts and chisels . . . attest to the working of wood, although no examples of the products survive." In addition to spindle whorls, bone awls and copper needles also prove the presence of spinning and weaving, as do impressions of woven materials found on the inside of pottery figurines. Unfortunately, the climate of coastal Ecuador, unlike that of certain very dry regions of coastal Peru, is not conducive to the preservation of such perishable remains as textiles or basketry.

It was during the Regional Development Phase that metallurgy was first introduced, and apart from copper needles a good many Guangala copper objects have been found, most of them of rather simple workmanship. These include fishhooks, tweezers, pins for fastening shawls, and nose rings. The latter were also made of shell. Beads and pendants of shell and stone, pierced for suspension, and mother-of-pearl ornaments, resembling those sewn to woven garments found in Peru, complete the surviving jewelry box of the Guangala people. Needless to say, if recent tropical forest Indians in Ecuador or the Amazon are any indication, there probably were many more kinds of personal adornments fashioned of bright-colored feathers, iridescent beetle wings, vegetable fibers, or flowers. Judging from the ceramic figurines, clothing was probably of minimal importance. One type, possibly female, is shown wearing a short, tight-fitting skirt. Another type, male, wears only a broad collar; another is also nude except for a tall cap. Many figurines have a kind of bulbous headdress, which, however, may be only an exaggerated representation of the common practice of head deformation. The figurines also wear ear ornaments apparently consisting of pellets, two for each lobe, one above the other.

As for burials, Bushnell found two kinds: primary burials where the skeleton is complete and extended, and secondary burials, frequently incomplete, where the bones are placed together in a disordered heap. These burials have been found in association, with the secondary ones for the most part stratigraphically deeper than the primary ones. They occur under mounds of refuse which, as suggested earlier, may have been house sites. Some are accompanied by grave-goods. Meggers (1966: 73) sees no conclusive evidence as to differential treatment based on status or rank, but she suspects some correlation with the sex of the deceased.

THE MANTEÑO CULTURE

THE TERRITORY of the Manteño in aboriginal times extended along the Ecuadorian coast from the Bahía de Caráquez in central Manabí down to and including the coastal parts of Guayas and Puná Island (Fig. 6). Because of the destructive climate and the ravages of the early Spaniards, very little remains to show that the Manteño had actually reached a relatively high level of urban civilization and cultural complexity. However, based on the archaeological record and on contemporary Spanish eyewitness accounts, some kind of picture can be pieced together.

Estrada (1962: 79) distinguishes three cultural-geographic subdivisions: Manteños of the North, Manteños of the South (los Huancavilcas), and the Punáes. The Manteño Culture was the last indigenous culture of pre-Conquest coastal Ecuador, terminating with the Spanish Conquest. Its origins are obscure. Bushnell (1952: 58), for one, believes it to have been intrusive: "The remains, especially pottery, and the distribution of the Manteño culture are so different from those of its predecessors in that area as to make it certain that it was introduced by an immigrant people." What is certain is that the Manteños do not owe their cultural achievements to the Inca, who made several attempts to conquer coastal Ecuador but were eventually forced to withdraw in the face of stiff resistance. In consequence, little or no Inca influence is found on the coast.

The Manteños were agricultural, but fishing and especially long-distance trade were of prime importance, so much so that Jijón y Caamaño (1945) calls them "la Confederación de los Mercadores." The art of navigation was highly developed. Manteño vessels were large rafts, so solid and well constructed that they were not restricted to coastal waters but ventured into open ocean as well. In an account written before 1528, Bartolomé Ruiz describes one Ecuadorian raft as being constructed of thick balsa logs, with masts of very fine wood and cotton sails, and having a capacity of about thirty tons (Estrada 1962: 108–09). This particular raft was carrying twenty men. Numerous artifacts of materials not naturally available in the Manteño region (jade, copper, etc.) attest to their trading activities. Crops included maize, beans, potatoes, and sweet manioc. The problem of water supply, which in some areas was precarious, was overcome by the Manteños with the construction of wells, some of considerable depth, with walls lined with stone. In some cases reservoirs were built.

With the economy capable of sustaining an increasingly larger sedentary population, several urban centers developed. Estrada (1962: 81–3) estimates, for A.D. 1500, a population of twenty thousand each for Manta, Charapotó, and Rocafuerte, and thirty thousand for Picoazá (Cerro de Hojas). Of Manteño administration and social stratification, Meggers (1966: 130–1) writes:

Differences in status and rank were manifested in differences in the size of houses and in the amount and kind of personal ornament. Puná was administered by seven secondary chiefs under a supreme chief, who was greatly feared and much respected by his subjects, and a parallel situation probably existed on the central Manabí coast with the capital at Manta. The great chief of Puná was surrounded by pomp and escorted by trumpeters and drummers whenever he left his residence. His wives were guarded by eunuchs. . . . Religion was formalized and public temples were tended by priests. Occupational specialization must have existed in arts and crafts also. Order and justice prevailed, according to the Spaniards, and towns were well laid out and maintained.

The Manteño was the only Ecuadorian culture to make extensive use of stone, both for utilitarian and artistic purposes. Of the first category there still remain stone-faced platform mounds, enclosures, and clusters of walled houses of which only the foundation outline is left. These stone foundations are called *corrales.* Saville (1907), who visited these ruins in 1906, before their complete destruction, describes some houses measuring one hundred ninety feet long and thirty-nine feet wide, with walls up to four and a half feet thick. Houses had from one to seven rooms. At Manta alone, he estimated hundreds of then-surviving house foundations, as well as an untold number already razed to the ground and built over with modern construction. Apparently not all houses were of stone, for Cieza describes some as being of wood, with thatched roofs (*in* Estrada 1962: 106). Shortly after the Conquest the population of Manta swelled briefly when the Spaniards forced the inhabitants of three nearby towns to abandon their homes and move to Manta, but rapidly decreased again due to the cruelties inflicted by the Conquistadores, who went to any length to extract gold and emeralds from the natives (Saville, *in* Estrada 1962: 102).

Manteño lithic art is especially famous for the U-shaped stone "seats" resting on crouching animals or human figures; there are also human statues, often stylized to the point of resembling columns, stone stelae with human figures carved in bas-relief and enclosed within panels of geometric design, animal effigies, and *incensarios*. These objects were confined to what probably were ceremonial centers, at Jaboncillo and Cerro de Hojas, away from populated areas, so that they escaped the eye of the early chroniclers.

There have been various attempts to explain the function of the stone carvings—especially the U-shaped "thrones"—in the aboriginal culture. Attributing the "functional" explanation to European bias, Feriz (1958) flatly rejects their interpretation as seats. Instead, he and Jijón y Caamaño (1945: 257) link them in some kind of ceremonial association to the rectangular slabs or stelae commonly found near them in the *corrales*. Feriz (1958: 396) suggests a comparison with southeast Asia, where similar constructions were used to attract the spirits of the dead and give them a place among the living. In support he cites skeletal finds within the *corrales*, and mentions that a small anthropomorphic effigy was found in one of the "thrones." He also proposes another possible interpretation, in which the "thrones" with their U-shaped form represent female sex symbols and the associated stone slabs phallic symbols. Jijón y Caamaño (1945: 269) was the first to suggest this explanation, which is to some degree supported by the frequent depictions on the slabs of nude females in

what appears to be a position of sexual intercourse. Also, there are cases of artifacts resembling the U-shaped "thrones" found buried in the ground with phallic monoliths placed vertically above them (Feriz 1958: 398). Estrada (1957a: 46–78) agrees with Jijón y Caamaño's interpretation and relates the stone seats and stelae to a whole complex of fertility rites, closely associated with life-and-death symbolism expressed in the carved figures on these stone objects as well as on other artifacts (notably spindle whorls).

Metallurgical skills were highly developed among the Manteño. Although few metal objects have been recovered the early Spaniards attest to their existence. Zárate (*in* Estrada 1962: 108) describes Manteño weapons: " 'Tiraderas, hondas, porras de plata y cobre, lanzas con el hierro de oro de baja ley.' " He also speaks of an island sanctuary where there existed " 'el retrato de una huerta con los arbolillos y plantas de oro' " (*ibid.*). " 'Y allí (Coaque) tomaron quince mil pesos de oro y mil quinientos marcos de plata. . . .' " (Zarate, *in* Estrada 1957b: 12). Copper beads have been recovered in Manteño sites, though in such small quantities that Holm (1963: 143), for one, sees this as an indication of the scarcity or high value of copper during this period. Minute pieces of gold have been found, some smaller than the head of a pin, which, when examined under a magnifying glass, turn out to have delicate, elaborate engraved designs that could only have been made with the help of some sort of lens (Verrill 1953: 147–8). Though beaten metal predominates, Manteño metal workers were clearly familiar with the art of casting. Copper implements include mold-made axes with stems, tanged knives and celts, digging-stick points, and a kind of spatula. Among gold and silver artifacts are armlets and leg-bands, belts, "crowns," diadems, tweezers, cups, leggings, pectorals, bells, and belts (Meggers 1966: 128–9). Gold was weighed with a steelyard. Based on contemporary accounts by the chronicler Cieza de León and other observers of Indian culture at the time of the Conquest, Holm (1963: 144–6) suggests that beads of jade and pink shell found among the Huancavilcas, or southern

Manteño, ma y have been used as a kind of primitive currency.

Compared with the earlier period of Regional Development, pottery-making underwent a qualitative and aesthetic decline in Manteño times, becoming more and more standardized as a result of large-scale production. Decoration is by burnishing, or often by stamping or punctating. Zoomorphic designs in the form of birds, felines, or other animals are common. Anthropomorphic vessels occur in various forms, as do pedestal-based jars (Meggers 1966: 129–30). Pottery whistles and figurines are also common. The latter, especially the so-called "Manteño solid" type, are quite stereotyped. Spindle whorls are found in great numbers, with excised geometric, anthropomorphic, and, above all, zoomorphic designs.

Cranial deformation was practiced as in the Guangala Phase, and the septum was perforated for dangling nose ornaments. Figurines wear a headdress consisting of a kind of tight-fitting cap, short in the back and long at the sides, similar to the cap worn by some Bolivian and Peruvian Indians today. The solid female figurines show in most instances a kind of necklace, most certainly of *chaquiras*, which hangs down to below the stomach. The necklace was fastened at the neck with a lock of shell. The necklaces of the male figurines hang only around the neck (Estrada 1962: 84). Contemporary Spanish accounts describe short, sleeveless shirts reaching to the navel, with the genital area covered by a loincloth which almost reached the ground (Estrada 1962: 106).

Burials were both primary and secondary. Two of the mounds excavated by Saville (1907) at Cerro Jaboncillo contained a number of burials of children and adults, both singly and in groups. This may possibly illustrate the custom of sacrificing women, children, and prisoners of war which prevailed in some parts of Manabí and on Puná Island. Sometimes burial was primary, below ground instead of in a mound, or secondary, in an urn or double urns (Estrada 1958: 16). Chiefs were buried in very deep shaft graves and sometimes embalmed with a kind of resin. They were interred with great ceremony, along with personal ornaments, arms, chicha, and sometimes with one of their wives (Thompson 1936: 110–11).

The burial practices of the coastal peoples clearly show that they believed in an existence after death, but apart from this very little is known about their religious beliefs. The most important temple was situated in Manta, about in the center of the Manabí coast. We are told that the doorway faced east and was covered with a cotton curtain. Inside were two images like black goats. There were also figures of serpents and large fish, the latter pertaining to the special cult of the fishermen. The Indians of Manta worshipped a great emerald, which was known as Umina. Hither came Indians from all parts to make offerings, particularly of small emeralds, to the great emerald. It was believed that the great emerald had powers of healing. . . . One early writer speaks of small shrunken heads in the temples. . . . (Thompson 1936: 111)

"In certain parts of Ecuador the deceased, accompanied by his widow and relatives, was carried to his final resting place in a litter. The procession advanced slowly, the mourners chanting lamentations and keeping time with a peculiar dance, in which a few paces were taken in a forward direction and then some backwards" (Thompson 1936: 101).

It is in the period of Integration, between A.D. 500 and 1000, that we get the first direct evidence of fabric production in Ecuador, although, as already noted, textiles are known to have existed in earlier cultures as well.

Biese (1960: 35) suggests that "the weaving of cloth . . . in most sedentary cultures seems to have developed shortly after the advent of pottery techniques." But in the case of Peru, where the oldest surviving textiles date back about 4,500 years, the art of textile making actually seems to predate the introduction of pottery by at least a millennium. As to the importance of weaving in early Peru, Bird (1968: 9) writes:

It is difficult for most of us today to visualize the role textiles have played in this region. For a thousand years prior to the appearance of pottery in the last half of the second millennium B.C., textiles seem to have been the major art medium. Even after other media were employed, textiles were important. In time, as more techniques were utilized, as the production of wool and cotton increased, and the dyeing process was perfected, many of the textiles were truly remarkable, both artistically and technically. Before the time of the Spanish conquest, textiles had become a measure of national wealth; they were collected as taxes, as contributions and gifts, were used in ceremonial sacrifices, and distributed as clothing for officials and for the armies.

The earliest surviving textile fragments from coastal Ecuador are six in number, all made of cotton. Some of these were found in graves (Estrada 1957a: 79–85). Cotton was apparently the most commonly worn material, although llama wool, imported from the highlands, was also used (Thompson 1936: 109).

"Textiles were produced in abundance and exported. . . . Flat and cylindrical pottery stamps with geometric patterns . . . may have been used for decoration of textiles. No traces survive of blankets, shawls, shirts, and other garments with bird, animal, fish and tree designs in brilliant . . . colours, described by the Spanish explorers" (Meggers 1966: 128).

In conclusion, it should be noted that all the surviving fragments of Manteño textiles have this in common: they are made of threads spun to the left (S-twist), a characteristic which may possibly have ritual significance.

Ecuador and Beyond

THE COAST OF ECUADOR, especially Manabí and Guayas, has a long and possibly unique position as a region of contact. Meggers (1966: 23–4) writes: "Geographically, Ecuador thus occupies a focal point. Drifting craft from south or north might be cast upon its shore by ocean currents. The intermontane corridors of Columbia form a ramp to its highland valleys, which are in turn accessible via easy passes to the Peruvian highlands or coast. This Andean route was the one most travelled during the colonial period and corresponds to the course of the Pan American Highway today." The same author also points out that climatically this area was easier for chance arrivals to adapt to than the Peruvian coastal deserts to the south or the Colombian rain forests to the north.

The earliest possible contact postulated so far may have occurred during the Machalilla Phase on the southern Manabí coast. This phase began about 2000 B.C. The Machalilla complex appears on the coast full-blown, with possible tropical forest origins but no local indications of its antecedents. Several of its pottery shapes and decorations appear to be closely related to Mesoamerican ceramics. The latter are of considerably later date, however (500–200 B.C.), so

that contact merely remains a possibility (Meggers 1966: 50–1).

Michael D. Coe (1960: 363–93) finds evidence overwhelmingly indicating connections between the region of La Victoria on the Guatemalan west coast and the Guayas basin, particularly during the Chorrea and Tejar Phases, the latter being a phase of Regional Development in this area. Coe bases his conclusions on ceramic evidence: technology, such as certain kinds of levelled rims, with decorations of iridescent paint, and form, such as whistling jars with bridge handle and single spout. In his opinion the direction of diffusion was in the main from north to south.

During the Regional Development Period there is strong evidence of Mesoamerican contact on the coast of Manabí and Esmeraldas, especially in the Tolita Phase in Esmeraldas. Borhegyi (1959) has prepared a list of sixty-four traits unique to Mesoamerica and Ecuador, most of which are found in the Tolita Phase. Some such traits are given by Meggers (1966: 116) as pottery masks, cylindrical and flat stamps, animal headdresses with gaping mouth, mold-made figurines with feather costumes, plaques depicting couples, family groups, or bound figures, demons and semi-anthropomorphic creatures, post-fired painting in green, black, white, yellow, etc. The above traits can be traced directly to Oaxaca and the Valley of Mexico.[1]

In the social and religious realm [of the Manteño period] . . . early Spanish explorers describe a number of Mesoamerican practices, especially in the Manteño region. Among these are burning of incense in temples, human sacrifice with the cutting out of the victim's heart, flaying of the body, shrinking of heads, and naming of children after the day of their birth. Some of these practices are also reported in the north highlands. In all probability, many are survivals of introductions made during the Regional Development Period. One new element of Mesoamerican origin, however, can be assigned to the Integration Period: ornamental gold inlay on the front of the upper incisor teeth. (Meggers 1966: 158)

Larrea (1958) suggests that the southern Manteño (who made the famous stone carvings) came to Esmeralda in migrations from Mesoamerica, beginning in the tenth century A.D. That the stone monuments date from approximately this time is confirmed by a radiocarbon date from the University of Michigan. Whether or not one wants to go so far as to accept mass immigration from the north, it is obvious from the highly developed watercraft and navigation techniques of the Manteño that migration was at least possible.

While we are discussing these prehistoric contacts between Ecuador and other parts of the New World, we might also briefly consider the relationships that may have existed between ancient Ecuador and Asia and that may account for several specific traits in Ecuadorian spindle-whorl art.

Estrada, Meggers, and Evans (1962) have postulated trans-Pacific contacts taking place in at least two cultural phases on the Ecuadorian coast: Valdivia and Bahía. The first is supposed to have occurred around 3200 B.C., resulting in the introduction of the con-

cept of pottery into Ecuador. They base their conclusions on similarities they perceive in vessel forms and decoration between Valdivia pottery and Jomon ware, produced by a contemporaneous culture of Japan, and on the fact that Valdivia pottery seems to have appeared on the Ecuadorian coast suddenly, fully developed, with no local traceable origin.

Estrada and Meggers (1961) propose an Asiatic origin for certain traits in the early Bahía Culture, starting around the first and second centuries B.C. These supposedly Asiatic traits generally persisted through the Bahía Phase and can occasionally be found in neighboring contemporary cultures, presumably spread by diffusion. By the beginning of the Manteño Phase these traits had largely disappeared. The presumed trans-Pacific traits are, briefly: pottery house models with raised gables, neck rests, raft navigation by sails and centerboards, panpipes graduated toward the center, rectangular pottery net weights, "golf tee" earplugs, seated figurines with double beards and necklaces with tusklike pendants, and figurines of warriors with oriental eyes.

In the context of the present study, it is especially intriguing that two spindle whorls from Manabí should add to the apparent evidence for trans-Pacific diffusion. One of these (Fig. 7) depicts a characteristically Asian method of burden carrying, the so-called "coolie yoke"; the other (Fig. 1) shows the aforementioned funerary procession. The artist responsible for the former was obviously acquainted with the fact that there existed two different ways of shouldering heavy loads. There are two panels on the whorl. The first depicts a bird-headed or masked woman wearing a skirt and carrying a large water jar by means of a band across the chest, a variation of the characteristic American Indian tumpline. This method of transporting jugs and other loads with a line across the chest or forehead may still be observed in Mesoamerica and the Andes. On the second panel there appears an anthropomorphic figure, possibly also female, carrying two loads balanced against one another at either end of what can only be described as a typically Asian coolie yoke, a method of carrying

[1] Krickeberg (1928: 381) observed close parallels between the pottery of highland Ecuador and figurines from Esmeraldas with similar ware from Mexico and the Maya region. He postulated an important gateway on the Ecuadorian coast through which Mesoamerican culture traits diffused into Ecuador and the highlands.

entirely foreign to New World tradition. (It might be noted parenthetically that despite the example set by countless Asian immigrants since the Conquest, American Indians as a whole have never forsaken the traditional tumpline in favor of the coolie yoke.) Whatever the significance of this curious scene, the ancient artist's deliberate juxtaposition of two decidedly different carrying techniques pertaining to opposite sides of the Pacific is certainly striking.

As for the second whorl (Fig. 1), the evidence is less convincing and is mentioned here only in passing. It consists of the fact that the birdman motif on this and similar Manabí spindle whorls has its almost identical counterpart on numerous rock carvings on Easter Island (Northern 1968: 14–20). In view of the widespread occurrence of bird symbolism and man-bird transformation, not only in the Americas but in many other parts of the world, including Polynesia, this may be only coincidence, explainable on the basis of common beliefs rather than direct contacts. That such trans-Pacific contacts might have taken place, nevertheless—or were at least physically possible—has been convincingly argued by several authors, among them Heyerdahl (1964) and, more recently, Jett (1971). Also, of course, there have been a number of successful accidental and deliberate trans-Pacific voyages in primitive watercraft, including balsa rafts similar to those in use off the Ecuadorian coast at the time of the Conquest. These are too well known to require discussion here.

Fig. 7 Spindle whorl. Black, conical. Max. height: 14.4 mm. Max. width: 11.6 mm. Diameter of holes: 2.9 and 3.2 mm.

21

Part II

Spindle Whorls and Techniques of Spinning

IT IS OBVIOUS by now that pre-Columbian spindle whorls in general, and those from the coast of Ecuador in particular, present far more complex problems for the culture historian than is suggested by their usual classification as economic artifacts or objects of material culture and primitive technology. Rather, they appear to have been intimately connected with concepts of life and death, not merely through the symbolic designs placed on them but through their primary role in the complicated and symbol-laden processes of weaving. To comprehend this more fully it is necessary first of all to discuss the function of spindle whorls and techniques of spinning.

Spindle whorls when found in archaeological contexts are usually taken as indicators of the presence of weaving in a particular culture. There are exceptions to this rule, as in the case of the Yanoama (Yanomamö) of Venezuela and Brazil, who have learned how to spin cotton but use the thread exclusively as body ornaments or for intertribal trading. Generally speaking, however, spinning is a preparation for weaving, the spindle serving as the tool to twist together and draw out massed short fibers, such as cotton or wool, into continuous thread (Emery 1966: 9).

The techniques of spinning and weaving are known to many South American Indians, although they are usually practiced only by agricultural Indians rather than by fishermen or hunters and food gatherers. The most basic material commonly used is cotton. Cultivated cotton (*Gossypium barbadense*) has been found in pre-ceramic shell midden deposits of coastal Peru dating to 3000 B.C. Threads and fabrics of cotton or bast fibers have been recovered by archaeologists from the remains of early cultures along the Pacific coast. In later times wool joined cotton as a basic textile material, with bast fibers and

hair being employed for special purposes. The llama, with its relatives, long a principal producer of wool in the pre-Columbian Andes, seems to have been introduced into Ecuador by the Inca, i.e., in late pre-Conquest times. After the Conquest the Indians adopted the goat and sheep as well, and the wool of these domesticated animals became the basic material used in weaving (Buitrón 1956: 287).

In South America

all spindles have whorls acting as balance wheels to steady the whirling motion. Materials and shapes vary; diameters are from 1 and 1½ to 2 inches. Most whorls are disks or discoidal forms; a few are rectangular. . . . More common materials . . . are wood, drilled pottery sherds, tortoise shell, raw or sun-dried clay forms, bone, stone, and rock. . . . Decorated whorls are not common. Some wooden whorls are carved or incised . . .; pottery is painted. Archaeological specimens from Peruvian sites are usually patterned with small geometric designs. (O'Neale 1949: 98–100)

There are two spinning techniques in South America.

(1) *The Bororo technique* (Fig. 8)

This is the older method, used by the ancient Peruvians and still in use among various tropical forest tribes. The spinner sits on the ground holding the spindle horizontally, with its upper end resting on a forked stick or between her toes, the lower end resting on her thigh or on a wooden block. With her right palm she rotates the lower end so that the motion gives a twist to the fibers which are attached below the whorl. With the left hand she draws out the fiber to elongate it. When it has sufficient twist it is wound on the upper part of the spindle.

(2) *The Bacaïri technique* (Fig. 9)

This technique is used by the Quechua and Aymará (the so-called Andean drop spindle). It is still wide-

Fig. 8 Panare woman spinning cotton; Bororo technique. (Photo L. T. Laffer.)

Fig. 9 Woman of the Peruvian highlands using a drop spindle; Bacaïri technique. (Photo de Rosner Productions.)

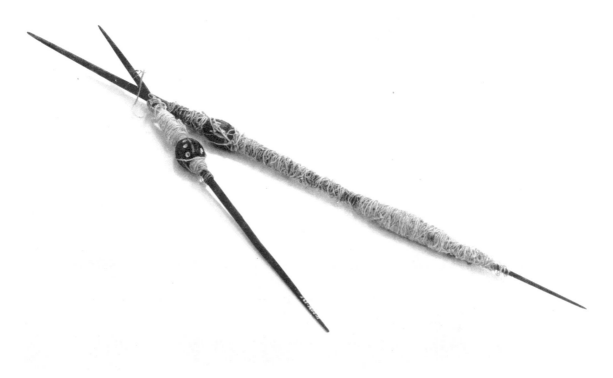

Fig. 10 Spindles from Peru showing the spindle whorls in place. (Photo P. T. Furst.)

spread in South America. The fiber is attached to the upper end of the spindle, which is held vertically. The spindle is given a rotating motion with the right-hand fingers or both palms, almost as in fire making. After being given a final vigorous twist it is allowed to fall, the whorl giving sufficient momentum to draw out and twist the fiber, which subsequently is wound around the spindle. When sitting down, Aymará women would twirl the stick in a small bowl, but the drop spindle was generally used by highland spinners while walking.

Funes Sánchez (1970: 158) has observed both techniques of spinning as being employed by Indians of the Ecuadorian highlands: the Bororo technique when the woman is walking, the Bacaïri technique when she is seated.

The Ecuadorian spindle whorls with which we are here concerned were used on slender eight- to twelve-

inch-long shafts with ends tapering to a fine point (Fig. 10). Whorls with representational anthropomorphic and zoomorphic decorations appear in the Regional Development Period and continue into the period of Integration, when they become very numerous in the archaeological record. Geometric designs seem to be rather less frequent during both these phases and, in any event, may not have appeared as abstract to the participants in the ancient cultures as they do to us.

The whorls are beadlike ceramic artifacts, occasionally flat but usually spheroid, semi-spheroid, barrel-shaped, oblong, or conical (Fig. 11). Funes Sánchez (1970: 158) found the forms and decorations of the whorls varying according to local culture and period. Thus, barrel-shaped whorls are most common on Puná Island, conical ones frequently come from Atacames in the province of Esmeraldas. Miniature sculptures in the shape of vases, pitchers, and pots are known from La Esperanza, near Machala. Zoomorphic, anthropomorphic, and cephaloform miniature sculptures occur as spindle whorls in various Manabí sites. From Esmeraldas come mushroom-shaped whorls, and from Portoviejo, Manabí, what Funes Sánchez (1970) calls "double- and triple-bodies." These whorls were fired in a reducing atmosphere which was not fully controlled, so that although intended colors might have been black and gray, occasionally whorls came out brown and orange. Spindles which have been recovered intact, i.e., with shaft, whorl, and yarn, show that the whorl was slipped over the shaft until it came to rest on the thicker lower third of the stick. The upper hole of the whorl is usually narrower than the lower and it is likely that the wet clay bead was decorated while being held on a stick or spindle shaft. The thread was wound around and over the whorl so that the designs remained hidden under the accumulating yarn. The oval-shaped ball of yarn was passed on the shaft through the weft and thus became a warper (Fig. 12).

Decoration was accomplished mainly by excision and incision. The excavated parts were filled with white lime and possibly other colors. Most frequently represented are such animals as the owl, pachota, pelican, bat, jaguar, monkey, opossum, fish, snake, iguana (crocodile), frog, slug, and anthropomorphic and zoomorphic representations of what appears to be a "Mother Goddess" figure, depicted in the well-known "hocker," or birthgiving position which may also stand for coitus. Admittedly, it is often difficult to identify the animals depicted beyond any doubt. Also, certain creatures may possess the attributes of two or more species (i.e., bat-jaguar) which may have been related conceptually in the classification system of the particular time and place, even if they appear genetically unrelated to us. Sculptured three-dimensional whorls have also been recovered but these have not been included in the present selection, except for one example depicting a lizard man. As noted by Snethlage (1930: 83), there exists a certain relationship between the decorations on Ecuadorian spindle whorls and those from Peru. Nevertheless, the style of these two Andean regions is distinctive and can easily be differentiated.

In view of the fact that spindle whorls have been found in such abundance in burials and in what appear to be ceremonial sites on the island of Puná and along the coast, there has been a good deal of speculation as to their actual function especially since, as is the case with many Peruvian spindle whorls, those

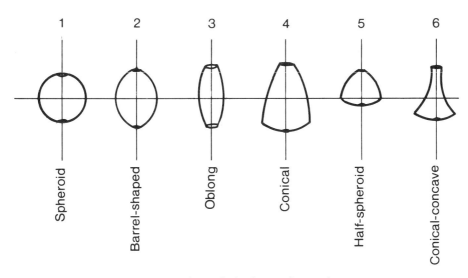

Fig. 11 Typology of whorls according to shape.

from Manabí tend to be extremely small, with such fine perforations that their utility for spinning has been placed in doubt. It has been suggested, for example, that the whorls were really employed as money, or as mnemonic devices similar to the Inca quipus. Another theory has it that the whorls were really beads for beaded skirts or necklaces; strings of them are regularly sold to tourists as "ancient necklaces." It may well be that the whorls were in fact strung together to be interred with the dead and that they did serve certain esoteric functions beyond their original meaning as spindle whorls. Also, it might be noted that many of the whorls show no or little evidence of use, suggesting that large numbers of them were specifically made as grave offerings. However, whatever their additional meanings, their identification as spindle whorls is certain; too many complete spindles and even excellently preserved baskets filled with spindles, woven thread, and other spinning paraphernalia have been found in archaeological sites in Peru to leave any doubt. Like those from Manabí, many Peruvian spindle whorls are also very small, with fine perforations. As Mason (1961: 244–5) suggested, it may simply be that the lightest whorls were employed to spin the finest threads and yarns, these in turn being used for the weaving of ritual and ceremonial fabrics.

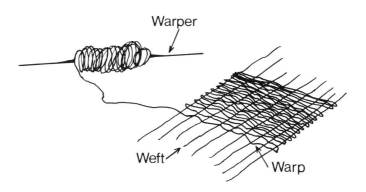

Fig. 12 The spindle used as a warper.

The Thread of Life

So much, then, for the technological side of the question. We turn now to the ideological. As mentioned earlier, all six surviving Manteño textile fragments were woven of threads spun to the left, a fact which, as noted, may be of ritual significance. Yarns may be spun in two directions, the spiral formed by twisting upward to the left being called the S-twist and that to the right the Z-twist by contemporary weavers. Now, according to Frödin and Nordenskiöld (1918: 49–62), the majority of all contemporary tribes for whom information was available employed the S-twist, i.e., spun to the left, a statement whose accuracy has since been questioned. As for ancient spinning, Bird (1954) has stated that, with a few exceptions in early times, the S-twist predominated on the Peruvian north coast and the Z-twist on the south coast, an apparent regional difference for which there is no explanation.[2] Interestingly, Frödin and Nordenskiöld speculated as to the possible connection of the spinning direction with "superstitious" beliefs. If a particular tribe was found to produce consistently thread spun to the right, they suggested, this might be due to some cultural dictum rather than a matter of conventional preference: perhaps the people associated misfortune with left-spun materials. This hypothesis finds support in the great body of folk beliefs and practices regarding left and right from all over the world, including North and South America. Frödin and Nordenskiöld conceded that they made only an unconfirmed guess, but some significant ethnographic evidence regarding the meaning of left and right in Andean spinning and weaving has recently come to light, augmenting that already available from early historical sources.

As is known, pre-Conquest Peruvians used beautifully shaped spindles of wood or bramble measuring from eight to sixteen inches in length. The whorls of pottery, stone, wood, or even metal were placed on the lower part of the shaft, and, although generally speaking contemporary whorls lack decoration, most archaeological specimens from Peru have at least geometric designs.[3] The Peruvian Indians used these spindles to produce right-spun thread "except in manufacturing articles to be used in sorcery" (Rowe 1946: 241). An Inca sorcerer who wanted to visit harm, sickness, and death on an enemy would "spin a thread of black and white wool, twisting it to the left (the reverse of the customary direction), and then place a noose of it on a path where the enemy might pass so that it would catch his foot" (Rowe 1946: 314).

That the magical significance of the left-spun thread has survived through time is shown in a recent study of spinning techniques in the region of Cuzco, Peru, where Goodell (1968: 7) found the right-hand or Z-twist to be the normal procedure, while the leftward, or S-twist, was reserved for magical purposes. After studying between forty and fifty rural communities, Goodell concluded that the use of the S-twist (the so-called *lloq'e*, from the Quechua word meaning "left" or "something different") is restricted to exceptional circumstances due to its supposedly supernatural properties. In some areas only the medicine man may spin *lloq'e*, but in most places anyone may use the S-twist when he needs *lloq'e* for medicinal or ritual-magical purposes. *Lloq'e* is be-

---

[2] Unless, of course, it is simply a matter of sampling. After all, what percentage of ancient textiles has survived, and of these, how many have been scientifically excavated and studied?

[3] The same reservation regarding the meaning of "representational" vs. "abstract" or "geometric" designs applies here as in the case of the Manabí whorls. Iconographic and symbolic studies of contemporary Indians and other non-Western art show that designs which to us look abstract or geometric may be no less "representational" to the native observer than those we would call "realistic."

lieved to be effective against various sicknesses, e.g., rheumatism; it makes for easier pregnancies; it protects against hexes and against accidents or bad influences in general. It is always included in the offerings to the earth deity in the annual harvest ceremonies. *Lloq'e* is also used for success in romances.

Similar practices are reported by Buechler and Buechler (1971: 101–02) from the Aymará community of Compi, situated on the shores of Lake Titicaca on the Bolivian high plateau. Not only is yarn that is "spun the wrong way" used in prophylactic rituals accompanying the birth of twins, but it plays an important role in curing ceremonies, especially for persons suffering from *susto*, or fright sickness, whose soul is thought to have become lost. According to the authors, "During the process of calling the soul, wool spun in reverse is also used. One tears small pieces and throws them to the wind, calling the soul as one throws. The next day this wool is burned and the patient must drink the ashes mixed with water. Yarn spun in reverse is also placed in the patient's hands and on the ground around him so that the soul may not escape" (Buechler and Buechler 1971: 102).

The left-spun or S-twist was also employed ritually in pre-Columbian Mexico, as is evident from the studies of Weitlaner Johnson (1966–67: 179–90), who analyzed miniature garments recovered from caves in the Mixteca Alta. She writes that miniature objects are typically associated with "birth and death ceremonies, curing or witchcraft practices, votive offerings or teaching devices." As for the direction of spinning, she writes, although "one could generalize and state that the Z-twist was *the* motor habit among spinners of cotton in Mesoamerica," the fact is that left-spun yarn was used for miniature garments from three different Mixteca caves and that S-twisted and Z-twisted yarn even occurred side by side in the same weaving.

Apart from the surviving fragments of Manteño textiles with their S-twisted fibers we have no direct evidence for the predominant direction in which the Manabí spindle whorls might have been used. However, it is likely that the orientation of spindle-whorl symbols is not arbitrary, and so might provide clues as to the direction of spinning.

Some brief concluding remarks are in order about the philosophical relationship between spinning and weaving on the one hand and life and death on the other. That such a symbolic relationship should have been recognized by the ancient Andeans is not surprising—it is nearly universal. Like any process, spinning and weaving have a beginning and an end. But not in all processes are beginning and end as plainly visible as here. When the Ecuadorian woman began to fill a fresh spindle, she fastened the beginning of the thread under the whorl. The accumulating yarn engulfed the whorl, and its symbolic meaning impregnated the spindle. When full, the spindle resembled a mandorla, the symbol of dualism and inversion. And, indeed, the spindle and the satisfaction of the spinner who finally held the full spindle in her hands were only transient. The law of *enantiodromia*, so well interpreted in Chinese mysticism, according to which *yang* at its optimum point converts into *yin*, its negative opposite, would soon also claim the fruit of her work. Her spindle which she patiently watched grow through the slow stages of waxing increment would soon wane and diminish again in the actual weaving, in the process of which the beginning of the thread would be converted into its own end.

But this sacrifice was made for a good cause: a piece of fabric was produced. Through the union of two basic elements (the warp and the woof) the "web of life" was created even as the spindle diminished and disappeared.[4] In the weaver's hands, passing along the horizontal axis of the loom and through the various (vertical) stages of its existence, the spindle spends itself developing the new form of life to its resplendent fullest.

---

4 The Araucanians believe that the soul of a woman on her way to the Otherworld has to pass a test which consists of weaving a cloth which shows her life (Casamiquela 1964: 224).

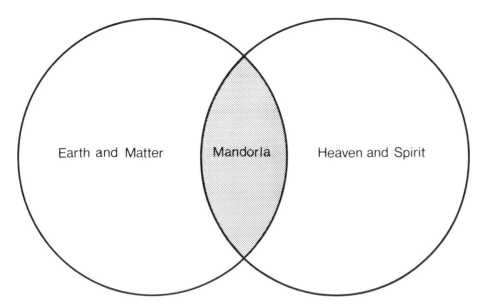

Earth and Matter   Mandorla   Heaven and Spirit

Fig. 13 The mandorla spindle of the Magna Mater.

The representations on Ecuadorian spindle whorls, as well as the insight of Estrada and others that spindle whorls belong to a prehistoric "cult of fertility" in Ecuador, leave no doubt that the ancient artist who created the designs and the woman who used them shared with many peoples, past and present, the symbolic meaning of the Magical Spinners, the Parcae, the Whirred Sisters, the Norns, and others. The dynamics of the ever-busy spindle and its dualistic nature were no secret to them. Almost universally the spindle-shaped mandorla (Fig. 13) is perceived as the product of the conjunction of the sphere of matter (left) and the sphere of spirit (right). Being a product of both, the mandorla section incorporates the essence of opposition and symbolizes all dualism—life and death, waxing and waning, appearance and disappearance, etc.[5] The two spheres are also understood as symbols of earth and heaven,

the mandorla being the result of their union and symbol of the creative power and the generative, mutual, and perpetual sacrifice of the parent spheres. The Magna Mater uses the mandorla as her spindle with which she spins the thread of life (Cirlot 1962: 194; Schneider 1946: 287).[6] Because of this intrinsic meaning of dualism and inversion of the spindle, it is to be expected that at least several of the zoomorphic and anthropomorphic creatures depicted over and over on the Manabí whorls should carry the message of life and death. I submit that they do this, either by themselves, stressing life or death, or else in combination, like two sides of the same coin.

The symbolic role of the spindle and other paraphernalia of weaving in Mesoamerican ritual makes this very clear. The Mother Goddess in her numerous manifestations was the spinner and weaver par excellence. Hence her sacrificial impersonators wore full

[5] The religious systems of ancient America were permeated with this same concept of dualism—the union of seemingly opposite attributes which assured renewal and survival. Dualism is especially apparent in Mesoamerican ritual art and mythology.

[6] Men among the Kogi Indians of Colombia sit in the sanctuary (the uterus of the Universal Mother) and spin thread which symbolizes the umbilicus by means of which they are attached to the Magna Mater (Reichel-Dolmatoff 1951: 2, 153).

spindles on the head as the identifying characteristics of the Magna Mater. At the Festival of Sweeping, called Ochpaniztli, in honor of Toci, Grandmother, the old Mother of the Gods and of the Earth, her impersonator was given bundles of maguey fibers which she spun into thread and wove into garments, because, Durán (1971: 233) tells us, that is how Toci supported herself and her children. In the codices, too, the various earth and fertility goddesses—essentially aspects of one another and of the Creator-Mother Goddess—are depicted with spindles and bunches of cotton. Likewise the Maya goddess Ixchel was patroness of spinning and weaving.

Many of the animals depicted on the Manabí spindle whorls are typically those which inhabit two or more planes of life: air, water, earth. For instance, the dualism of life and death was easily attached to the bat, so frequently depicted in pre-Columbian art. We know that this "animal of the twilight" symbolized birth and fertility in Zapotec art, and death and the Underworld in Maya. In Ecuadorian spindle-whorl art the bat is often combined as a symbol of darkness with the jaguar, predominantly the symbol of light and the Sun. Then there are such ambiguous birds as the pelican, which in diving moves from one plane to another, and the owl, the bird of the night. Among mammals there is the opossum which feigns death and which for the Ecuadorian Indians carried the message of the "Thread of Life."[7] It is this ambiguity that may, in part at least, explain why these animals above all should have been selected for depiction on the spindle whorls and other ceremonial art believed to have been related to a "fertility cult."

Yet another thought concerning the symbolic meanings of the spindle arises from the image of the accumulating thread coiling itself like a snake around the shaft. This symbol has been understood as one of mediation between earth and heaven. Hermes, the psychopomp of Greek mythology, carried it, as did the Roman messenger-god Mercury. Even today the staff with its coiling snake—the caduceus—symbolizes the medical profession and the doctor's role of intermediary in life-crisis situations. Besides these more hidden meanings of dualism and intermediacy, the spindle and its parts demonstrate in a more direct way the subtle conditions of fertility, in that the spindle shaft can be seen as a phallus penetrating the female whorl. From this union comes the thread, the warp and the woof of the Web of Life.

A good example of this symbolic context was recorded by Reichel-Dolmatoff (1951: 218–19) from the Kogi Indians of Colombia where "the man [who deflowers the girl], the *máma* [shaman], sets up a small hut (called *nyuíji hubé* or 'bat house'), wherein the first coitus is to occur. A day prior to this event, the *máma* hands the girl a spindle whorl and a spindle shaft made of deer bone (sometimes made of antler), explaining that these two objects represent the male and the female organs of reproduction. Both objects are deposited in the hut and, subsequent to the coitus, picked up and guarded carefully by the girl as her . . . marriage license."

Finally, we cannot overlook the fact that a full spindle appears not only in the shape of a mandorla but also in that of a vagina. With it the Magna Mater creates new life from the female body. This symbolic relationship between spindle and vagina, and loom and woman's body, respectively, finds clear expression in a myth from Middle India where a supernatural being instructs a man to spin cotton thread for the first time. Obeying the command the man then "made his wife lie down and tied a stick across her breasts. From this he stretched his yarn. He took out her vagina and used it as a shuttle. The cloth he made was long and narrow, narrow as the distance between a woman's breasts" (Verrier 1949: 473). The many fish representations on Ecuadorian spindle whorls may be related to such symbolism.

7 Similarly for the Huichol Indians of Mexico, the opossum is both a guardian of the Underworld, symbolic of death, and, as Bringer of Fire, the guarantor of life (Furst 1967: 70–1).

Spindle Whorls and Their Decoration

BIRDS AND BIRD SYMBOLS

IF OUR INTERPRETATION of the symbolic meaning of spindle-whorl art is correct and it does indeed relate to the life-and-death cycle, then it is not surprising to find certain birds prominent among the themes depicted on the whorls. Owls and pelicans are especially frequent, suggesting that their symbolic function was of considerable importance to the ancient Ecuadorians.

The bird has been a symbol of spiritual transcendence from time immemorial. Cave paintings dating to the Upper Paleolithic show shamans wearing bird masks, and, like their antecedents of thirty thousand years ago, the shamans of the Siberian tribes, the *taltos* of the Hungarians, and medicine men in many parts of the world emphasize bird symbolism in relation to the passage from this to the Otherworld. The Egyptian god Toth had the head of an ibis and was the judge of the birdlike souls in the Underworld. The souls in the Babylonian Hades wore headdresses of bird feathers and, according to Homer, the souls of the dead chirp like birds. Mercurius, the divine patron of Roman merchants and travelers, was winged. Bird spirits and the Thunder Bird permeate North American Indian religion, just as the transcendental role of the great King Vulture in the ancient religions of Panama and Costa Rica found expression in countless castings of precious gold. The souls of Aztec warriors were transformed into hummingbirds. Christians symbolize the Holy Spirit, the font of all spiritual life and renaissance, in the form of a dove, as do the Huichol their divine Mother of Maize. The list could be extended almost indefinitely.

Besides the general meaning of transition from matter to spirit through death or metamorphosis, birds have been identified also as phallic symbols. The pachota bird, depicted on so many Ecuadorian spindle whorls, is said to be the bird that deflowered the primordial woman. Folk tales of many other Indian groups tell of birds fulfilling a similar function.

On the spindle whorls, diving birds—especially the pelican—seem to symbolize mainly fertility and transition of life between different planes. The owl most probably stands for darkness and the end of terrestrial life. It is interesting also that the head of the owl is frequently depicted alone, very likely as a symbol of death. Here again duality is evident, for the Indians—ancient and contemporary—conceptualized the head as the seat of life and the soul. Of mantic significance are flocks of birds which sometimes crowd a spindle whorl. On a very beautiful example, a flock of birds, perhaps symbolizing darkness and the Underworld, is chased by a jaguar, who here might be interpreted as a being of the Sun and light. Another magnificent piece depicts an anthropomorphic pachota bird adorned with a biblike poncho, in juxtaposition with a jaguar wearing a collar, as though the symbols of death and fertility were facing each other in dynamic awareness. A disk next to the head of the bird may represent the Sun.

An interesting parallel in Ecuadorian spindle-whorl art to the art of the Olmec in Mesoamerica is the abstraction of the bird to its barest essential—the wing. Many spindles are decorated with wing designs, sometimes naturalistic, sometimes almost geometric, which, like the complete bird, probably symbolize spirituality, enlightenment, and sublimation.

Fig. 14 Spindle whorl. Black, conical. Max. height: 13.7
mm. Max. width: 12.9 mm. Diameter of holes: 3.2 and
3.5 mm.

Fig. 15 Black, conical (concave). Max. height: 13.5 mm.
Max. width: 18.6 mm. Diameter of holes: 3.3 and 4.5 mm.

Fig. 17 Brown, conical. Max. height: 15 mm. Max. width: 15.9 mm. Diameter of holes: 3.1 and 3.2 mm.

Fig. 16 Black, barrel-shaped. Max. height: 14.5 mm. Max. width: 9.8 mm. Diameter of holes: 2.3 and 2.5 mm.

Fig. 18 Gray, conical. Max. height: 13.7 mm. Max. width: 14.4 mm. Diameter of holes: 3 and 3.1 mm.

35

Fig. 19 Gray, conical. Max height: 14.7 mm. Max. width: 14.8 mm. Diameter of holes: 3.9 and 4.2 mm.

Fig. 20 Black, conical. Max. height: 12.5 mm. Max. width: 15 mm. Diameter of holes: 4 and 4.3 mm.

Fig. 21 Gray, spheroid. Max. height: 12.8 mm. Max. width: 14.5 mm. Diameter of holes: 3.5 and 3.7 mm.

HEAD PORTRAIT OF DEATH—THE OWL

JUST AS "trophy heads" of slain enemies or the preserved heads of deceased ancestors are believed to
assure fertility,[8] so the many representations of disembodied heads on Ecuadorian spindle whorls may
be related to the symbolic system Estrada called
"fertility cult." In many cases these heads are un-
questionably owls, in others they resemble human
skulls. Head portraits of this kind are found not only
on spindle whorls but also on other ceramic artifacts,
such as vessels and pottery stamps, as well as on
ceremonial copper axes. An interesting feature that
the Ecuadorian heads share with Olmec representations of the were-jaguar is a V-shaped cleft at the
crown; sometimes the center cleft is flanked by additional clefts, but these may also represent feathers. In
any event, there is archaeological evidence that such
heads and *tzanzas* as symbols of death prevailed for
centuries over a wide area of Ecuador (Estrada
1957a: 52; 1957b: 12; 1957c: 11).

The heart-shaped form of these "head portraits of
death" is reminiscent of the face of the barn owl,
Tyto alba, and it may well be that this owl served as
prototype for the head design on the whorls. There
is also another native Ecuadorian bird, the valdivia,
which is diurnal rather than nocturnal but which
otherwise closely resembles ordinary owls. Both the
owl and the valdivia are popularly associated with
death, their calls being considered as omens of impending evil and doom. So persistent are these ancient associations that even today, when an Ecuadorian mother hears the call of these birds close to
her house she will hide her unbaptized child to pre-
vent it from being taken away (Estrada 1957a: 61).

This association of owl with doom and death,

though not precisely universal (e.g., the owl as emblem of ancient Athens) is certainly widespread
throughout the world. In the Americas, among the
Aztecs, for example, the *tecolotl* was an omen of
death, as was the Maya *cui*, the owl messenger and
companion of death. In contemporary Latin America
the owl is frequently identified with witches and
malevolent sorcerers. In Manabí art, representations
of the owl occur in association with cult objects that
seem to pertain to shamanism. In short, there is little
question that the prehistoric Ecuadorians shared the
owl with other peoples as symbol and harbinger of
death—death not as oblivion but as the comple-
mentary opposite of life.

What is remarkable in spindle-whorl representations of owls is that despite their minute size and
frequent conventionalization, young birds can actually be differentiated from mature ones. Nestlings are
recognized by their white down feathers, adults by
stripes and circles. Most characteristic of Manabí
owls is the large head with the above-mentioned V-
shaped cleft or a depression with soft contours at the
top of the head. The characteristic frontal eyes of
the bird are also emphasized. Rather infrequently
chicks are conventionalized, with outspread wings
and only one eye, as if to suggest the initial blindness
of newborn birds. Disembodied owl heads are sometimes surrounded by what seems at first glance to be
a kind of headdress but what may also be either a
conventionalized representation of wing and tail
plumage, raised and puffed up in characteristic threat
posture, or else might be rays, intended to emphasize
the transcendental nature of the head symbol. With
the possible exception of the birdmen on the funerary
whorl (Fig. 1), I have not come across any anthropomorphized owls on spindle whorls, although the
owls depicted in flight with their legs shown prominently give a somewhat anthropomorphic impression.

[8] For example, the well-known shrunken heads or *tzanzas*
of the Jivaro Indians of Ecuador.

Fig. 22 Black, conical. Max. height: 13.2 mm. Max. width: 16.1 mm. Diameter of holes: 3.7 and 4.4 mm.

Fig. 23 Black, barrel-shaped. Max. height: 15.1 mm. Max. width: 10.7 mm. Diameter of holes: 3.8 and 4 mm.

Fig. 24 Gray, conical. Max. height: 11 mm. Max. width: 14.1 mm. Diameter of holes: 3.6 and 4 mm.

Fig. 25 Black, conical. Max. height: 16 mm. Max width: 16.9 mm. Diameter of holes: 3.5 and 3.9 mm.

Fig. 26 Black, grooved. Max. height: 17.2 mm. Max. width: 13 mm. Diameter of holes: 3.1 and 3.3 mm.

Fig. 27 Black, conical. Max. height: 13.5 mm. Max. width: 13.8 mm. Diameter of holes: 3.3 and 3.6 mm.

Fig. 28 Gray, conical. Max. height: 12.1 mm. Max. width: 13.4 mm. Diameter of holes: 3.5 and 3.6 mm.

Fig. 29 Gray, conical. Max. height: 14.1 mm. Max. width: 14.4 mm. Diameter of holes: 3.5 and 3.8 mm.

Fig. 30 Black, conical. Max. height: 14.4 mm. Max. width: 15.3 mm. Diameter of holes: 3.5 and 3.9 mm.

Fig. 31 Black, conical. Max. height: 16.6 mm. Max. width: 14.3 mm. Diameter of holes: 4.3 and 4.5 mm.

Fig. 32 Black, conical. Max. height: 13 mm. Max. width: 13.7 mm. Diameter of holes: 3.3 and 4 mm.

Fig. 33 Brown, barrel-shaped. Max. height: 13.8 mm.
Max. width: 11 mm. Diameter of holes: 4 and 4 mm.

Fig. 34 Gray, conical. Max. height: 18.1 mm. Max. width:
18.7 mm. Diameter of holes: 3.6 and 3.8 mm.

THE PACHOTA

THE SO-CALLED PACHOTA is a heronlike bird with a long, narrow, and powerful beak. It occurs not only on Manabí spindle whorls but also on ceremonial objects that Estrada (1957a: 61–2) relates to the prehistoric cult of fertility. If, as he suggests, the pachota is indeed the Ecuadorian version of the widespread South American motif of the bird that de-flowered the primordial woman, its symbolic association with the concept of fertility would, of course, be most appropriate.

Unlike certain other animals, on the spindle whorls the legendary pachota is never shown with human attributes but always appears as pure bird, either as a young chick or as a mature specimen. Occasionally two birds facing each other are joined, sharing, as it were, the same beak.

Fig. 35 Black, barrel-shaped. Max. height: 15.9 mm. Max. width: 11.2 mm. Diameter of holes: 2.9 and 3 mm.

43

Fig. 36 Black, barrel-shaped. Max. height: 16.2 mm. Max. width: 12.6 mm. Diameter of holes: 3.4 and 3.8 mm.

Fig. 37 Brown, conical. Max. height: 13.2 mm. Max. width: 12.5 mm. Diameter of holes: 3.2 and 3.4 mm.

Fig. 38 Brown, conical. Max. height: 15.2 mm. Max. width: 13.5 mm. Diameter of holes: 3.2 and 4 mm.

Fig. 39 Black, conical. Max. height: 16.1 mm. Max.
width: 11.3 mm. Diameter of holes: 2.7 and 3.2 mm.

Fig. 40 Gray, conical. Max. height: 13.4 mm. Max.
width: 13 mm. Diameter of holes: 3.5 and 4 mm.

Fig. 41 Gray, spheroid. Max. height: 10.9 mm. Max. width: 13.6 mm. Diameter of holes: 3.8 and 4.3 mm.

Fig. 42 Black, barrel-shaped. Max. height: 14.5 mm. Max. width: 10.5 mm. Diameter of holes: 2.8 and 3.2 mm

THE PELICAN

Judging from the frequency with which it was depicted in spindle-whorl art alone, the pelican had a peculiar fascination for the ancient inhabitants of the Ecuadorian coast. Not only is it depicted more often than almost any other subject, it also appears in a greater variety of designs. It is pictured on other ceramics, as well as in stone. In fact, pelican representations are so abundant in the Manteño culture of the Santa Elena peninsula that Bushnell (1951: 136) considers this bird almost emblematic for this culture. According to Estrada (1957b: 43), the pelican also represents one of the basic religious concepts of the Huancavilca-Manteño.

It may be of course that the frequency with which the pelican (*Pelicanus occidentalis*) appears in Manabí iconography reflects primarily the fact that this bird is the predominant creature of the Ecuadorian littoral, as Jijón and Bushnell point out. I would suggest, however, that the explanation is more complex, and that the relatively large number of pelican images on the spindle whorls as well as in other art is somehow related to the pelican's symbolic attributes as a creature at once of the heavens, the earth, and the mysterious realm of watery darkness. Like waterfowl in general, it is an intermediate creature: comfortable on land, it is both a superb flyer and an excellent swimmer. Completely released it soars seemingly without effort above earth and sea, and to feed itself dives like a dart from the sky into the water.

The great variety of pelican representations—on the ground, on the water, under water, in flight with open wings—suggests that the Manabí artist was conscious of this "grand design of transcendence." There are depictions of adult birds and chicks, naturalistic as well as conventionalized to the point of abstraction. Although some of the apparently abstract and geometric designs in Manabí art may well symbolize pelicans, on all the whorls we have examined, the designs clearly recognizable as pelicans are exclusively zoomorphic, without either human characteristics or attributes associated with other animals, and often include considerable realistic detail.

The representations of adult pelicans looking backward, as if arranging or preening themselves, are exceptionally graceful. These are commonly carved on oblong or barrel-shaped whorls, a form which forces the somewhat plump bird into a rather graceful stance that makes it appear superficially less like a pelican and more like some other waterfowl. The spearlike beak is usually well represented and on some whorls one can even see the enormous throat pouch. Also visible are the characteristic feather markings of young animals and adult specimens. In fact, chicks are mainly recognizable as such by white notches representing tufts of immaculately white down that in nature grows all over the black skin of the young bird. Representations of adult birds sometimes also show, in addition to body feathers, the typical long plumes that project from the rear of the pelican's head and neck. Also quite characteristic of pelican representations are short legs and a stubby, wide, and rounded tail. When depicted on land, the bird's totipalmate feet are usually emphasized by the artist to counterbalance tail, wings, and beak.

In nature the pelican chick is a rather grotesque, ungainly creature. Its club-shaped head, weighed down by the immense beak, appears too heavy for the weak neck. So long is the beak in proportion to the rest of the body that in some cases the artist, unable to contain it down to the hooked tip within his design, had to shorten it a bit. Despite this divergence from the natural model, other characteristics leave no doubt of its identity. Swimming pelicans are usually depicted with great simplicity, both in form and style. Especially remarkable are those whorls on which several birds are shown swimming in closed single-line formation. On several pieces the pelicans are interconnected, tail to beak, making for a peculiarly dynamic picture of birds floating effortlessly on the waves. Diving pelicans, their bodies streamlined and stylized to the point that they resemble fish more than birds, are nevertheless recognizable by their heads and characteristic beaks.

Based on these and other artistic representations

47

and the archaeological contexts in which they are found, Estrada (1957b: 43) speaks of the "adoration of the pelican" in Huancavilca-Manteño culture. Unfortunately, the evidence does not permit us to say more than that the pelican occupied an important symbolic position in belief and ritual, the precise nature of which, in the absence of historical traditions, eludes us.

We are more fortunate concerning ancient Mexico, where the great chronicler Sahagún (1963: 29–30) set down some of the beliefs of the sixteenth-century Aztecs about the pelican. To the Aztecs the pelican was "the heart of the lake," leader and master of all waterfowl. Like Ecuadorian Indians the Aztecs did not normally eat this bird. Only on ceremonial occasions did they make an exception to this rule, and then the pelican was eaten only ritually, not as food. Fishermen would pursue the pelican on the lake in order to obtain a precious green stone or feather from its gizzard. The stone or feather was a charm that guaranteed its owner continued luck in fowling and fishing. After the hunt the fishermen assembled for a ritual meal in which each ate a small piece of the slain bird. Pelicans commanded the storm which they would summon to drown any fisherman who for four days had unsuccessfully tried to stalk them. A successful hunter who caught the bird within the specified time but who, instead of the green stone or feather, found a piece of charcoal, would interpret this as an omen of impending death. Thus, according to Sahagún, the fishermen "consider it [the pelican] as the mirror. For there they see what each is to merit in their profession as water folk."

These Aztec beliefs and rituals relating the pelican to life and death appear to fit rather well into the symbolic and ritual complex at Manabí; no claim is made, of course, that they corresponded in detail.

Fig. 43 Orange, oblong. Max. height: 14.5 mm. Max. width: 8.5 mm. Diameter of holes: 2.9 and 3.7 mm.

Fig. 44 Black, conical. Max. height: 19.9 mm. Max. width: 15.1 mm. Diameter of holes: 4 and 4.4 mm.

Fig. 45 Gray, conical. Max. height: 15.2 mm. Max. width: 15.3 mm. Diameter of holes: 3.2 and 3.8 mm.

Fig. 46 Black, conical. Max. height: 13.7 mm. Max. width: 13.6 mm. Diameter of holes: 3 and 3.2 mm.

Fig. 47 Gray, conical. Max. height: 16.7 mm. Max. width: 16.5 mm. Diameter of holes: 2.9 and 3.4 mm.

Fig. 48 Gray, conical. Max. height: 14.1 mm. Max. width: 16 mm. Diameter of holes: 3.2 and 3.4 mm.

Fig. 49 Black, conical. Max. height: 13.9 mm. Max. width: 14.3 mm. Diameter of holes: 2.9 and 3.1 mm.

Fig. 50 Brown, spheroid. Max. height: 13.1 mm. Max. width: 13.5 mm. Diameter of holes: 3.9 and 3.9 mm.

Fig. 51 Black, conical. Max. height: 16.3 mm. Max. width: 15.1 mm. Diameter of holes: 3 and 3.8 mm.

Fig. 52 Black, barrel-shaped. Max. height: 13.5 mm. Max. width: 12.6 mm. Diameter of holes: 3.9 and 4 mm.

Fig. 53 Brown, conical. Max. height: 14.5 mm. Max. width: 13.5 mm. Diameter of holes: 3 and 3.5 mm.

Fig. 54 Orange, conical. Max. height: 15.4 mm. Max. width: 16.5 mm. Diameter of holes: 3.3 and 3.9 mm.

Fig. 55 Black, half spheroid. Max. height: 8.8 mm. Max. width: 11.7 mm. Diameter of holes: 2.8 and 3 mm.

Fig. 56 Black, conical. Max. height: 13.7 mm. Max.
width: 13.1 mm. Diameter of holes: 3.5 and 3.8 mm.

Fig. 57 Black, conical. Max. height: 13 mm. Max. width:
12.6 mm. Diameter of holes: 2.8 and 3.2 mm.

THE BAT

FEW CREATURES in the animal kingdom have been so shrouded in magic, mystery, and folk belief as the bat. Four-thousand-year-old Egyptian tomb paintings dating to the Twelfth Dynasty, the "bat gods" of the ancient Maya, Count Dracula, and Batman all attest in their way to the fact that since time immemorial the "Winged Hunter of Darkness" has tracked man's soul through the obscure corners of his unconscious. In the European tradition, especially, the bat has been imbued with all sorts of negative attributes—death, witchcraft, dark forebodings, gloom. Many non-Western peoples also identify the bat with death, the souls of the deceased, and the Underworld, as might be expected of a creature that lives in caves and other dark places and comes to life only at dusk. Significantly, it is in Asia, notably China and Japan, that we find the bat viewed most positively, as symbol not of death and gloom but of prosperity (Lessing 1934–35: 22). In Japan, *komori*, the bat, stands for happiness and plenty, a concept that reached Japan from China, where this belief seems to be very ancient. However, the identification of the bat with good fortune may only be due to a phonetic coincidence, for both in Japanese and Chinese the characters for "good luck" and for "bat" are pronounced alike, *fu* and *fuku*, respectively (Volker 1950: 18). A bat alone or holding a coin or snail shell is a popular subject of the Japanese miniature carvings in wood and ivory known as *netsuke*.

Like medieval European alchemists, who associated the meaning for bat with those of dragon and hermaphrodite, primitive naturalists have been greatly impressed by the bat's ambiguous nature. Here is a mammalian species that flies like a bird but has teeth and parturates like a mammal. However, unlike other mammals it does not have several pairs of active nipples but, humanlike, suckles its young with but a single pair. At sunrise it retires to sleep—upside down—and at sunset it emerges to pursue its quest for food. During cold parts of the year it hibernates. While most bats live on insects, many are fruit-

eaters. Some are carnivorous and a few species even imbibe the blood of animals and humans, a habit that inspired the Dracula legend of Transylvania. More than any other creature that flies, and certainly any beast of the forest, the bat would seem to be a misfit par excellence. As ancient Latin lore recalls, "when the birds in council passed an edict to exile a certain one, the bat said he was a mouse; again, when another law was proclaimed against mice, he declared that he was a bird" (Gesner 1555, *in* Allen 1967: 4). But where some peoples might have been made uneasy and fearful of the bat because it defied classification, for others—notably the ancient peoples of Mesoamerica and South America—it was probably its very ambivalence, its apparent embodiment of the qualities of several diverse species, that gave it exalted status as living proof of the validity of dualism and transformation.

Throughout the fifty million years of their history, bats have made good use of their wings and successfully invaded the tropical and subtropical belt of the entire globe. Of the six New World families of bats, two in particular have attracted the Indians' imagination, the vampires (*Desmodontidae*) and the leaf-nosed bats (*Phyllostomidae*). It was especially the prominent teeth of the vampire and, of course, the bloody feeding habits that fascinated man. Leaf-nosed bats grow an erect and fleshy "leaf" from the tip of their nose, a membrane which has been linked to spearheads, swords, and, in the case of Mexican picture writing, to flint knives. This leaf, together with the alert eyes and big upright ears, give leaf-nosed bats a certain fierce en garde appearance. By combining the vampire's blood-seeking teeth and the leaf-nosed bat's aggressive air with a human body, the Indian artist succeeded in creating a powerful symbol of numinous qualities. Whether written as a hieroglyph, painted on pottery, modeled in clay and stucco, carved in stone, or depicted in oral literatures, the symbol of the bat played an important religious and social role from Mexico to Peru and from the Circum-Caribbean area to the tropical forest of South America. In the former area the bat was even elevated to the highest possible level and ranked among the supernatural demigods and deities. Along the north coast of South America, in the Venezuelan Andes and on several Caribbean islands, bat ornaments are found in association with death ritual (Wagner 1971: 23–5). The Ur-Bat of tropical forest Indians in the Mato Grosso will eventually devour the Sun (Nimuendajú 1914: 318).

In the Nahuatl language the bat was referred to as *Zinacan*, the Zapotec called it *Piquite ziña*, and the Maya, *Zotz*. Apparently whole tribes counted themselves among the bat deity's followers. There were the Zotzil (Tzotzil), for instance, a Cakchiquel subgroup of highland Guatemala, whose generic name meant "belonging to the bat." The Tzotzil Maya of Chiapas used to call themselves *Zotzil uinic*, "bat men," and supposedly had a stone bat as their patron deity. Aztec merchants referred to the chief town of these batmen as *Zinacantlan*, "the place of the bats"; it is still known as Zinacantan, Mexico. Yet another Zinacantlan is situated in the deep southeast of Guatemala, and bats figure prominently as temple decorations and on sculpture at Copán, in Honduras.

The Zapotec of Oaxaca also seem to have had a bat deity. In fact, judging from the frequency with which the bat is depicted in their art at Monte Albán, it is more than likely that this animal symbolized one of the most important deities of the Zapotec pantheon. The bat-nahual of this god appears often in association with the jaguar but also with the God of Maize. The latter relationship is of particular significance for the overall life-and-death symbolism of our spindle-whorl art, because it links the bat with birth, fertility, and prosperity (reminiscent of its meaning in China and Japan). Beyond this, however, its association with maize (life) among the ancient Zapotec-speakers seems to conflict with its obvious association with death and the Underworld in the ritual art of the Maya. This opposition may, of course, be more apparent than real, i.e., we may be looking at only one side of the coin. For example, bat symbolism is very prominent in association with the Sun God of the Night on the well-known cylindrical *incensarios* from Palenque and other lowland Maya sites. Here the Underworld association is unmistakable. But of course the Night Sun is merely the other side—the alter ego—of the Day Sun, guarantor of life and prosperity, giving the bat an added dimension as well.

Why the fourth *uinal* (twenty-day month) of the Maya calendar should have been represented by the bat glyph is not known. But in keeping with the bat's symbolic meaning, the Maya could not have made a more fortunate choice than the inverted head portrait of the animal at rest to suggest finiteness and the end of a time period's burdensome journey (Berlin 1964). It may be that the Ecuadorian artist meant to express the same symbolic meaning on those spindle whorls on which the bat appears in an alternating pattern of inversion (viz., Funes Sánchez 1970: Pl. 15, Fig. 68).

The most diagnostic physical features that help identify the bat on the whorls are the wings and the nasal membrane of the leaf-nosed bats. As to species, both vampire and the leaf-nosed bat seem to be depicted in the present collection. The wing markings of some of the vampire bats also suggest the tropical species *Diaemus youngi* (Fig. 58). Beyond that, it should be noted that the Ecuadorian artist depicted bats not only as ordinary animals but also as nonordinary, or chimeral, beings that combine typical bat characteristics with those of man as well as other animals, notably the jaguar (e.g., Fig. 69; cf. Estrada 1957b: 53, Pl. 118). Some of the anthropomorphic bats are also distinguished by an erect phallus, thereby not only identifying the sex of the bat demon but also relating it unequivocally to fertility (e.g., Figs. 70, 71). One is also reminded of the phallic symbolism at Uxmal, Yucatan, and of certain Mesoamerican Maya texts that deal with the birth of the bat (Barthel 1966: 106–07). According to one Mexican tradition, recorded in the Codex Magliabecchiano (f. 61r; cf. Franco 1954: 112), the bat was born out of the semen ejaculated on a stone by the masturbating Quetzalcoatl. The bat became the messenger of the gods and master of the Underworld. This same tradition has it that the bat was sent to remove from the goddess Xochiquetzal "that what she had in her vagina." If

Barthel (1966: 107) is correct in his interpretation of this passage that this refers to the *vagina dentata*, the bat's relationship to fertility becomes all the more explicit, for it was through the removal of the vaginal teeth in the primordial women that intercourse, hence fertility, became possible.

As to bat-jaguar association in spindle-whorl art, in one instance the phallus of a bat man appears threatened by a jaguar or puma lying on its back (Fig. 72). On the same whorl there also appears a perching pelican. A very similar composition on a pottery stamp from Ecuador was published by Parducci (1970), except that in that instance bat man, jaguar, and pelican are joined by an opossum (Fig. 77). The jaguar has an upturned batlike nose, as does the opossum, whose phallus is also visible.

On some whorls in our collection, the jaguar is shown side by side with the head of a leaf-nosed bat. On another example a mythological animal combines the head and wings of a bat with the body and front legs of a jaguar. Sometimes the feline features predominate over those of the bat, the latter being indicated only by a typical nose-leaf and an amorphously added wing symbol.

Considering the jaguar's symbolic relationship to the Sun and the cycle of day and night, both in South America and Mesoamerica, its inconographic linkage with the bat is not altogether surprising. One is also reminded of the association of jaguar and bat in shamanism among certain hunting and gathering societies in South America. Among the Yanoama of Venezuela the shaman known as *hewīawan* is initiated by a supernatural jaguar who strips him of his human flesh and re-covers his skeleton with the flesh of a supernatural bat—hence his name, which literally means "bat man" (Wilbert 1963: 222). In any event, whatever the reason, bat and jaguar are as closely associated in Ecuadorian spindle-whorl art as they are in the ritual art of Mesoamerica.

A most peculiar-looking anthropomorphic creature one comes across repeatedly is a leaf-nosed bat with long head appendages in the back which resemble elephant ears (Fig. 75). On one whorl this creature appears with what I believe to be an upside-down vampire (Fig. 75). A similar personage can also be seen on a pottery seal or stamp from Manabí (Edwards 1970: 7). Here he is seated as a high-ranking personage or culture hero on a throne or dais in the aft section of a watercraft, holding a fish or a fishlike paddle, centerboard, or club (Fig. 76). He is confronted by a standing personage holding a paddle. This person's head, as well as the entire second half of the watercraft, has been lost. Only a fish or a fishlike paddle, centerboard, or club in a third (lost) person's hand remains, as does the phallus.

Several of the bats presented in this section hold staffs or objects in their hands which might also represent paddles or centerboards, and one highly stylized anthropomorphic bat even holds a fish or a fishlike paddle similar to the one in the hand of the dignitary of the craft (e.g., Fig. 78). The head of the stylized bat also appears as a boat decoration on the gunwales of a second boat which comes also from a Manabí pottery stamp (Edwards 1970: 6).

Some of the anthropomorphic-zoomorphic representations of the bat on the spindle whorls are reminiscent of certain Mesoamerican and Andean masks on which the upper lip appears rolled backward. I have interpreted this striking feature uniformly as representing the nose leaf of a bat.

Finally it should be noted that whereas there is little doubt as to the identification of the more "realistic" bats on the whorls, the identification of the anthropo-zoomorphic representations is much more difficult. A few of the anthropomorphic creatures I have included under the heading "bats" bear a certain resemblance to the so-called "lizard demons" or "fox demons" of Moche art and students of Andean iconography may prefer to see them as such, rather than as bats. I have no quarrel with such interpretations. Because of the high degree of conventionalization in some of the designs, unequivocal zoological classification is not possible and must remain a matter of personal choice and probability rather than of proof. The same stricture applies, of course, to some other classifications in these pages.

Fig. 58 Black, spheroid. Max. height: 10.5 mm. Max. width: 11.8 mm. Diameter of holes: 3.8 and 4.4 mm.

Fig. 59 Brown, conical. Max. height: 11.3 mm. Max. width: 11 mm. Diameter of holes: 3 and 3.2 mm.

Fig. 60 Black, conical. Max. height: 13 mm. Max. width: 13.5 mm. Diameter of holes: 4.1 and 4.4 mm.

Fig. 61 Gray, conical. Max. height: 12.9 mm. Max. width:
14.1 mm. Diameter of holes: 3.8 and 4 mm.

Fig. 62 Gray, conical. Max. height: 13.7 mm. Max. width:
12 mm. Diameter of holes: 3.3 and 3.9 mm.

Fig. 63 Gray, conical. Max. height: 13.8 mm. Max. width: 13.2 mm. Diameter of holes: 3.2 and 3.4 mm.

Fig. 64 Black, conical. Max. height: 14.4 mm. Max. width: 15.3 mm. Diameter of holes: 2.9 and 3.4 mm.

Fig. 65 Black, conical. Max. height: 14 mm. Max. width: 12.5 mm. Diameter of holes: 3 and 3.1 mm.

Fig. 66 Brown, conical. Max. height: 14.9 mm. Max. width: 13.2 mm. Diameter of holes: 2.9 and 3.5 mm.

Fig. 67 Black, barrel-shaped. Max. height: 14.3 mm. Max.
width: 12.1 mm. Diameter of holes: 4 and 4.4 mm.

Fig. 68 Black, barrel-shaped. Max. height: 14 mm. Max.
width: 9.1 mm. Diameter of holes: 2.8 and 2.9 mm.

Fig. 69 Black, conical. Max. height: 14.4 mm. Max. width: 12.8 mm. Diameter of holes: 2.8 and 2.9 mm.

Fig. 70 Brown, barrel-shaped. Max. height: 14.9 mm. Max. width: 10.7 mm. Diameter of holes: 3.2 and 3.3 mm.

Fig. 71 Orange, oblong. Max. height: 15.9 mm. Max. width: 8.9 mm. Diameter of holes: 2.2 and 2.8 mm.

Fig. 72 Black, conical. Max. height: 13.5 mm. Max. width: 12.7 mm. Diameter of holes: 3.2 and 3.4 mm.

Fig. 73 Black, spheroid. Max. height: 11.3 mm. Max.
width: 13.1 mm. Diameter of holes: 3.8 and 4.2 mm.

Fig. 74 Brown, spheroid. Max. height: 11.4 mm. Max.
width: 11.5 mm. Diameter of holes: 3.4 and 3.7 mm.

Fig. 75 Brown, conical. Max. height: 13.1 mm. Max. width: 11.1 mm. Diameter of holes: 3.5 and 3.8 mm.

Fig. 76 Pottery seal or stamp, Manabí Province. (Photo courtesy H. Wagner and Olaf Holm.)

Fig. 77 Pottery stamp from Manabí. (Parducci 1970.)

Fig. 78 Spindle whorl. Black, conical. Max. height: 16 mm. Max. width: 13.5 mm. Diameter of holes: 2.2 and 2.4 mm.

Fig. 79 Pottery seal or stamp, Manabí Province. (Photo
courtesy Olaf Holm.)

Fig. 80 Spindle whorl. Gray, spheroid. Max. height: 13.2
mm. Max. width: 13.1 mm. Diameter of holes: 3.6 and
4 mm.

THE JAGUAR

As might be expected from its pervasive role in South American shamanism and its prominence in the art of the high cultures of the Andes, the jaguar is one of the animals most frequently depicted on the spindle whorls of the Ecuadorian coast. We do not know the precise nature of the jaguar's position in the mental universe of the ancient Ecuadorians. But if, in addition to sheer quantity, the care lavished on these minute jaguar representations offers any clue, the great spotted feline of tropical America must have been of major ideological importance. That the jaguar motif occurs in connection with other symbols related to the so-called "fertility cult" complex suggests that as in Mexico, Central America, and the Andes the Ecuadorian jaguar was symbolically linked with earth, fertility, night and moon, the Otherworld, and more indirectly with the Sun. The jaguar's relationship with the fertility cult becomes apparent also in northern Manabí and in Esmeraldas, where the god Cocijo is represented not only with feline characteristics but with the bifurcated tongue of the snake (Parducci 1966: 125). According to Estrada (1957b: 150–1, Figs. 113, 115) this represents a merging of feline and serpentine characteristics akin to that of the Mexican deity Quetzalcoatl. Also indicative in this connection is the practice of the Huancavilcas who, when preparing their fields, or when their chiefs fell ill, propitiated their jaguar god with human hearts (Cieza de León, *in* Estrada 1957c: 13).

Deification—or, more correctly, the identification or merging of the jaguar with one or another deity —appears to have been restricted mainly to the high civilizations and those societies with temple cults. But the identification of the jaguar with the shaman is an almost universal theme in South America. The shaman *is* the jaguar, and vice versa, and consequently an actualizing principle between the supernatural and mankind. "The supernatural jaguar," writes Furst (1968: 145), "may be master of the air, of his own species, of all animals and all good plants; he may be bringer of rain, devourer of the planets, foster parent and antagonist of the mythical twins, guardian of sacred places and of gods, and (almost universally) avatar of living and deceased shamans. But he is rarely elevated to the status of 'deity' in the true sense of the term, much less the principal deity, even in cultures where we can speak of a pervasive 'jaguar cult.'" Directly or indirectly almost all these characteristics are reducible to such major features as we have mentioned: earth, fertility, night, the planets, and otherworld. In at least one case, i.e., among the Kayapo (Brazil), the jaguar taught the Indians how to spin (Lukesch 1968: 131). Considering the wide distribution in Central and South America of this dominant theme, it would be surprising if the Manabí jaguar would not fit into a similar symbolic syntax.

The jaguar representations on the whorls are aesthetically some of the finest in the collection. Most are zoomorphic, but on some examples the feline is seen standing manlike on his hind legs or seated like a person, reminiscent of anthropomorphic felines or "were-jaguars" in the art of the Andes or Mesoamerica (Figs. 89, 98, 99). Occasionally the animal is depicted on its back (Fig. 94). Head and teeth are generally accented, and the tip of the nose often bent upward like the membrane of the leaf-nosed bat. The massive elongated body suggests great strength and the powerful paws are given great prominence. The tail is characteristically rolled in at the tip and the fur shows simple spots or more elaborate rosettes with central spots as markings.

Fig. 81 Gray, conical. Max. height: 14 mm. Max. width: 13.5 mm. Diameter of holes: 2.5 and 2.9 mm.

Fig. 82 Black, spherical. Max. height: 11.2 mm. Max. width: 13.2 mm. Diameter of holes: 3 and 3.2 mm.

Fig. 83 Gray, conical. Max. height: 10.2 mm. Max. width:
11.2 mm. Diameter of holes: 3.1 and 3.2 mm.

Fig. 84 Black, barrel-shaped. Max. height: 14.2 mm. Max.
width: 10.6 mm. Diameter of holes: 3.2 and 3.7 mm.

Fig. 85 Gray, conical. Max. height: 12.3 mm. Max. width: 14 mm. Diameter of holes: 3.2 and 3.6 mm.

Fig. 86 Brown, conical. Max. height: 13.2 mm. Max. width: 14.3 mm. Diameter of holes: 3.3 and 3.7 mm.

72

Fig. 87 Brown, spheroid. Max. height: 17.3 mm. Max. width: 17.6 mm. Diameter of holes: 3.3 and 3.4 mm.

Fig. 88 Black, conical. Max. height: 15 mm. Max. width: 15 mm. Diameter of holes: 2.5 and 3.5 mm.

Fig. 89 Gray, barrel-shaped. Max. height: 14 mm. Max. width: 12.3 mm. Diameter of holes: 3.4 and 3.6 mm.

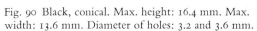

Fig. 90 Black, conical. Max. height: 16.4 mm. Max. width: 13.6 mm. Diameter of holes: 3.2 and 3.6 mm.

Fig. 91 Gray, conical. Max. height: 13 mm. Max. width: 11 mm. Diameter of holes: 3.4 and 3.7 mm.

Fig. 92 Brown, conical. Max. height: 10.6 mm. Max.
width: 10.2 mm. Diameter of holes: 2.9 and 3.5 mm.

Fig. 93 Gray, barrel-shaped. Max. height: 14.6 mm. Max.
width: 9 mm. Diameter of holes: 2.7 and 2.9 mm.

Fig. 94 Black, spheroid. Max. height: 12.2 mm. Max. width: 13.4 mm. Diameter of holes: 4.3 and 4.5 mm.

Fig. 95 Brown, spheroid. Max. height: 11.1 mm. Max. width: 12.9 mm. Diameter of holes: 3.5 and 3.6 mm.

Fig. 96 Black, barrel-shaped.Max. height: 11.5 mm. Max.
width: 10.2 mm. Diameter of holes: 3 and 3.1 mm.

Fig. 97 Brown, conical. Max. height: 15 mm. Max. width:
15.2 mm. Diameter of holes: 3.1 and 3.5 mm.

Fig. 98 Black, barrel-shaped. Max. height: 16.1 mm. Max. width: 10 mm. Diameter of holes: 2.9 and 3.1 mm.

Fig. 99 Black, barrel-shaped. Max. height: 13.5 mm. Max. width: 12.5 mm. Diameter of holes: 2.7 and 3.1 mm.

THE MONKEY

ALTHOUGH MONKEYS are plentiful in tropical America, represent an important part of the native diet, and are the subject of many folk tales and religious beliefs wherever they occur in nature, they form a clearly secondary motif, though an important one, in Ecuadorian spindle-whorl art, especially that of the Manteño culture. Most often the animal is shown in climbing position. Great care is usually given by the artist to achieve a balanced spatial distribution. Although at first glance the animal might also be interpreted as a cat, the shape of the head, with its leveled-off top and ears too close to the skull to be visible, clearly identifies it as simian. The tail too is more typically simian than feline, with the artist stressing its prehensile nature by accentuating the digitlike tip. In some instances there is even a handlike appendix. The spindle-whorl monkeys are usually pictured from the side, with the head turned to stare directly at the viewer. The eyes are usually indicated by the common circle and dot, but in one case the pupils are almond-shaped horizontal excisions (Fig. 103).

In the absence of information on the monkey's role in the life-and-death symbol complex of the Ecuadorian coast, the following data from Mesoamerica is of interest for comparative purposes. As in most other Middle American calendars, the eleventh day of the calendar of Yucatan was named after the monkey, here called *chuen*. The name is also related to the word for Spider Monkey, who was considered the brother of Howler Monkey. Both monkeys were believed to be especially skilled in arts and crafts, and the God of Art and Craft may be represented in monkey form. As such he corresponds to one of the chief deities of the Manche Chol, described by las Casas (1909: ch. 235) as the creator of heaven and earth and of fire and water. Together with his brother he created man. The importance of the monkey-faced god of the Maya can thus scarcely be overstated (Thompson 1970: 322).

Also among the Maya the monkey appears frequently in association with the Moon Goddess. Like the Moon, the monkey is liberal in matters of sex. The Moon Goddess and her lover, the Sun, had the first sexual intercourse, an event which lies at the core of life-death symbolism in Maya ideology, a subject too complex to discuss adequately in these pages. Suffice it to add that the Moon, symbol of sexual intercourse and birth, is also the patroness of spinning and weaving, and is sometimes depicted as a weaving woman in Maya art.

In Costa Rica and Nicaragua the monkey has been recognized by Lothrop (1926: 163) as one of the important motifs occurring in the ceramic art of the Pacific region. It is of course also prominent in the art of ancient Mexico and northern Peru.

Fig. 100 Brown, barrel-shaped. Max. height: 14.1 mm. Max. width: 9.2 mm. Diameter of holes: 2.8 and 3.2 mm.

Fig. 101 Black, barrel-shaped. Max. height: 12 mm. Max. width: 9 mm. Diameter of holes: 3.1 and 3.3 mm.

Fig. 102 Brown, barrel-shaped. Max. height: 12.8 mm. Max. width: 11.5 mm. Diameter of holes: 3.6 and 3.6 mm.

Fig. 103 Black, conical. Max. height: 13.2 mm. Max. width: 13.2 mm. Diameter of holes: 3.2 and 3.9 mm.

Fig. 104 Black, conical. Max. height: 10.5 mm. Max. width: 12.6 mm. Diameter of holes: 4 and 4.2 mm.

THE OPOSSUM

IN AMERICAN INDIAN folklore the opossum occupies an ambiguous position which relates it at once to birth and to death. Although we know that supernatural attributes ascribed to many animals are frequently entirely unrelated to physical facts, in the case of the opossum it may well have been the peculiar characteristics and habits of this unique New World marsupial that gave rise to such dualistic identification.

The female opossum gives birth to two litters a year, each with eighteen to twenty-five young. These are considerably less developed at birth than the young of most mammals; in fact, they are normally only about half-an-inch long and weigh less than 1/2800 of a pound. Gestation lasts only thirteen days and birth of the entire litter takes place in five minutes. Once born the young crawl into the maternal pouch where they remain for sixty to sixty-five days, firmly attached to one of the mother's thirteen nipples. Those undeveloped fetuses unable to reach a nipple do not survive. As the scientific term for opossum, *Didelphidae*, implies, the female has a paired uterus. The male has a forked penis, "hence the belief, attested throughout the whole of North America, that the animal copulates through the nostrils, and that the female sneezes its young into its marsupial pouch" (Hartman 1921: 321–3; Lévi-Strauss 1969: 171). Apart from the belief in superabundance of ejaculated sperm or fetuses by the male there are other recorded Indian traditions according to which the female opossum is capable of conceiving its young without the intervention of the male.

With its rapid gestation and large families the opossum would seem to be a rather obvious symbol of life and fecundity. Also, it resembles man in two important respects—its hind legs are shaped very much like the human hand, and it is omnivorous.

The semantic meaning of the opossum as it relates to death may be partly due to the fact that it is nocturnal, hiding by day in caves or holes in the earth or in trees, and, above all, that it is in the habit of "playing possum." This apparent ability to feign death at will is said to be due to paralysis of the breathing center in the brain when the animal is confronted with danger. Once the danger is removed the opossum quickly recovers consciousness, thereby giving the appearance of having died and come to life again. Perhaps more important than any of these characteristics is the fact that the opossum emits a highly disagreeable, putrid odor. This smell, which is offensive to most other animals and therefore serves as a kind of defense, may be the principal reason why the opossum has been causally linked in Indian folklore with man's loss of immortality, i.e., death. Lévi-Strauss (1969: 249–50; cf. 164–95) writes, "The opossum is characterized by ambiguity: as a nursing mother, it serves life; as a foul-smelling or rotten beast, it anticipates death." It might be noted in this connection that most predators shun the flesh of the opossum, whereas the opossum, in turn, will eat any carrion. The peculiar odor of opossum meat is also a factor in the opossum's role as a guardian of the Underworld in the funerary mythology of the Huichol Indians of Mexico (Furst 1967: 70–1). As the mythological bringer of fire (i.e., life as human beings) to the first (animal) people to inhabit the world, the opossum is sacred to the Huichol and its flesh is taboo. To enforce this prohibition, Opossum stands guard in the Underworld, operating a stone trap in which to crush any soul whose owner violated the taboo in life. Opossum discovers this "sin" by examining the inside of the dead person's mouth with his keen sense of smell. The ambiguity of the opossum's symbolic meaning to the Indians is also apparent in the figure of the Quiché-Maya creator deity and mythological hero Hunahpu. He was considered to be male and female at the same time, the male part, *hunahpu vuch*, corresponding to the opossum.

To deduce the symbolic meaning of the opossum in ancient Ecuador either from its mythological role in Mesoamerica or from its biological characteristics is, of course, conjectural at best. Unfortunately, though Estrada (1957b: 155) believed the opossum representations of Esmeraldas and Manabí to be comparable to Tlacuache, a "god of fecundity" of Oaxaca, on the basis of his own field work in coastal Ecuador, there is little other evidence from Ecuadorian sources on which to base an interpretation.

On the spindle whorls the opossum is usually depicted with a large, almost doglike head, exaggerated long pointed ears, prominent eyes, and a ferocious-looking set of teeth (the opossum in fact has fifty teeth—more than any other mammal). The long tail projects from a rather elongated body, and as though to emphasize its prehensibility the tail is either strongly curved or depicted holding a baby opossum (Fig. 108). "Playing possum" may be indicated by depicting the animal in a dorsal position (Figs. 110, 111). It may be that different species of opossum are

represented and that, in addition to the common American species, *Didelphis marsupialis*, there are representations also of the semi-aquatic "water opossum," or yapok (*Chironectes minimus*), which is distinguished by white stripes along the flanks and which has webbed feet in place of the three prominent independent middle claws of its terrestrial and arboreal cousins (Figs. 109, 111). The aquatic opossum also lives on land but dives into streams and ponds in search of fish and shellfish. The symbolic association of diving into the waters with the journey to the Underworld has already been mentioned elsewhere. Water opossums also give off an even viler odor than their cousins, a characteristic that would seem to strengthen further the identification of this animal with death and the Underworld.

Fig. 105 Black, conical. Max. height: 14.3 mm. Max. width: 16.1 mm. Diameter of holes: 3.7 and 4.1 mm.

Fig. 106 Brown, conical. Max. height: 13.9 mm. Max. width: 14.2 mm. Diameter of holes: 3.2 and 3.8 mm.

Fig. 107 Brown, spheroid. Max. height: 10.2 mm. Max. width: 14.2 mm. Diameter of holes: 3.5 and 3.6 mm.

Fig. 108 Black, conical. Max. height: 11.9 mm. Max. width: 13.6 mm. Diameter of holes: 3.4 and 3.5 mm.

Fig. 109 Brown, barrel-shaped. Max. height: 14.5 mm. Max. width: 10.9 mm. Diameter of holes: 3.2 and 3.7 mm.

Fig. 110 Gray, conical. Max. height: 12.2 mm. Max.
width: 14 mm. Diameter of holes: 4.1 and 4.3 mm.

Fig. 111 Black, conical. Max. height: 12.7 mm. Max.
width: 14.7 mm. Diameter of holes: 4 and 4.3 mm.

FISHES

CONSIDERING the strong maritime orientation of the peoples of the Ecuadorian littoral, it is not surprising to find fishes among the prominent motifs of spindle-whorl art. Nevertheless, we should not assume that fish were depicted solely because of their economic importance; as elsewhere in the world, the fish probably had symbolic significance far beyond its culinary value.

As a fertility symbol the fish is widely distributed throughout the tropical forest area of South America. It occurs in ritual song, in narratives, as masks, costumes, body paint, and amulets. It decorates baskets, boats, and paraphernalia. Wooden bull-roarers are made in the shape of fish and so are ceremonial clubs, etc. However, no matter how varied the shapes and forms in which the fish symbol occurs, it carries one basic message—that of fertility (Kunike 1912). Accordingly, fish are believed by many Indians to be able to impregnate and to deliver the women, and, on the Xingú, women fashion their bast pubic covers to represent the meréschu-fish (Schmidt 1905: 395). Also for indigenous Mexico, Seler (1904: 275) refers to the fish as the animal of fertility. In Ecuador, large effigies of fish were kept in such a prominent place as the temple at Manta, a fact which Thompson (1936: 111) relates to the presence of a special religion or cult of fishermen.

It is of course natural that people who spent much of their life on the water and depended heavily on the products of the ocean for survival should have come to worship the sea and to have chosen fish as a symbol to represent it in their ceremonial art and ritual. Worship of the sea and of fish is well known, for example, from neighboring Peru, to the south. According to Garcilaso de la Vega, the Inca ". . . of the coast made the sea their god, which in their language they call Mamachoca [sic], and is as much as to say the mother-sea; the whale for its prodigious bigness was in no less veneration than the rest, and every sort of fish which abounded amongst them was deified, because they believed that the first fish in the world above them always takes care to provide them with a number of the like sort or species sufficient to maintain and nourish them" (Mead 1909: 127).

The symbolic identification between the sea and the Magna Mater is by no means peculiar to Peruvian coastal Indians. Even agricultural peoples living some distance from the sea and lacking a maritime tradition are known to worship the ocean as a mother goddess; to cite one example from Mesoamerica, the Indians of the Sierra Madre Occidental in Western Mexico worship the Pacific Ocean as "Our Mother Haramára" and make pilgrimages to the coast to ask for fecundity and rain in shoreline ceremonies. Fish and fish blood are also prominent among the offerings made to the various supernaturals that govern fertility. Fish worship is also known from Asian, Oceanic, Near Eastern, European, and other peoples. Schneider (1946: 289) refers to the fish as the Mystic Ship of Life, which may change here and there in specific form "but at all times it is the *spindle spinning out the cycle of life* after the pattern of the lunar zodiac" (italics added).

Because of their spindle-shaped form and its consequent association with mandorla symbolism, fish have a dualistic meaning: they are phallic as well as purely spiritual and uterine. But in either case they symbolize fecundity at its fullest—one need only think of the enormous numbers of eggs they deposit. Inhabiting and arising from the unfathomable depths of the Mother Sea, fish become the bearers of numinous, chthonic messages of transcendental meaning.

On the spindle whorls, fish are depicted in a naturalistic side view, showing scales, fins, gills, and other detail. Fish are seen swimming to the right and to the left, and upward as well as downward. Some of the fish representations are done in the so-called X-ray style, showing the outer form as well as the spinal column. Certain designs also appear to depict dead and decaying fish.

Fig. 112 Black, conical. Max. height: 14.3 mm. Max.
width: 14 mm. Diameter of holes: 3.4 and 3.6 mm.

Fig. 113 Black, conical. Max. height: 14.1 mm. Max.
width: 15 mm. Diameter of holes: 4 and 4.1 mm.

Fig. 114 Brown, spheroid. Max. height: 12.3 mm. Max. width: 12.3 mm. Diameter of holes: 3.4 and 3.4 mm.

Fig. 115 Gray, spheroid. Max. height: 10.6 mm. Max. width: 13.4 mm. Diameter of holes: 4 and 4 mm.

Fig. 116 Gray, spheroid. Max. height: 11.5 mm. Max. width: 14 mm. Diameter of holes: 4 and 4.3 mm.

Fig. 117 Orange, barrel-shaped. Max. height: 12.6 mm. Max. width: 11.7 mm. Diameter of holes: 3.6 and 3.7 mm.

Fig. 118 Gray, conical. Max. height: 13.4 mm. Max. width: 12 mm. Diameter of holes: 3.7 and 4 mm.

Fig. 119 Gray, conical. Max. height: 13.2 mm. Max. width: 11.5 mm. Diameter of holes: 3.4 and 3.6 mm.

Fig. 120 Gray, conical. Max. height: 13.8 mm. Max. width: 13.9 mm. Diameter of holes: 4 and 4.1 mm.

Fig. 121 Black, conical. Max. height: 16.4 mm. Max. width: 17.4 mm. Diameter of holes: 3.9 and 4.6 mm.

REPTILES: SNAKE AND LIZARD

SERPENT SYMBOLISM in religious traditions and ritual art the world over attests to man's eternal fascination with the snake. The symbolic meaning of snakes varies from place to place, but, if one may generalize, on the whole it is ambiguous, symbolizing good and evil, life and death, etc. The snake's identification with fecundity and perennial life is generally assumed to be due to its striking habit of periodically shedding its skin, and with it—so it is widely believed—old age and death. Seemingly in possession of the secret of eternal life, the snake became the hoped-for companion of the shaman as he entered upon the cure of the patient—just as contemporary physicians are still identified by the ancient Greek emblem of the caduceus, with its serpent coiled around the staff. In the time of Moses the brazen serpent gave new life to those who lifted their eyes to it, and Moses' divining rod was transformed into a serpent to swallow the lesser snakes of the sorcerers of Pharaoh. As phallic symbol the snake became the embodiment of fertility and life and was worshipped as such from early dynastic Egypt through the Near East to India. To the Greeks and Romans it was a guardian spirit; the snake kept in the cage in Athena's temple in Athens was considered the guardian spirit of the temple. China and Japan are full of traditions that treat the snake as a phallic symbol and relate it to fertility: "In old Japan it was sometimes taken that the whole population of a certain village was descended from a snake that in human form had got a woman with child" (Volker 1950: 144). In Africa, too, "the most fundamental ideas of all kinds of African snake beliefs are those of resurrection and fecundity" (Hambly 1931).

Basically the same serpent symbolism prevails also throughout the New World. Many North American Indians attribute to snakes supernatural powers to influence rain, thunder, and lightning. To the Huichol, the Rain Mothers appear as serpents, as does the sea. Rainstorms are believed caused by a giant serpent lashing the world. In the pre-Columbi-an art of Mexico and Central America the snake is omnipresent: "Nowhere else in the world are so many carvings of snakes to be found as on the temples and monuments of the Toltecs, Aztecs, and Mayans" (Morris and Morris 1965: 38). Here as elsewhere serpent symbolism revolves around the fundamental theme of life and death and rebirth, as exemplified by Coatlicue, She of the Serpent Skirts, Mother of the Gods, and divine patroness of the earth, life, and death; Tlaloc, God of Rain; and, of course, Quetzalcoatl, the Plumed Serpent, creator and master of life.

Moving south we find practically the same symbolism throughout indigenous South America. It is because of this universality of beliefs about the snake that we are safe in assuming that the prehistoric Ecuadorian Indians also recognized the snake as a powerful symbol of mankind, connected with fecundity, life, death, and rebirth. What Roth (1915: 369–70) says of snake symbolism among many northern South American tribes may well hold also for the Ecuadorian coast—e.g., the snake as progenitor of man, symbol of perennial life, rain, fertility, and also as potential lover of women. In fact, according to Funes Sánchez (1970: 163), there is some evidence that Ecuadorian Indians recognized "snakes as symbol of power, wisdom and fertility." Dignitaries and shamans from Manabí and Imbabura, therefore, used serpents as symbols of command, as crowns, and as scepters. An early Colonial account by Augustín de Zárate (n.d.: 518) also speaks of effigies "of large serpents which they worshipped" in the temples of the people of Manabí (Parducci 1966: 125; cf. Cieza de León 1862: 403, in Estrada 1957b: 13).

In spindle-whorl iconography, reptiles—especially snakes, iguanas, and crocodiles—are somewhat less common than birds and lizards, but they are nevertheless prominent motifs. As elsewhere, the symbolic meaning of reptilian creatures—iguanas, crocodiles, snakes, and "dragons"—tends to blend. In Ecuadorian pre-Columbian art, including that of the spindle whorls, these reptiles occur in close association, and seem to fit well into the symbolic syntax of the "fertility cult" complex. The same applies to Mexican and Central American ideology and art.

Some snakes, of course, could also be interpreted as eels, and, likewise, some of the iguanas might be alligators or crocodiles. This applies especially to one of the naturalistic "iguanas" included here (Figs. 124, 126). Both creatures have a serrated back but vary considerably in the shape of the head, one being blunt like that of the iguana, the other more pointed,

like that of the crocodile. There is also one exquisite anthropomorphized standing crocodile adorned with a wide necklace (Fig. 125).[9] The anthropomorphic spindle whorl depicting a chimeral creature with joined hands (Fig. 127) is reminiscent of lizard-man representations of the Milagro Phase.

[9] This creature could also be interpreted as a fox, but the serrated back leads me to include it under the present heading.

Fig. 122 Orange, flattened spheroid. Max. height: 10 mm. Max. width: 10.4 mm. Diameter of holes: 3.2 and 3.5 mm.

Fig. 123 Black, conical. Max. height: 12.4 mm. Max. width: 10.9 mm. Diameter of holes: 3 and 3.3 mm.

Fig. 124 Brown, spheroid. Max. height: 10.8 mm. Max.
width: 12.7 mm. Diameter of holes: 3.7 and 4.4 mm.

Fig. 125 Black, barrel-shaped. Max. height: 14.2 mm.
Max. width: 11.5 mm. Diameter of holes: 2.8 and 3.2 mm.

Fig. 126 Gray, spheroid. Max. height: 11.7 mm. Max. width: 14.8 mm. Diameter of holes: 3.2 and 4 mm.

Fig. 127 Black, grooved. Max. height: 11.7 mm. Max. width: 9.4 mm. Diameter of holes: 3 and 3.3 mm.

FROGS, TOADS, AND SLUGS

APART FROM certain insects—which as a whole are absent from spindle-whorl iconography—few creatures embody the concept of metamorphosis and transition better than the frog. Extraordinarily fertile, born in water, it passes from egg to a wholly aquatic stage in which it resembles a fish before transforming itself into an air-breathing, four-legged amphibian as well adapted to water as it is to land. Little wonder that the frog has long been a symbol of transformation (in this connection one need only recall the many folktales of the frog and the prince). The world over, the frog is also closely associated with rain and the related symbolism of fecundity and the Moon. In Mexico frogs were the companions of the rain god Tlaloc, and the Chac ceremonies of the Maya likewise emphasized the association of the frog with rain and fertility. At the same time, we cannot overlook the fact that in Central and South America certain frogs, especially those belonging to the family *Dendrobatidae*, are highly poisonous—indeed, one has been found to secrete the most powerful natural poison known to man. Some Indians have long employed frog poison for their weapons, and hunters of more than one Amazonian tribe rub frog poison into self-inflicted wounds to induce a violent illness followed by trances in order to achieve supernatural power for the hunt (Daly and Myers 1967: 970–3; Carneiro 1970: 340).

Whether the amphibians depicted on the Ecuadorian spindle whorls (Figs. 128, 129) are meant to be frogs or toads is not certain. The rows of white dots might represent warts, in which case the creature would probably be a toad, or else they might depict the characteristic exudations of certain poisonous frogs that figure in hunting ritual and other magic. On the other hand, toads are also venomous, secreting poison from glands in the skin. In fact, the poison of one species, *Bufo marinus*, has been found to contain bufotenine, a hallucinogen also present in certain plants.

A differentiation between toads and frogs in spindle-whorl art is not insignificant, in light of the important mythological and cosmological role of the toad in South America as well as Mesoamerica. In a recent paper on this problem, Furst (1972: 37–46) demonstrates a basic similarity between toad symbolism in Mexico and South America, where aboriginal inhabitants shared the concept of the toad as the monstrous, and indeed cannibalistic, animal manifestation of the Mother Goddess or Earth Mother. The Aztec earth monster Tlaltecuhtli, with her jaguar claws and fangs, was shown to be essentially the same being as the toad-jaguar foster mother of the Hero Twins of South American tropical forest tradition, or the Earth Mother in her form as a large *Bufo* toad among the Tacana of Bolivia. Even the Aztec name, Tlaltecuhtli, and the Tacana name for the Earth Mother as toad, Eaua Quinahi, mean the same thing —Owner or Master of the Earth.

We cannot, therefore, assume that toad or frog symbolism in Central and South American art is always related only to fecundity or rain; the symbolism may vary according to its context, or it may be ambivalent.

The snails and slugs of Ecuadorian coastal iconography are assigned by Estrada (1957a: 40) to the symbol complex of the fertility cult; in fact, slugs are often identified in folk literature with the snake as symbols of fertility, the origin of life, and the male seed. The naturalistic examples in the present collection represent elongated and biconical forms of the shell-less slug; the biconical form, according to Estrada, is characteristic of the Manteño Culture. As for snails, it may be that the "geometric" spirals on certain non-representational spindle whorls are actually conventionalized snail shells as symbol of the origin of life and the circle of life and death.

Förstemann (1904: 427) connects the snail in Maya tradition with the winter solstice which occurs in the eighth month of the Maya year, the month of the death and rebirth of the Sun. In Aztec manuscripts the sea snail also maintains a close relationship with the gods of death. In connection with Förstemann's idea of a relationship between snail and winter solstice in Maya tradition, it is interesting to note that according to Cirlot (1962: 285) the slug symbolizes "the silent tendency of darkness to move towards life," as is so well expressed in Egyptian mythology. In Maya ideology, the snail, as an animal related to the water and the subterranean region, appears as the symbol of the Great Mother, the Moon Goddess, who is the goddess of earth and water. In Central Mexican cosmology the snail connects Quetzalcoatl with the surface of the earth. The snail was also related to Xolotl, who guided the Sun through the Underworld, and to Tepeyollotli, god of mountains and caverns.

Fig. 128 Black, conical. Max. height: 12.9 mm. Max. width: 10.7 mm. Diameter of holes: 3.5 and 4.2 mm.

Fig. 129 Black, conical. Max. height: 14.4 mm. Max. width: 14.2 mm. Diameter of holes: 3.2 and 3.5 mm.

Fig. 130 Black, conical. Max. height: 13.1 mm. Max.
width: 14.5 mm. Diameter of holes: 3.5 and 3.8 mm.

Fig. 131 Black, conical. Max. height: 11.7 mm. Max.
width: 13.7 mm. Diameter of holes: 3.8 and 4 mm.

97

THE HOCKER OR "SPLAYED CREATURE"

A FREQUENT REPRESENTATION in spindle-whorl iconography is a figure shown with knees apart of the type sometimes described as the "hocker" motif. Similar figures can be found in the Manteño Culture, carved in low relief and on stone slabs where "the upper end of one surface is dominated by a human or animal figure with the legs and arms bent to each side. The head often fits into a niche in an ornamental frieze with a repetitive geometric pattern. A pair of birds, disks, or monkeys often accompanies the principal figure" (Meggers 1966: 126).

The Ecuadorian motif bears a striking resemblance to what Fraser (1966), in an article seeking to trace the diffusion of an apparently complex pattern, calls the "heraldic woman," familiar in Oceanic art. Many theories have been advanced for the meaning of this figure: woman, monkey, iguana, frog, and even insect. The various designs may in fact represent different anthropomorphized animals as well as humans, but, as Muller (1971: 67) points out in a critique of Fraser's diffusion theory, the splayed, or bilaterally symmetrical, position is "one that occurs very widely in childbirth. Furthermore, in Oceania, where this design seems to have its most continuous distribution, very similar positions are among the most common for coitus" (Ford and Beach 1951: 24).

In Mexico, the Earth Mother as monstrous toad (Tlaltecuhtli), is depicted in the same "hocker" position, emphasizing her creative, birth-giving function just as her claws and fangs symbolize the other side of her dualistic life-death nature. That the "hocker," or squatting position, is in fact symbolic of birth— i.e., creation—is overwhelmingly clear from the depiction of the goddess Tlazolteotl in the Codex Borbonicus, where she is shown in the act of giving birth to the young maize god Centéotl.

If this interpretation of the "hocker" or splayed figure as a female receptive to coitus or about to give birth is correct, then of course it does not matter whether the particular figures shown on the spindle whorls are human or animal (e.g., Tlazolteotl is represented in human form whereas Tlaltecuhtli is a monstrous animal). What counts, in ancient Ecuador, as in Mexico, is fertility, of which the Magna Mater is the archetype.

Some of our spindle-whorl "hockers" are executed in the X-ray style, emphasizing the spinal column (Figs. 133–8) and even internal organs or a fetus within the body of the mother (Fig. 132). In several designs the artist, by indicating the external female genitalia between the legs either by a cleft (Fig 133) or a circle (Fig. 137), leaves no doubt about the figure's sex.

Fig. 132 Black, oblong. Max. height: 13.8 mm. Max. width: 7.7 mm. Diameter of holes: 2.7 and 3.8 mm.

Fig. 133 Black, conical. Max. height: 15.3 mm. Max. width: 13 mm. Diameter of holes: 4 and 4.2 mm.

Fig. 134 Black, conical. Max. height: 12.3 mm. Max. width: 12.2 mm. Diameter of holes: 3.7 and 3.9 mm.

Fig. 135 Black, conical. Max. height: 11.6 mm. Max. width: 12.9 mm. Diameter of holes: 3.7 and 4 mm.

Fig. 136 Black, conical. Max. height: 11.9 mm. Max. width: 12.1 mm. Diameter of holes: 3.5 and 3.6 mm.

Fig. 137 Brown, conical. Max. height: 13 mm. Max. width: 11.3 mm. Diameter of holes: 2.6 and 2.7 mm.

Fig. 138 Gray, conical. Max. height: 13.2 mm. Max. width: 13.7 mm. Diameter of holes: 2.7 and 3.4 mm.

Fig. 139 Black, conical. Max. height: 12.5 mm. Max. width: 13.7 mm. Diameter of holes: 3.7 and 3.9 mm.

GEOMETRIC DESIGNS AND OTHERS

GEOMETRIC and abstract designs are very common in spindle-whorl art and, as has been stressed before, probably carried as intelligible a symbolic message for the native observer as any of the representational decorations. Unfortunately, we lack the necessary insights to unlock the meaning of the non-representational designs; all we can do from our cultural vantage point is to enjoy them aesthetically and attempt to interpret them according to their degree of resemblance to familiar objects. Thus, the common zigzag band with parallel lines may appear to us like a snake, or the diamond-shaped meander like the scales of reptiles. The oft-repeated spiral looks like a snail shell, but whether that is what the prehistoric artist meant to portray we will never know. In contemporary Mesoamerican Indian art spirals are often snakes used as water symbols, but they can also mean long ritual journeys with a return to the beginning. It is best, perhaps, to refrain from interpretation of these esoteric symbols, remembering only with Lumholtz (1903) that no primitive artist ever made a meaningless design.

Fig. 140 Black, conical. Max. height: 15.8 mm. Max. width: 14.9 mm. Diameter of holes: 2.6 and 3.3 mm.

Fig. 141 Gray, spheroid. Max. height: 16.1 mm. Max. width: 19.1 mm. Diameter of holes: 3.6 and 4.2 mm.

Fig. 143 Gray, biconical. Max. height: 16.7 mm. Max. width: 20.1 mm. Diameter of holes: 3.7 and 3.8 mm.

Fig. 142 Gray, biconical. Max. height: 17.1 mm. Max. width: 17.7 mm. Diameter of holes: 3.3 and 3.5 mm.

Fig. 144 Black, conical. Max. height: 16.9 mm. Max. width: 17.5 mm. Diameter of holes: 4 and 4.3 mm.

Fig. 145 Black, conical. Max. height: 9.5 mm. Max. width: 11.6 mm. Diameter of holes: 3.5 and 3.8 mm.

Fig. 146 Gray, conical. Max. height: 13.5 mm. Max. width: 13.8 mm. Diameter of holes: 3.5 and 4.1 mm.

Fig. 147 Gray, conical. Max. height: 16 mm. Max. width: 12.8 mm. Diameter of holes: 3.5 and 3.5 min.

Fig. 148 Gray, conical. Max. height: 14.1 mm. Max.
width: 14.9 mm. Diameter of holes: 3.8 and 3.9 mm.

Fig. 149 Black, conical. Max. height: 10.8 mm. Max.
width: 13.8 mm. Diameter of holes: 3.9 and 3.9 mm.

Fig. 151 Gray, spheroid. Max. height: 12.6 mm. Max. width: 12.8 mm. Diameter of holes: 3.1 and 3.3 mm.

Fig. 150 Black, spheroid. Max. height: 11.6 mm. Max. width: 13.2 mm. Diameter of holes: 3.9 and 3.9 mm.

Fig. 152 Gray, conical. Max. height: 14.7 mm. Max. width: 16.1 mm. Diameter of holes: 3.6 and 4.1 mm.

Fig. 153 Brown, spheroid. Max. height: 13.3 mm. Max. width: 13.8 mm. Diameter of holes: 3.4 and 3.5 mm.

Fig. 154 Black, conical. Max. height: 15.9 mm. Max. width: 12.9 mm. Diameter of holes: 2.9 and 3.2 mm.

Fig. 155 Gray, conical. Max. height: 11.8 mm. Max. width: 12.8 mm. Diameter of holes: 3.1 and 3.2 mm.

Fig. 156 Gray, conical. Max. height: 14.7 mm. Max. width: 13.1 mm. Diameter of holes: 3.6 and 4.4 mm.

Fig. 157 Gray, conical. Max. height: 9.5 mm. Max. width: 15.5 mm. Diameter of holes: 2.9 and 3.1 mm.

Bibliography

ALLEN, GLOVER MORRILL
1967 Bats. Harvard University Press, Cambridge, Mass.

ANDERS, FERDINAND
1963 Das Pantheon der Maya. Akademische Druck- und Verlagsanstalt, Graz.

ARMILLAS, PEDRO
1945 Los dioses de Teotihuacán. *Anales del Instituto de Etnología Americana*, vol. 6, pp. 35–61. Universidad Nacional del Cuyo, Mendoza.

BARTHEL, THOMAS S.
1966 Mesoamerikanische Fledermausdämonen. *Tribus*, vol. 15, pp. 101–124. Linden-Museum für Völkerkunde, Stuttgart.

BERLIN, HEINRICH
1964 El glifo "zotz invertido." *Antropología e Historia de Guatemala*, vol. 16, no. 1, pp. 1–7. Ministerio de Educación Pública, Guatemala.

BIESE, LEO P.
1960 SpindleWhorls from Panamá Viejo. *Panama Archaeologist*, vol. 3, no. 1, pp. 35–45. Archaeological Society of Panama, Balboa, Canal Zone.

BIRD, JUNIUS B.
1968 Handspun Yarn Production Rates in the Cuzco Region of Peru. *Textile Museum Journal*, vol. 2, no. 3, pp. 9–16. The Textile Museum, Washington.

BIRD, JUNIUS, and LOUISA BELLINGER
1954 Paracas Fabrics and Nazca Needlework. The Textile Museum, Washington.

BORHEGYI, STEPHAN F. DE
1959 Pre-Columbian Cultural Connections between Mesoamerica and Ecuador. *Middle American Research Records*, vol. 2, no. 6, pp. 141–156. Middle American Research Institute, Publication 18. Tulane University, New Orleans.

BUECHLER, HANS C., and JUDITH-MARIA BUECHLER
1971 The Bolivian Aymara. Case Studies in Cultural Anthropology. Holt, Rinehart and Winston, New York.

BUITRÓN, ANÍBAL
1956 La tecnificación de la industria textil manual de los indios de Ecuador. *In* Estudios antropológicos publicados en homenaje al doctor Manuel Gamio, pp. 287–293. Sociedad Mexicana de Antropología, Universidad Nacional Autónoma de México, Mexico.

BUSHNELL, G. H. S.
1951 The Archaeology of the Santa Elena Peninsula in South-West Ecuador. *Occasional Publications of the Cambridge University Museum of Archaeology and Ethnology*, I. Cambridge University Press, Cambridge.

1952 The Stone Carvings of Manabí, Ecuador. *In* Proceedings of the Thirtieth International Congress of Americanists, Cambridge, pp. 58–59. The Royal Anthropological Institute, London.

CARNEIRO, ROBERT L.
1970 Hunting and Hunting Magic among the Amahuaca of the Peruvian Montaña. *Ethnology*, vol. 9, no. 4, pp. 331–341. University of Pittsburgh, Pittsburgh.

CASAMIQUELA, RODOLFO M.
1964 Estudio del nillatún y la religión araucana. Universidad Nacional de Sur, Bahía Blanca.

CASAS, BARTOLOMÉ DE LAS
1909 Apologética historia de las Indias. Bailly, Baillieré e hijos, Madrid.

CASO, ALFONSO, and IGNACIO BERNAL
1952 Urnas de Oaxaca. *Memorias del Instituto Nacional de Antropología e Historia*, II. Mexico.

CIRLOT, JUAN EDUARDO
1962 A Dictionary of Symbols. (Trans. from the Spanish by Jack Sage.) Philosophical Library, New York.

COE, MICHAEL D.
1960 Archaeological Linkages with North and South America at La Victoria, Guatemala. *American Anthropologist*, vol. 62, no. 3, pp. 363–393. American Anthropological Society, Washington.

DALY, JOHN W., and CHARLES W. MYERS
1967 Toxicity of Panamanian Poison Frogs (Dendrobates): Some Biological and Chemical Aspects. *Science*, vol. 156, pp. 970–973. American Association for the Advancement of Science, Washington.

DURÁN, FRAY DIEGO
1971 Book of the Gods and Rites and the Ancient Calendar. (Trans. and ed. by Fernando Horcasitas and Doris Heyden.) University of Oklahoma Press, Norman.

EDWARDS, CLINTON R.
1970 Possibilities of Pre-Columbian Maritime Contacts among the New World Civilizations. *Latin American Center Pamphlet Series*, no. 8. University of Wisconsin, Milwaukee.

EMERY, IRENE
1966 The Primary Structure of Fabrics: An Illustrated Classification. The Textile Museum, Washington.

ESTRADA, VÍCTOR EMILIO
1957a Ultimas Civilizaciones Pre-Históricas de la Cuenca del Río Guayas. *Publicación del Museo Víctor Emilio Estrada*, no. 2. Guayaquil.
1957b Prehistoria de Manabí. *Publicación del Museo Víctor Emilio Estrada*, no. 4. Guayaquil.

1957c Los Huancavilcas. Ultimos Civilizaciones Pre-Históricas de la Costa del Guayas. *Publicación del Museo Víctor Emilio Estrada*, no. 3. Guayaquil.

1958 Las Culturas Pre-Clásicas, Formativas o Arcaicas del Ecuador. *Publicación del Museo Víctor Emilio Estrada*, no. 5. Guayaquil.

1959 Arte aborigen del Ecuador: sellos y pintaderas. *Humanitas, Boletín Ecuatoriano de Antropología*, vol. I, no. 2. Editorial Universitaria, Quito.

1962 Arqueología de Manabí Central. *Publicación del Museo Víctor Emilio Estrada*, no. 7. Guayaquil.

ESTRADA, VÍCTOR EMILIO, and BETTY J. MEGGERS
1961 A Complex of Traits of Probable Transpacific Origin on the Coast of Ecuador. *American Anthropologist*, vol. 63, no. 5, pp. 913–939. American Anthropological Association, Washington.

ESTRADA, VÍCTOR EMILIO, BETTY J. MEGGERS, and CLIFFORD EVANS
1962 Possible Transpacific Contact on the Coast of Ecuador. *Science*, vol. 135, pp. 371–372. American Association for the Advancement of Science, Washington.

FELTER, JAMES WARREN
1967 450 diseños del 500 D.C. OCEPA, Quito.

FERIZ, HANS
1958 The Problem of the Stone "Thrones" of Ecuador and the Stone "Yokes" of Tajin. *In* Proceedings of the Thirty-second International Congress of Americanists, Copenhagen, pp. 395–401. Munksgaard, Copenhagen.

FORD, CLELLAN STEARNS, and FRANK A. BEACH
1951 Patterns of Sexual Behavior. Harper & Row, New York.

FÖRSTEMANN, E.
1904 Aids to the Deciphering of the Maya Manuscripts. *In* Mexican and Central American Antiquities, Calendar Systems, and History (trans. by Charles P. Bowditch), *Bureau of American Ethnology, Bulletin 28*, pp. 397–472. Smithsonian Institution, Washington.

FRANCO, JOSÉ LUCIANO
1954 Un notable ejemplar de arte individual en cerámica azteca con una breve discusión sobre el Xochimecatl y Quetzalcoatl. *Yan*, no. 3. Centro de Investigaciones Antropológicas de México, Mexico.

FRASER, DOUGLAS
1966 The Heraldic Woman: A Study in Diffusion. *In* The Many Faces of Primitive Art (Douglas Fraser, ed.), pp. 36–99. Prentice-Hall, Englewood Cliffs.

FRÖDIN, OTTO, and ERLAND VON NORDENSKIÖLD
1918 Über Zwirnen and Spinnen bei den Indianern Südamerikas. *Göteborgs Kungl. Vetenskaps- och Vitterhets-Sámhälles Handlingar*, Band 19. W. Zachrissons Boktryckeri Aktiebolag, Göteborg.

FUNES SÁNCHEZ, MARÍA ANTONIETA
1970 Arte precolombino ecuatoriano: las fusaiolas o torteras del litoral. Editorial Casa de la Cultura Ecuatoriana, Núcleo de Guayas, Guayaquil.

FURST, PETER T.
1967 Huichol Conceptions of the Soul. *Folklore Americas*, vol. 27, no. 2, pp. 39–113. Los Angeles.

1968 The Olmec Were-Jaguar Motif in the Light of Ethnographic Reality. *In* Dumbarton Oaks Conference on the Olmec (Elizabeth P. Benson, ed.), pp. 143–178. Dumbarton Oaks, Washington.

1972 Symbolism and Psychopharmacology: The Toad as the Earth Mother in Indian America. *In* Religión en Mesoamerica, XII Mesa Redonda, pp. 37–46. Sociedad Mexicana de Antropología, Mexico.

GESNER, KONRAD
1555 Historiae animalium liber III. Apud C. Froschoverum, Tiguri.

GOODELL, GRACE
1968 A Study of Andean Spinning in the Cuzco Region. *Textile Museum Journal*, vol. 2, no. 3, pp. 2–8. The Textile Museum, Washington.

HAMBLY, WILFRID DYSON
1931 Serpent Worship in Africa. *Field Museum of Natural History, Publication 289, Anthropological Series*, vol. XXI, no. I. Chicago.

HARTMAN, CARL
1921 Traditional Belief Concerning the Generation of the Opossum. *Journal of American Folklore*, vol. 34, no. 133. American Folklore Society, New York.

HEYERDAHL, THOR
1964 Feasible Ocean Routes to and from the Americas in Precolumbian Times. *In* Actas del XXXV Congreso Internacional de Americanistas, Mexico, vol. 1, pp. 133–142. Mexico.

HOLM, OLAF
1963 Cámara funeraria No. 5 "Bellavista" (Ecuador). *Cuadernos de Historia y Arqueología*, años 12–13 (1962–63), vols. 11–12, nos. 28–29, pp. 129–157. Casa de la Cultura Ecuatoriana, Núcleo de Guayas, Guayaquil.

JETT, STEPHEN C.
1971 Diffusion versus Independent Development: The Bases of Controversy. *In* Man across the Sea: Problems of Pre-Columbian Contacts (Carroll L. Riley, J. Charles Kelley, Campbell W. Pennington, and Robert L. Rands, eds.), pp. 5–53. University of Texas Press, Austin.

JIJÓN Y CAAMAÑO, JACINTO
1945 Antropología Prehispánica del Ecuador. La Prensa Católica, Quito. (Reprint 1951.)

KRICKEBERG, WALTER
1928 Mexikanisch-peruanische Parallelen: Ein Überblick

und eine Ergänzung. *In* Festschrift Pater Wilhelm Schmidt (W. Koppers, ed.), pp. 378–393. Mechitharisten-Congregations-Buchdruckerei, Vienna.

KUNIKE, HUGO
1912 Der Fisch als Fruchtbarkeitssymbol bei den Waldindianern Südamerikas. *Anthropos*, vol. 7, pp. 206–229. Vienna.

LARREA, CARLOS MANUEL
1958 El misterio de las llamadas sillas de piedra de Manabí. Editorial Casa de la Cultura Ecuatoriana, Quito.

LEHMANN, HENRI
1962 Pre-Columbian Ceramics. (Trans. by Galway Kinnell.) Elek Books, London.

LESSING, FERDINAND
1934–35 Über die Symbolsprache in der chinesischen Kunst. *Sinica*, 1934–35, pp. 22–25. China Institut zu Frankfurt am Main, Frankfurt.

LÉVI-STRAUSS, CLAUDE
1969 The Raw and the Cooked. (Trans. from French by John and Doreen Weightman.) Harper and Row, New York.

LOTHROP, SAMUEL KIRKLAND
1926 Pottery of Costa Rica and Nicaragua. 2 vols. *Contributions from the Museum of the American Indian*, vol. VIII. Museum of the American Indian, Heye Foundation, New York.

LUKESCH, ANTON
1968 Mythos und Leben der Kayapo. *Acta Ethnologica et Linguistica*, no. 12, Series Americana 2. (E. Stiglmayr, ed.). Vienna.

LUMHOLTZ, CARL
1903 Unknown Mexico. 2 vols. MacMillan and Co., Ltd., London.

MASON, J. ALDEN
1961 The Ancient Civilizations of Peru. 2nd edition. Penguin Books, Baltimore.

MEAD, CHARLES W.
1909 The Fish in Ancient Peruvian Art. *In* Putnam Anniversary Volume: Anthropological Essays, pp. 126–136. G. E. Stechert & Co., New York.

MEGGERS, BETTY J.
1966 Ecuador. Frederick A. Praeger, New York and Washington.

MORRIS, RAMONA, and DESMOND MORRIS
1965 Men and Snakes. McGraw-Hill, New York.

MULLER, JON
1971 Style and Culture Contact. *In* Man across the Sea: Problems of Pre-Columbian Contacts (Carroll L. Riley, J. Charles Kelley, Campbell W. Pennington, and Robert L. Rands, eds.), pp. 66–78. University of Texas Press.

MUSEUM OF PRIMITIVE ART, NEW YORK
1965 Ancient Peruvian Textiles from the Collection of the Textile Museum, Washington, D.C. Introduction and notes by Mary Elizabeth King. The Museum of Primitive Art, New York.

NIMUENDAJÚ, CURT
1914 Die Sagen von der Erschaffung und Vernichtung der Welt als Grundlagen der Religion der Apapocúva-Guaraní. *Zeitschrift für Ethnologie*, vol. 46, nos. 2–3, pp. 284–403. Berliner Gesellschaft für Anthropologie, Ethnologie, und Urgeschichte, Berlin.

NORTHERN, REBECCA T.
1968 The Birdman Bead. *Américas*, March, pp. 14–20. Division of Cultural Relations, Pan American Union, Washington.

O'NEALE, LILA M.
1949 Weaving. *In* Handbook of South American Indians (Julian H. Steward, ed.), vol. 5, pp. 97–138. *Bureau of American Ethnology, Bulletin 143*. Smithsonian Institution, Washington.

OSBORNE, HAROLD
1968 South American Mythology. Paul Hamlyn, Feltham, Middlesex.

PARDUCCI, RESFA
1966 Sellos zoomorfos de Manabí (Ecuador). *Cuadernos de Historia y Arqueología*, años 12–13 (1962–63), vols. 11–12, nos 28–29, pp. 123–128. Casa de la Cultura Ecuatoriana, Núcleo de Guayas, Guayaquil.
1970 Representación de casa en los sellos triangulares de Manabí. *In* Diskurs 70: Culturas en las costa del Ecuador. Colegio Alemán Humboldt, Guayaquil.

REICHEL-DOLMATOFF, GERARDO
1950–51 Los Kogi: Una tribu de la Sierra Nevada de Santa Marta, Colombia. 2 vols. Bogotá.

ROTH, WALTER E.
1915 An Inquiry into the Animism and Folk-Lore of the Guiana Indians. *Thirtieth Annual Report of the Bureau of American Ethnology (1908–1909)*, pp. 103–386. Government Printing Office, Washington.

ROWE, JOHN HOWLAND
1946 Inca Culture at the Time of the Spanish Conquest. *In* Handbook of South American Indians (Julian H. Steward, ed.), vol. 2, pp. 183–330. *Bureau of American Ethnology, Bulletin 143*. Smithsonian Institution, Washington.

SAHAGÚN, FRAY BERNARDINO DE
1963 Florentine Codex: General History of the Things of New Spain. Book 11: Earthly Things. (Trans. by Charles E. Dibble and Arthur J. O. Anderson.) *Monographs of the School of American Research and the Museum of New Mexico*, no. 14, part XII. The School of American Research and the University of New Mexico, Santa Fe.

SANDERSON, IVAN T.
1961 Living Mammals of the World in Color. Third edition. Hanover House, Garden City.

SAVILLE, MARSHALL H.
1907 The Antiquities of Manabí, Ecuador: A Preliminary Report. *Contributions to South American Archaeology*, vol. 1. Irving Press, New York.

SCHMIDT, MAX
1905 Indianerstudien in Zentralbrasilien. Verlag von Dietrich Reimer, Berlin.

SCHNEIDER, MARIUS
1946 El origen musical de los animales-símbolos en la mitología y la escultura antiguas. *Instituto Español de Musicología, Monografías, no. 1*. Barcelona.

SELER, EDUARD
1904–09 Codex Borgia: Eine altmexikanische Bilderschrift der Bibliothek der Congregatio de Propaganda Fide. Hrsg. auf Kosten Seiner Excellenz des Herzogs von Loubat, Berlin.

SNETHLAGE, E. HEINRICH
1930 Form und Ornamentik altperuanischer Spindeln. *Baessler-Archiv*, vol. 13, pp. 77–95. Verlag von Dietrich Reimer, Berlin.

THOMPSON, J. ERIC S.
1936 Archaeology of South America. *Leaflet no. 33*. Field Museum of Natural History, Department of Anthropology, Chicago.
1966 The Rise and Fall of Maya Civilization. University of Oklahoma Press, Norman.
1970 Maya History and Religion. University of Oklahoma Press, Norman.

UHLE, MAX
1902 Types of Culture in Peru. *American Anthropologist*, vol. 4, pp. 753–759. American Anthropological Association, Menasha.

VERRIER, ELVIN
1949 Myths of Middle India. Oxford University Press, Madras.

VERRILL, ALPHEUS HYATT, and RUTH VERRILL
1953 America's Ancient Civilizations. G. P. Putnam's Sons, New York.

VOLKER, T.
1950 The Animal in Far Eastern Art. E. J. Brill, Leiden.

WAGNER, ERIKA
1971 Alte Zeremonialgeräte aus den Venezolanischen Anden. *Antike Welt*, vol. 2, no. 4, pp. 19–27. Raggi-Verlag, Zürich.

WEITLANER JOHNSON, IRMGARD
1966–67 Miniature Garments Found in Mixteca Alta Caves, Mexico. *Folk*, vol. 8–9, pp. 179–190. Essays Presented to Jens Yde on his 60th Birthday. Dansk Etnografisk Tidsskrift, Copenhagen.

WHITE, TERENCE HANBURY, ed.
1954 Bestiary: The Book of Beasts, being a Translation from a Latin Bestiary of the Twelfth Century. G. P. Putnam's Sons, New York.

WILBERT, JOHANNES
1963 Indios de la región Orinoco-Ventuari. *Fundación La Salle de Ciencias Naturales, Monografía no. 8*. Instituto Caribe de Antropología y Sociología, Caracas.

ZÁRATE, AUGUSTÍN DE
n.d. Descubrimiento y conquista del Perú. Edición de textos originales, revisados y anotados por Dr. Julio de Riverend. Editorial Nueva España, Mexico.

A FURTHER EXPLORATION
OF THE ROWE CHAVÍN SERIATION
AND ITS IMPLICATIONS FOR
NORTH CENTRAL COAST CHRONOLOGY

PETER G. ROE

Dumbarton Oaks   Trustees for Harvard University   Washington, D.C. 1974

Contents

Introduction	5
Methodological Considerations	5
The Structure of Chavín Art	7
Explanation of the Feature Lists	9
The Feature Lists	
Period AB	11
Period C	13
Period C–D	14
Period D	15
Period EF	17
Explanation of the Seriation Charts	19
The Phases	
Phase AB	19
Phase C	20
C–D Transition	21
Phase D	22
Phase EF	25
Extensions of the System	
Pacopampa	26
Kotosh	27
Kuntur Wasi or La Copa	27
Monte Calvario, Catache	28
Lambayeque	28
Alto de la Guitarra	29
Chicama and the North Coast	29
Ancón	30
Ica	31
Huara	33
Casma	33
Huaylas	36
Nepeña	37
Explanation of the Illustrations	38
Illustrations	40
Charts	69
Bibliography	75

A Further Exploration of the

Rowe Chavín Seriation and Its Implications

for North Central Coast Chronology

Introduction

AS THE TITLE INDICATES, I intend this seriation to act as a supplement to, rather than a replacement of, John Rowe's analysis. However, the present study was done as independently as possible of Rowe's exact procedure, a task facilitated by his previous exposition of the Chavín style (Rowe 1962, 1967), which delineated the main characteristics of its evolution and was not intended to provide an exhaustive discussion of all diagnostic criteria. The primary aim here is to make the content of each period more explicit. Thus I hope that it will now be easier to make precise statements about the dating of a particular piece, by employing some of the features and organization developed here, than was possible by using Rowe's published works alone. While agreeing with Rowe (1967:77) that "it is not necessary to be able to place every piece," I have tried to assign more pieces to specific periods than he did, with the hope of detecting patterns from the resultant array of dated specimens.

The relative dating of the Chavinoid centers of the North Central Coast will be a unifying problem of this exercise. Immediately relevant, then, is a seriation of the human figure, a task not undertaken by Rowe. Donald Lathrap has assembled some notes on the subject which he was kind enough to let me

examine. A similar examination of the chronological implications of the snake motif is a further requirement in this study. Here, too, the discussion follows Lathrap's notes quite closely, although I hope that enough original observations will follow so as to make this more than a clerical exercise in judicious plagiarism. At this point in the history of research in the problem area, this paper can be regarded as no more than an argument in relative dating that will either be supported or refuted by future stratigraphic work.

Methodological Considerations

SERIATING across topography and distance, as I will attempt to do here, is at best a hazardous undertaking. However, Rowe has demonstrated that the Chavín style was sufficiently rigid in the control and application of its canons to warrant qualified comparisons with a coastal valley as far away as Ica (Rowe 1967: 73–4; Menzel, Rowe, and Dawson 1964:4). To obviate the confusion of geographical (regional) and chronological variables, I will try to keep them as separate as possible, following Rowe's lead in limiting the first version of the seriation to Chavín de Huantar itself. "When we say that an object from some other part of the country is decorated in the Chavin style we mean that it is substantially the same style as the sculpture at Chavin" (Rowe 1967:72). Only later will distant manifestations of the Chavín style be related to the sequence at Chavín de Huantar with the necessary qualification that their inclusion is indeed an extension of the system.

Chavín is located at 3,135 meters above sea level near the town of that name situated at the entrance of the Callejón de Conchucos on the eastern flanks of the Andean Cordillera Blanca. The site itself is between two rivers. The larger river, the Puchka, runs from the south eventually to drain into the Marañón to the northeast. In addition to Chavín de Huantar itself, the smaller Puchka basin sites of Qaucho or Oshnu, near the temple; Gotush, 5 kilometers to the southwest; Waman-wain near the pueblo; and Olayan or Yura-yako will be considered as one sample. All of these smaller sites are near Chavín de Huantar and, given the importance of the latter, intimate contact was assured (geographical data from Lumbreras 1967:49; Rowe 1967:72; Tello 1960:149–52). The site of Yauya to the north, just off the Marañón, is also included in the sample, largely because it is usually grouped with the sculpture from Chavín, and because of its relative proximity.

Regarding absolute chronology, I will follow Rowe's dates of roughly 1200 to 300 B.C. (1967:73) with the proviso that the upper range limit may be extended in the future. Luis Lumbreras (1970:133) gives a date of 1200 B.C. for the ceramics from the Rocas gallery at Chavín based on a radiocarbon determination. He remarks on the stylistic similarities of this pottery with the Lanzón, the type specimen for Rowe's earliest AB Phase. Therefore, there is evidence to assign this date to the first manifestations of this culture at Chavín. For the site of Kotosh in the Huánuco basin, Izumi and Sono (1963:154) cite a C-14 date of 3000±150 B.P., approximately 1000 B.C. for the Kotosh Kotosh ceramics and an identical date for the Kotosh Chavín ceramics at the site, which should be later. At Chavín de Huantar, the Ofrendas galleries yielded a C-14 date of 750 B.C. (Lumbreras 1970:132) for the Ofrendas pottery style which is beyond doubt attributable to the period in the evolution of the stone sculpture represented by

the Tello Obelisk (Lumbreras 1970:143), the type specimen for Rowe's Period C. The above data can be used for the following correlation.

CHAVIN DE HUANTAR

Sculpture (Rowe 1967:74)		Ceramics (Lumbreras 1967:58–60, 1970:41)
1200 B.C.	AB	ROCAS
750 B.C.	C	OFRENDAS
	D	MOSNA
	EF	

An argument will be presented later in justification of the D dating of Mosna, but suffice it to say here that the independent evidence from the pottery corresponds to the stylistic evolution evident in the stone sculpture.

In addition to the variables of space and time, there exists the variable of material. The original Chavín seriation was limited primarily to subtractive stone carving. It could be argued that the principles evident in the seriation can be extended to processes analogous to stone sculpture. I do not maintain here that working in stone is exactly like working in ceramics, only that incising on the surfaces of pottery that runs from a dry to a leather-hard state calls for the same kinds of procedures and orientations to visual problem-solving (one way of looking at artistic creation) as does incising on prepared stone. Naturally the more obdurate material calls for more physical effort and greater "control" on the part of the artist, which *may* tend to result in a kind of pictorial rigidity. A more pliant material tends to encourage more "freedom," yielding a relatively cursive result. It is not proposed here that material is either a necessary or sufficient cause of a certain kind of representation, only that it offers broad parameters within which any art style has to operate and to which some styles will respond more than others. Chavín art seems to offer such a case of the interplay of media and execution.

Between ceramics and stone, the differences do not appear very significant, especially when both categories are incised, as are the majority of specimens in this style. However, differences do appear when the ceramics bear a painted design. In this event, they become more nearly comparable to painted textiles which often tend to be highly cursive and exhibit a margin of looseness not found in the stone sculpture. Examples that come readily to mind, which will be dealt with in greater detail later, are the important Mosna bottle design (Lumbreras and Amat 1966: Fig. 13b) and the Ica painted textiles (Figs. 12–19; Rowe 1962: Figs. 29, 30).

The classes of artifacts least amenable to direct comparison with stone sculpture are weaving and metalwork. The piece of cloth from Ancón illustrated by Willey and Corbett (1954: Pl. 24) is a perfect example of how weaving introduces a tendency to rectangularity, dictated by the tyranny of warp and weft, which makes a visual first impression that the piece is more "advanced" than a contemporary piece of ceramic within the same phase of stylistic evolution. In metallurgy, things become still more complex. Chavín metalwork, though including a variety of techniques not again rivaled until the Moche tradition, was still primarily concerned with embossing and repoussé. These techniques, by their very nature, seem to impose a tendency for simplification and stylization represented in its most extreme form by the curious specimens from the Lambayeque Valley illustrated by Samuel Lothrop (1941: Fig. 28a and b); the technical limitations make them appear more alien and later than they really are. Other works in metal seem more directly comparable to those executed in stone. One piece from the Bliss (formerly Simkhovitch) Collection, attributed to Chavín de Huantar, does "illustrate a metallurgical technique not hitherto recorded in the New World . . . working from the front and driving in the background to produce the pattern. The result is called champlevé, the normal manner in which Chavín motives were produced on flat stone surfaces such as the famous Raimondi panel" (Lothrop 1951:227). It is necessary to take into account the material of objects represented in the disembodied drawings floating around in the literature. This is done in this paper by noting the medium on the charts, and by discussing the implications of material in the summary sections.

The Structure of Chavín Art

ROWE'S ANALYSIS of meaning in Chavín art is accepted here and forms the basis of the following discussion. Accordingly, my usage of such terms as "kennings," "agnathic," etc., is derived from the same source (Rowe 1967:79). The concept of "modular width," first suggested by Lawrence Dawson and used by Rowe (1967:77), gives a label to an obvious device that the Chavín artist used extensively.

The Chavín artist may have used another formal device related both to the above-mentioned "modular width" and "angular modularity" concepts. Using *Webster's Seventh New Collegiate Dictionary*, "modular" will be employed here as a "standardized dimension," and "template" as a pattern or mold used as a guide to the form being made. Design elements will be defined as the irreducible constituent elements of a whole design. The resultant construct is "modular design-element templates."

It is obvious that in addition to being rigidly conceptualized, Chavín art is rigidly executed. The curves are regular, the lines straight, as if they had been ruled. Moreover, the design elements themselves are often so nearly alike that they look as if they were copied, if not from one another, then from an independent model. In fact, something like that may have happened. The so-called "Lintel of the Jaguars" is a crucial piece in this regard (Fig. 9; Rowe 1967: Fig. 19). It is rather late, a baroque work. Figure 9 is a rendering that was constructed in a fully architectual fashion using templates. Since this is the way I did the drawing, and since the result is very close to the original—a piece very hard to draw accurately because of its complexity—I suggest that this was the way the Chavín artist originally executed the work.

In this hypothetical reconstruction, the artist had a few modular design-element templates which he had earlier drawn freehand. These templates were the following: the double-snake group below the lower lip (Fig. 10g); a mouth-band segment (Fig. 10e); the head complex containing the eye, nose, and above-the-nose fold (Fig. 10a); the small swirl head (Fig. 10i); a front-face agnathic mouth supplied with nostrils (Fig. 10j); a leg unit, either front or rear, since front and rear are identical (Fig. 10h); the curl-ear element (Fig. 10f); the behind-the-neck agnathic profile jaw and associated eye (Fig. 10d); and two back filler templates (Fig. 10b and c). These ten basic design-element templates are all that are needed to generate the entire complex cayman figure! Just to take one step as an example, the artist made the first double-snake profile-head group below the jaw, and then drew two more simply by sliding the original template back and repeating the whole procedure. The beauty of this system is that it makes possible the potentially endless replication of like elements, minimizing inevitable human error. Instead of two opposed cayman figures, I could have produced fifty! In a word, it is mass production.

In the early part of the sequence, it is hard to find such transparent cases of mechanized drawing except where the artist was called upon to execute a whole series of nearly identical works as part of a frieze (see Carrión Cachot 1948:28, Fig. 3). The cat/bird AB cornice figures (Fig. 1a and b; Rowe 1967: Figs. 11, 12) are good examples of such a case. Figure 1b differs from 1a only in a few details such as the small scallop below the cere on the bird mask of Figure 1b which is absent in 1a, and the fact that the wingspan of Figure 1b is greater. This lengthening of the wingspan provided space for the insertion of the small filler heads between the continuing mouth band at the base of the wings and the volute-jaws near the wing tips, so characteristic of this phase. The span of the wings was increased by the method just outlined. Both bird-guardians were derived from a single set of modular design-element templates. The Figure 1b specimen was created simply by sliding the wing units out a sufficient distance to leave space for the filler-head template to be replicated eight times.

The exact mechanism for this procedure is, of course, unknown. Thin cloth or hide with the design drawn on one side and smeared with charcoal on the other is one possibility. By tracing the design on the cloth with a hard stylus, it would be transferred to the surface of the stone previously smoothed to accept the image. Recent finds at Cerro Sechín (Mendoza and Román 1969:33) show that the figure to be incised in the stone was first indicated in charcoal, the chisel following the marked lines. Whatever the case, one can be certain that the Chavín artist did not compose his very complex renderings by starting out to chisel on a perfectly blank stone surface without any mechanical aids to his efforts. Even if a physical template was not always used, a mental one certainly was.

Valid statements about seriational chronology, such as Rowe's (1967:78) assertion that "the accommodation of designs to modular banding became increasingly strict in Late Chavín art, the curved lines of earlier designs being replaced in Phase EF by straight ones which interrupted the banding less," can now be made using the modular design-element template concept. As the EF Phase is approached, its use increases. The already mentioned tendency to rectangularity, generated by an increasing adherence to a strict modular-width concept, also made it easier to replicate like elements in a similar modular fashion. The two trends are not unconnected.

Though the general validity of the preceding observations of Rowe and of the author is clear, it is not always easy to implement these observations in terms of the dating of an individual specimen. In particular, Terence Grieder (personal communication 1970) has shown that a fully operational and quantitative implementation is difficult and in some cases ambiguous. Proceeding from that point, Lathrap (personal communication 1970) has suggested that "the best implementation of the modular design concept for the more classic Chavín specimen might be in terms of the number of lines in the design which can be considered part of a rectilinear grid imposed on the design field and the width of the most frequently occurring band." Clearly more detailed and fully quantitative studies of the problem are needed.

Explanation of the Feature Lists

As ROWE (1967:77) notes, "Chavín art is basically representational, but its representational meaning is obscured by the conventions which govern the Chavín style and, in many cases, by the fact that representational details are not expressed literally but in a figurative or metaphorical fashion." This *managed realism* is basically zoomorphic or anthropomorphic. Julio C. Tello (1960:164) leaned to the interpretation that the characters of Chavín art were "monstrous." Rowe (1967:82) also asserts that, while in the majority of cases the representations were simply portrayals of natural forms, some part-human, part-animal monstrous forms such as the examples portrayed on the Black-and-White Portal columns do occur. These are real compounds, a human figure that has taken on some feline traits, claws replacing nails, feline feet, and a feline head. Over the face of these guardians there is "the bird's beak and cere . . . attached to the profile like an ill-fitting mask" (Rowe 1967:80). Along the body, which is human in shape, sprout wings with four sets of primary feather elements as in all Chavín depictions of this figural type. The feathers do not, however, form an integral part of the body, implying that what is represented here is a Cat-Icarus figure.

On the other hand, this distinction does not justify creating a separate iconographic category, for these are the same divinities as those depicted in Figure 1a and b, where they are simply birds with cat attributes. The presence of "hawk markings" (Yacovleff 1932) on the north column (Rowe 1962: Fig. 10) reinforces this notion of identity. What exists here is one character, a bird-feline guardian angel that becomes, through time and with the increasing frequency of anthropomorphic representation in later Chavín art, a truly monstrous form.

The main iconographic figures in Chavín art besides the bird-feline (man) guardian angel already dealt with are the cayman (fish-feline) and the human-feline. The last category has been subdivided by Rowe into his "Staff God" and "Smiling God" figures. The precise religious significance of each of these beings is the subject of a literature (Carrión Cachot 1959; Tello 1923) which will not be treated here.

Another usage should also be defined, the distinction between mythical and non-mythical human beings. The former term denotes human representations with a feline mouth supplied with prominent canines, while the latter stands for purely naturalistic depictions. These are perhaps unfortunate terms because we do not know the significance of the figures to the people who created them; but since they have been employed primarily as a stylistic distinction, they will be retained.

This paper will employ in a systematic fashion Rowe's (1967:82) distinction between principal and subsidiary figures. A host of human and animal characters such as monkeys, hawks, owls, and snakes can act as subsidiary figures. The subsidiary figures are usually portrayed without the elaborate kennings that accompany the main divinities discussed above. As Tello (1923) suggested, these may represent mythical analogues when they appear with a major deity form, as on the Tello Obelisk. For example, the realistic eagle on the Tello Obelisk may represent the Guardian Bird-Angel. When these secondary figures appear alone or are, in turn, accompanied by subsidiary figures, they become, by definition, primary figures, and must be treated as such. There is, of course, some intergradation between these two categories. Body parts of the subsidiary figures like eyes and mouths, which are as sensitive indicators of stylistic change as any others, are often simplified versions of the same parts on a major figure (Features 1 and 2, 40 and 41, 46 and 47, and 126 are just several examples of this tendency). There are even cases where the major figure has borrowed a body part from a subsidiary or even a filler-figure. The eye form of the Phase D "Smiling God" (Rowe 1967: Fig. 21) is ultimately derivable from the eye (Feature 7, see Chart III) associated with an agnathic mouth on the body of an AB cat representation (see Rowe 1962: Cover).

However, the primary/secondary-figure distinction is general in Chavín art. The conventions of representing body parts differed according to whether they belonged to a primary or secondary figure. The two categories also had slightly different rates and directions of evolution within the same general stylistic trend. For example, the evolution of the eye feature on a main figure must be separated from and treated differently than the evolution of the same feature on a subsidiary figure.

The serpent is a perfect illustration of this necessity for observing the primary/secondary distinction. It is the only subsidiary figure that does not occasionally appear as a primary figure. The form of the snake head is also more conservative, changing more slowly, than the major figures with which it is associated. Nevertheless, at one point in the sequence it changes radically and becomes more advanced than the major figure to which it is affixed. Beyond these various changes there is a major directional trend followed by the snake head that allows it to be used as a sensitive chronological indicator. It is also the feature most consistently explicable in terms of Rowe's metaphorical interpretation of Chavín art.

One difficulty in using any one of the major figures as the sole standard indicating evolutionary changes is their sporadic pattern of occurrence through the sequence. It may be just an accident of preservation that the cayman deity appears to be exclusively a Phase C and Phase D phenomenon. However, the fact that the Chavín artist took the trouble to portray the cayman differently than the cat, and did so only in certain periods of the style, seems to indicate that more was involved than sampling error. The difficulty of discontinuous distribution is obviated if the serpent is used. Besides the feline mouth and generalized felinid characteristics, the serpent is the ubiquitous symbol of the Chavín art style. It occurs throughout the sequence.

While Rowe recognized the temporal significance of change in the execution of the simple snake form,

he did not regard the distinction between it and the elaborate collared cat-snake as being anything more than functional. In this paper, this distinction will be treated as a temporal variable. But first, some definitions are in order. The several varieties of snakes tend to polarize into two major categories, the "simple snake" and the "collared cat-snake." In the first stage of its development, the former is portrayed realistically. The eye is drawn separately from the nostril, which usually is supplied with a nostril hole. The mouth is represented by a single and separate line that forms an upward scallop different from the nose line. In its later variant, the mouth becomes a continuation of the eyebrow line as Rowe observed (1967:74). The collared cat-snake is characterized by a cat ear projecting behind the head as well as a collar and a feline mouth with indicated canines. It may also be supplied with a forked tongue extending beyond the lips or a single-wing tongue projection.

Now that a definition of terms used in the following feature lists has been accomplished, it is time to turn to the mechanics of the lists themselves. Each piece extant in the literature has been broken down into its diagnostic parts. Each part so treated then becomes a feature, defined for the purposes of this paper as a stylistically discernible unit. A preliminary seriation was then run on the defined features. After comparing the results with the Rowe seriation, the features were listed below and defined. Of course, many of the features were shared by more than one period so they are pictured in association with the period in which they first appeared at Chavín de Huantar. A drawing of each feature provides a visual summary of the characteristics of each period. In the right of each column there is a short explanatory note telling what kind of a figure the feature originally occurred with—whether primary, secondary, filler, or decorative motif—and its significance.

The Feature Lists

PERIOD AB

1 Feature 1 is a main-figure eye form. The brow projection ends in a serpent head which is the more complex form of the early simple-snake type. The projection itself may be straight or curved, although the latter form is more common.

2 Feature 2 is also a main-figure eye form. It is obviously derived from the form above, the brow projection becoming a plain curl. The entire appearance of this feature is not unlike the geometric volute also used in the style.

3 Feature 3 is a subsidiary-figure eye form where only the line of the upper lid is indicated, extending beyond the pupil as a single line only. The basically round eye is here cut lower to form a lenticular shape.

4 Feature 4 is a subsidiary-figure eye form. It hangs on the end of a swirl that may be considered a simplification of the brow projection of Features 1 and 2 above. Note how the whole image is one of a circle.

5 Feature 5 is a subsidiary eye form almost perfectly circular in outline. It is essentially the eye form of Features 1 and 2 above, but simplified in the respect that it either stands alone or with a vestigial lid line indicated. As always, the pupil hangs on the top edge.

6 Feature 6 refers to the AB tendency to make every fold into an eye by the addition of a central pupil.

7 Feature 7 is a subsidiary-figure eye form that is markedly rectangular, but yet is relatively wide in comparison to its length. The bottom corners are rounded off.

8 Feature 8 is an elaborate above-the-nose fold that forms an undulating line. The same treatment can also appear associated with the head and on the bodies of serpents. It occurs on main figures and accompanying figures.

9 Feature 9 is the subsidiary-figure counterpart of Feature 8. In a simpler variant the nostril is formed by a single scroll.

10 Feature 10 is a main-figure nose form related to the one above, but here all the elements are separate. The nostril sits in the middle.

11 Feature 11 is a main-figure mouth form. The broad canines come only from the top. As Rowe has suggested, the upper portion of the mouth conforms to the agnathic mouth type.

12 Feature 12 is also a main-figure mouth type. Here the tips of the canines are cut off by the lower line of the lip. The front teeth spread outward.

13 Feature 13, a main-figure form, is agnathic and has two canines descending in paired fashion from the upper lip. Note the mouth corner transformed into an eye and the general manner in which the mouth conforms with circular lines.

14 Feature 14 is a subsidiary mouth type where the canine follows the upturned lip, like the extension of a circle. The teeth are scalloped.

15 Feature 15 is a continuing mouth band which is actually an extended version of Feature 14. Characteristic of this period, the mouth is equipped with short, broad-based canines, the other teeth being scalloped. The canine follows around the mouth line in a circle.

16 Feature 16 shows the tendency for mouths to form circles. As noses were indicated with swirls, and eyes were pendant from them, so the mouth emerges from a swirl. Note that the canine is cut.

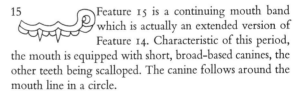

17 Feature 17 depicts how all non-canine teeth are indicated as a scalloped line. These teeth can be regarded as half-circles.

18 Feature 18 shows the typical sabre-like canines of the AB Phase. They are curved but yet not very long. The base is broad.

 19 Feature 19 is the kind of tooth found in continuous and continuing mouth bands. Note that it is not very long with regard to its base.

 20 Feature 20 represents scales that perform a filler function within a figure. Each scale is broad and stubby. Furthermore, they only progress in a straight or only slightly curving line and do not change direction.

 21 Feature 21 is a series of angular frets which Lothrop has plausibly derived from the intertwined bodies of snakes. Note the central space between contiguous units.

 22 Feature 22 represents some of the pelage markings on cat figures characteristic of this phase.

 23 Feature 23 shows an early appearance of the "pelt convention" when applied to a series of double or dual faces that share a common lip band. It occurs as a subsidiary, decorative element on major figures.

 24 Feature 24 is the forked-tongue as it appears issuing from the serpent's mouth. It has a triple point instead of only two.

25 Feature 25 is a volute that often appears on the body of main figures. The central parts of the design have been converted into eyes.

26 Feature 26 is a set of head curls, each one forming a circular swirl, presumably representing feathers and/or fur.

27 Feature 27 indicates the simple presence of repeated swirls that can be used for a multitude of functions besides and including those already specified.

28 Feature 28 consists of a series of bands parallel to each other with a central dip, all pointing in the same direction. It is used as a filler element much as in the manner of Feature 20 above.

 29 Feature 29 is a decorative element that appears on the body of a primary figure. While the details of the interior fill vary, the outline remains the same.

 30 Feature 30 is a primary-figure hand. The hand is rounded and naturalistic, the fingers stubby and the fingernails are long. In all cases, the number of digits is anatomically correct. The bracelet is plain.

 31 Feature 31 is the main-figure foot form. The heel is fully rounded, the number of toes is complete and they possess long toenails that curl upward to give the impression of fitting into a circle.

 32 Feature 32 is a subsidiary-figure collared cat-snake with double head curl. The mouth projection or tongue is single-winged and points upward. Note that the canine is truncated.

 33 Feature 33 is a subsidiary-figure simple snake head. The eye is separate from the nostril line which now has a nostril hole. The one-scallop mouth is also present.

 34 Feature 34 indicates that all the simple snake heads emerge from a ring on the body of the main figure.

 35 Feature 35 is a subsidiary-figure front-view agnathic mouth. The teeth are rounded, as indicated before. The general proportions are squat. The presence of the central fang is questionable; while it is shown on the drawing this was taken from (Rowe 1962: Cover), it does not occur on the photo in Tello (1960: Pl. XXIXa).

36 Feature 36 is a true continuous mouth band which is used only to mark the central axis of the body, the backbone. Again, the canines are short.

 37 Feature 37 is a main-figure ear form. The bottom is obscured, but presumably it follows the top in outline. The earring forms an integral part of this feature.

38 Feature 38 is a main-figure ear type. It is the zoomorphic counterpart of the anthropomorphic Feature 37 above. The ear takes the form of a single upcurling element.

39 Feature 39 is a main-figure pleated skirt. The lower edges are perfectly scalloped.

PERIOD C

40 Feature 40 is a main-figure eye form. The eyebrow extension is here simplified to exclude the zoomorphic snake. Multiple lines surround the eye, indicating its importance. On the top edges there are points.

41 Feature 41 is a subsidiary-figure eye. Note that on the variant it is merely the main-figure eye of Feature 40 minus the brow extension. There is a tendency for the lines to bend upward.

42 Feature 42 is a subsidiary-figure eye that results from Feature 7 simply turning upside-down. To distinguish it from earlier forms, the pupil rests on the bottom of the eye, as do the ones above.

43 Feature 43 is a main-figure eye characterized by its lenticular shape. The pupil is round and floats freely in the center. Both ends are sharp points.

44 Feature 44 is a subsidiary-figure eye. A simple circle, it has an L-shaped projection.

45 Feature 45 is a decorative device consisting of a constellation of Feature 3 eyes. It is their grouping, not their form, which is a unique feature of this period.

46 Feature 46 is a main-figure nose form. The nostril here floats in the center and is not attached to the lower line. The back is outlined twice to show its importance. Like the eyes, the contours of the nose bend upward.

47 Feature 47 is a subsidiary-figure nose. It is slightly more bulbous in relation to later variants, but is chiefly distinguished by the concave upper line above the nostril.

48  Feature 48 is a conservative secondary-figure nose form in that it is defined by a swirl. The lines have, however, become double.

49 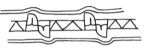 Feature 49 is a main-figure mouth form which, being primary, is outlined twice to show its importance. Note the points that appear above the base of the blunt canines on either side of the lip line.

50  Feature 50 is a continuous mouth band associated with a major figure. The lip curls in a rounded fashion above the tips of the canines. The teeth are represented in saw-fashion.

51 Feature 51 is a subsidiary-figure mouth which is curved downward. A single canine projects from the upper lip, like earlier agnathic mouths, but here the lower jaw is indicated.

52 Feature 52 is a subsidiary-figure mouth type. As all subsidiary forms are simplifications of major forms, this one is patterned after Feature 49 in the points above the base of the canines but lacks a double line.

53 Feature 53 is a subsidiary-figure mouth form which bends downward and is characterized by no externally indicated teeth.

54 Feature 54 is a subsidiary-figure agnathic mouth and is distinguished by the line that runs down the middle of the lip. The canine projects outward and does not follow the lip line to form a circle as it did in AB specimens.

55 Feature 55 is a canine form associated with the primary-figure mouths already discussed. It has line modifications of varying patterns on its interior. It is broad and blunt. The line in front curves, while the back-line is straight.

13

56

 57

Feature 56 is a primary-figure extremity. It can function as either a foot or a hand depending on orientation. The fingers are elongated, as are the fingernails. The latter, however, project straight forward and do not curve. The formerly plain bracelet becomes a simple twined snake. Feature 57, a foot, differs only in being shorter.

 58

Feature 58 is a secondary-figure hand form. Note the realistic rendering with all five digits present. Note also how the hand increases in width as the tips of the fingers are approached.

 59

Feature 59 is a secondary-figure foot form. Here again the shape is a "U" spreading apart toward the tips. The number of toes may be variously reduced.

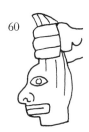 60

Feature 60 indicates the first iconographic evidence of the existence of the trophy-head cult. Small severed heads are carried in the hand of mythical or non-mythical human figures.

 61

Feature 61 depicts the first appearance of weapons, more specifically, atlatl and darts. As above, this feature appears in the hand of a human figure.

 62

Feature 62 is an elaborate version of the collared cat-snake. The bulbous quality of the mouth and nose is characteristic.

 63

Feature 63 is a subsidiary-figure simple snake-head variant. Note that all the anatomical features are separate.

64

Feature 64 marks the first appearance of the exceedingly simplified snake head in the Chavín sequence. The mouth becomes the extension of the eyebrow line, disappearing as a separate element, and the nose is omitted.

65

Feature 65 is an elaborate hair arrangement. The hair is indicated by vertical lines and is piled up.

 66

Feature 66 is an abstract, geometric, decorative motif, developed out of the pelage markings of AB Feature 22 by the addition of a central hole. Apparently, they are no longer exclusively pelt markings since they can appear independently.

 67

Feature 67 is an angular fret motif that has developed out of Feature 21 by the loss of the interstitial spaces.

 68

Feature 68 is a stylized spinal column that appears to be bifurcated by a straight line.

 69

Feature 69 is a decorative motif/filler figure which consists of a series of rays with recurved tips. The shank is not exceedingly long in relation to the curl. There is a space where the tip recurves.

70

Feature 70 is a peculiar finger-ray that appears as part of a secondary figure.

PERIOD C-D

 71

Feature 71 is a primary-figure eye form. While the eyebrow element is derived from earlier prototypes, differing in that it has two projections, the earlier simple lower line has become a projection extending above the eye proper.

 72

Feature 72 is a main-figure continuing mouth band. It differs from the earlier Feature 14 in having another canine interrupt the smaller rounded teeth.

 73

Feature 73 is a primary-figure mouth form. Note the lips projecting at right angles to the mouth and the conservative points in the lip above the bases of the canines.

74

Feature 74 is a human-like hand where, however, talons have replaced fingernails to give a zoomorphic effect.

 75

Feature 75 evolves out of Feature 20. Here the scales, instead of continuing in a straight line, form a right angle, indicating an increase in complexity and plasticity.

PERIOD D

76 Feature 76 is essentially Feature 7 with the addition of a correspondingly rectangular frame that has its origins in the earlier eyebrow projection. It is one of the most diagnostic features of this period.

77 Feature 77 is, like the one above, a main-figure eye form. By a process similar to the one above, it is formed by adding a bi-projecting eyebrow element to an old form, in this case Feature 5.

78 Feature 78 takes Feature 76 and, in a conservative fashion, makes the rear eyebrow projection end in a snake head à la Period AB. It is a primary-figure form.

79 Feature 79, also a primary-figure form, takes a modification of 78 and adds a projecting tooth above the eye. Notice that while the rear projection has lost its snake head it is still elongated.

80 Feature 80 retains a conservative projection ending in a snake head and combines it with the lower element of Feature 71 to create an upward projection in the back only. Sometimes the rear projection is plain.

81 Feature 81, a primary-figure eye form like the above, is merely a variant of 80. The only distinguishing feature is that this one is without a pupil.

82 Feature 82 is a primary-figure eye that elaborates the principles of Feature 80, retaining the round eye form with the centrally located round pupil.

83 Feature 83, a main-figure eye form, is a development of Feature 43. While it is still basically a football shape, the end points have become rounded. The pupil is stretched out from a circle.

84 Feature 84, a main-figure mouth form, is simply Feature 73 with the addition of decorative corner points, a diagnostic trait of this period, as Rowe has indicated. Note that it has also lost the points above the base of the canines that Feature 73 possessed.

85 Feature 85 is a nose form that has notches on the upper section, originally indicating wrinkles.

86 Feature 86 is a main-figure mouth analogous to Feature 84, but without the decorative point. The mouth line curves downward.

87 Feature 87 is a primary-figure mouth type with the mouth line curving upward in this case. In other examples, the mouth can go downwards, the important trait being the continuation of the lip into the canine.

88 Feature 88 is a primary-figure mouth type with the upper lip extending to form a serpent. In other cases, the lower lip is the one to become transformed.

89 Feature 89 is a subsidiary filler element similar to Feature 54. Note, however, that it is much more rectangularized, the canine becoming an "L."

90 Feature 90 is the typical canine form for this period. It is blunt and bent in a right angle like an "L." The device was adopted to make the once-projecting canine compatible with the increasing rectangularization of Period D portrayals.

91 Feature 91 is a main-figure mouth form that is an elaboration of Feature 73. The width of the lip band decreases in comparison with earlier examples.

92 Feature 92 shows how the decreasing lip-band width, coupled with teeth depicted in a saw pattern, becomes ever longer in a narrow decorative band.

93 Feature 93 is the canine depiction at the opposite extreme from the L-shaped canine. Here the canine becomes very long and rapier-like in comparison with earlier short ones, as in Feature 19.

94

Feature 94 is a continuing mouth band. It has the conservative trait of twin points above the base of the canine with Feature 92 teeth depiction. Its general outline is reminiscent of a bat-wing.

95

Feature 95 is a subsidiary-figure mouth form. Its upper lip has multiple short fangs descending from it. The mouth itself is agnathic.

96

Feature 96 is a subsidiary-figure mouth form similar in function to Feature 54. What differentiates it is that the teeth have now begun to climb the lip line as it bends upward.

97

Feature 97 is a subsidiary mouth type which demonstrates the same pattern of the teeth following up the front, but here this tendency includes only the smaller teeth.

98

Feature 98 continues the tendencies of Feature 97 to the exclusion of all canines in an abstract pattern. It functions as a decorative device.

99

Feature 99 is a continuous mouth band. Note the loss of both the points above the canines and the curl of the lip around their tips as the lip becomes very rectangular and straight.

100

Feature 100 is a subsidiary-figure front-view agnathic mouth that differs from earlier examples in the degree to which it has been compressed and hence widened.

101

Feature 101 is a subsidiary filler head that often takes the place of earlier plain anklets. It has a characteristic double-ended bar element over the brow.

102

Feature 102 depicts the ear as portrayed in certain instances in Period D. It has been divided into two parts with similarly shaped internal elements.

103

Feature 103 is the primary-figure head shape that is a transparent rectangle if the facial features are taken out.

104

Feature 104 represents the above-the-nose fold of skin that in earlier periods had been plain but is now elaborated by a central inclusion.

105

Feature 105 shows how, as the lip was made to end in a snake head, the above-the-nose fold does also.

106

Feature 106 is an above-the-nose fold that is not very elaborate but which does hang out over the nose rather than line up with it as had been the case earlier.

107

Feature 107 is a major-figure ear form in which both ends curl inward, but where the back line remains straight.

108

Feature 108 is an example of how the increasing tendency to fill all spaces manifests itself in filling in a "hawk marking" just as the above-the-nose fold was filled in.

109

Feature 109 is a main-figure hand. It is rectangular in general form and the fingers have been reduced.

110

Feature 110 is also a main-figure hand, but in this case more fingers are indicated than above, but the number still is not anatomically correct. Note that a nail is indicated on only one digit.

111

Feature 111 is the foot form of a main figure. The whole appearance shows a flattening and consequent horizontal stretching.

112

Feature 112 is a main-figure foot type. Again note that the toes are reduced with no indication of nails. The toes are delineated with a single line.

113

Feature 113 is a collared cat-snake. It is distinguished by an ear that projects straight backwards.

114

Feature 114 is a variant of the simple snake. There is a rib that extends through the middle of the body terminating in a perpendicular line behind the neck.

115 Feature 115 shows how the ultra-simplified version of the snake tends to be used in great profusion on a main figure; here it is combined with recurved rays as a bordering fringe.

 116 Feature 116 is a characteristic subsidiary head of a double-ended snake with a curl on either end of the rectangular head. The teeth are broken down into separate rectangles.

 117 Feature 117 is a subsidiary filler head distinguished by the elaborate treatment of the head that ends in a number of prongs.

 118 Feature 118 is a small subsidiary "hammer-headed falcon" characterized by two identical projections from the head at right angles to each other.

 119 Feature 119 is an abstract zigzag design that is used as a filler element.

120 Feature 120 is made up of the same stacked rays with recurved tips as Feature 69. However, here the stems become more plastic in the directions in which they bend as they become longer.

 121 Feature 121 depicts a common device that is termed here the "flayed-pelt convention" where the subject is visually laid out on a flat surface as if it had been cut by a line running down the middle and both halves splayed out.

122 Feature 122 is the stylized spinal column represented in Feature 68 with the difference that here the other half is indicated. The details of the interior fill are variable, but generally the lines inside are parallel with the outer edges.

 123 Feature 123 is the usual dress of mythical and non-mythical humans in later Chavín art, consisting of a G-string with paired serpent appendages. (It continues into Moche iconography.) It replaces the earlier pleated skirt seen as Feature 39.

124 Feature 124 is a small front-view circular head that is generally found in a subsidiary position in a central part of the main figure.

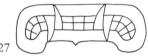 125 Feature 125 is a subsidiary eye form that continues the same type as Feature 7 to the logical extreme of flattening and rectangularization. The top and bottom are now completely straight, the corners sharp.

 126 Feature 126 is a primary-figure ear form. The first, being on a more important piece, is elaborated over the second, which instead of having intertwined snakes merely has lines. The ear differs from Feature 107 in that the rear line extends through the middle of the ear, cutting it in half.

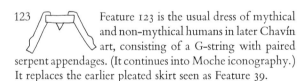 127 Feature 127 is a primary-figure mouth type viewed from the front and in profile. The smaller teeth are indicated by intersecting lines at right angles to each other, thus producing teeth that are little squares. The corners of the mouth turn down. The canines do not project beyond the lip line.

 128 Feature 128 is the same primary-figure mouth seen in profile.

 129 Feature 129 is a front-view agnathic mouth that differs from Feature 100 in having an extra set of canines projecting from the top.

 130 Feature 130 presents a difficulty. Due to differences in the depictions in the literature of the Raimondi Stela, from which this was taken, this subsidiary/filler mouth may or may not be agnathic. If not, the lower jaw is like the top. The teeth are square.

131 Feature 131 is a front-view agnathic mouth which may possess a central fang. Note the rectangular quality of the lip line.

132 Feature 132 is a front-view agnathic subsidiary mouth like the one above, only in this feature the corner canines are transformed into rays with recurved tips.

133 Feature 133 is a continuous mouth band. The salient feature here is that the canines have themselves been reduced to rectangles ending in a flat tip.

134 Feature 134 is a front-view nose characterized by extreme flattening and consequent widening.

135 Feature 135 is a profile main-figure nose. Note how the entire nose could easily be encompassed within a rectangle and how the nostril has been lost through simplification.

136 Feature 136 consists of main-figure hand types. Again, the rectangularity is evident. The fingers are indicated only by straight lines.

137 Feature 137 is a main-figure foot type that differs from Feature 111 by the addition of a swirl indicating the heel.

138 Feature 138 is a primary-figure foot type. The heel has now become a complete rectangle, the toes are indicated only with straight single lines and are reduced in number.

139  Feature 139 indicates stylized blood gushing from the severed neck of a trophy head. The streams are represented by straight bars whose square tips are separated from the body by a horizontal line.

140  Feature 140 is a convention for the depiction of hair elements analogous to those above, but differentiated from them by having pointed rather than blunt or rectangular tips. The strands of hair are looped in this case.

141 Feature 141 is a collared cat-snake of a type later than but similar to Feature 113. Notice, however, that the face has taken on the characteristics of simple snake portrayal, including the eyebrow line forming a nose.

142 Feature 142 is the last variant of the simple snake. This includes the appearance of a form with a pointed snout.

143 Feature 143 shows how the simple snake is intertwined to form a nested pattern.

144 Feature 144 is a method of drawing a naturalistic cat head in profile that treats the ear as a forward-pointing element, convex in its outer line and concave on the inside.

145 Feature 145 is a double-winged eye that developed out of a Feature 3 eye form by the thickening of the upper line and the reduction of the eye in the center to a single line. It is a primary-figure element.

146 Feature 146 is a method of using a single mouth as a shared element between two sets of eyes and noses, thus creating two different faces, one right-side up and the other upside-down.

147 Feature 147 is the ray element with recurved tip familiar from Feature 120. The stem now becomes longer in relation to the curl, which is used with greater frequency, and the hole where the tip recurves is absent.

148 Feature 148 is a cross-hatched decorative-element panel.

Explanation of the Seriation Charts

THE FULL DISTRIBUTION of the various features on works illustrated in the literature is depicted here. The numbers that were assigned in the feature lists are ranged along the horizontal axis in order of their appearance. The Phases in the Rowe chronology are then indicated above the horizontal axis, with their divisions marked by a thick vertical line. The specimens themselves, represented by the citations in the literature in which they are illustrated, are ranged along the vertical axis in the order of their presumed antiquity. To the left of this category is a space marked with an "M" which stands for media. In it a notation indicates the material in which the figures appeared, and something about the manner of execution. The notation consists of letters which have the following correspondences:

WT = Woven Textile
M = Metallurgy
S = Carved or Incised Stone
G = Carved or Incised Gourd
SH = Carved or Incised Shell
W = Carved or Incised Wood
B = Carved or Incised Bone
C = Carved or Incised Ceramics
MC = Modeled Clay
PC = Painted Ceramics
PT = Painted Textile
WP = Wall Painting

To the left of this column are the figure numbers in this paper. To the right of the figure category is listed a synoptic estimate of the relative dating of the figure. Chart I depicts all of the original sample for the seriation, primarily the material from Chavín de Huantar, the nearby smaller Puchka River Basin sites, and Yauya. Chart II shows the various extensions of the system such as the published sculpture from La Copa, Cerro Sechín, Pacopampa, the wall-paintings from Catache, etc. Some areas or sites have numerous illustrations of works attributed to them. When there is good evidence that all such works were contemporary, as is the case with the reliefs at Cerro

Sechín, they will be represented as a single, composite entry. Often it is not easy to make such a determination, especially in the case of rock-paintings which offer no sound associational data and which could have been added to over an extended period of time. Monte Calvario seems stylistically uniform but is given individual entries as a conservative solution.

To aid in reference, the more famous and therefore more familiar pieces and those which are particularly crucial to this discussion are given a special number which is inserted after the synoptic phase designation. In order of antiquity these are:

1. The Lanzón (Tello 1960: Fig. 30)
2. The Pennsylvania Mortar (Tello 1960: Fig. 128)
3. The Tello Obelisk (Tello 1960: Fig. 31)
4. The Lintel of the Jaguars (Rowe 1967: Fig. 19)
5. The Yauya Stela (Rowe 1962: Fig. 31)
6. The Columns of the Black-and-White Portal (Rowe 1962: Figs. 9 and 10)
7. The Head-Bearer (Tello 1960: Fig. 81)

The Phases

PHASE AB

THE EARLIEST PHASE in Chavín art is by far the easiest to seriate. Most of the known examples represent a tight-knit unity. For example, the mouth on the isolated cat figure (Rowe 1962: Cover) is identical to the one on the bird-cat guardians (Fig. 1a and b). At first I was skeptical of Rowe's statement (1967:84) that the mouth on the Lanzón was possibly originally agnathic and the lower jaw a later addition. After comparing it to the mouths of the tenoned heads of this period and realizing the general preference for the agnathic-mouth type at this time, I was convinced of the plausibility of the interpretation. Perhaps the present mouth was added to the Great Image when the rectangular framed wall plaque of the "Smiling God" was executed in Period D (Lumbreras 1967:53; see also Chart V). If so, the process of emulation was not all one-way, for a close modeling of the later image on the earlier would go a long way toward explaining a number of curiously conservative elements on the Phase D piece.

My main interest here is in the human figure,

although there is little to work with in this phase. It seems as though non-human animals were more important in this phase than in any of the following, since most of the representations are of natural forms without the admixture of human traits. The only usable exception to this statement is the Lanzón itself. However, to use it to extrapolate directly to less transformed and less sacred human depictions is dangerous. Therefore, in Chart IV it has been separated from the example of more naturalistic human extremities. Nevertheless, it is possible to make some qualified observations. In keeping with the general cursive character of line in this phase, the hands are rounded and naturalistic. Very long fingernails are added, but it should be pointed out that they are not claws. The bracelet is unadorned. The feet are long and the heels are distinctly rounded. The number of fingers and toes is complete and anatomically correct. All of these characteristics are important for an understanding of later non-mythical human depictions.

Regarding the snake motif, the two defined types are present. The collared cat-snake may be observed behind the leg of the Great Image (Tello 1960: Fig. 30). Above, on the spire of the statue, there is another variant of the same type, this form having an equally curled nose and ear. Another variant has a double set of ear- and eyebrow-extension curls and possesses the pelt markings of a cat; it can be seen on the carved lintel of the southwest corner along with the cat already cited (Kauffmann Doig 1971: Fig. 263). The simple snake is also present and equally well developed. At this end of the stylistic continuum, the form has a full complement of features, including a nose drawn separately with the nostril sitting on top of the line. While the simple snake is present, the point to note in this phase is the importance of the collared cat-snake, occurring as it does on quite a few specimens.

Concomitant with the naturalistic tendencies of AB art is its transparent structure. A form may be elaborated (as in Fig. 1a and b), but all detail is encompassed within the outlines of the subject and subordinated to it.

Yet another general characteristic of this phase is the degree to which all lines tend to be curved and the manner in which smaller filler elements and subsidiary figures conform to circles (see the swirl heads on Rowe 1962: Cover, Feature 16, or the agnathic mouth on the Pennsylvania mortar in Tello 1960: Fig. 128).

PHASE C

IT IS CLEAR that this phase is a transitional one, Rowe himself admitting that, "only a few other fragments of sculpture can be assigned to this phase" (1967:76). Now, however, the sample can be increased, and it no longer seems possible to question the validity of the phase on the basis of small sample size. A glance at Charts III, IV, and V demonstrates that, to paraphrase Voltaire, if the Tello Obelisk did not exist, it would be necessary to invent it. This is particularly evident in the case of the evolution of the mouth in Chavín art (see Chart V). It would be impossible to have generated the points above the base of the canines on later mouths without the example of the Tello Obelisk.

It is in the area of the human figure, however, that the crucial character of this piece is demonstrated. The hand forms that occur on both the mythical and non-mythical humans that function as subsidiary figures on the body of the cayman (see Fig. 2a–c) are fully derivable from those on the Lanzón. The mythical characters have similar hands, but have feet bearing a reduced number of toes. Chief differences between these figures and the Lanzón are a shortening of the length of the fingernails and a C hand-shape that widens perceptibly toward the fingertips. The feet undergo a similar process although, as mentioned, the toes are reduced, usually to three. Identical hands appear on a monkey (Fig. 4a; Ayers 1961) which can be placed in this period. The monkey has a new eye type (Feature 43), characteristic of this phase, which will continue nearly to the end of the style, with later derivations. The slight difference in foot form undoubtedly stems from the simian character of the principal figure here. The evidence from the associated snake heads is consistent with this ascription. A stone mortar is now dated to this phase on the evidence of the figure's elaborate coiffure (Fig. 3a) which also appears on the humanlike figures of the Tello Obelisk (Fig. 2b). The presence of the constellation of disembodied eyes (Feature 45)—another feature shared with the Tello—the mouth style, and the hands, which are of C type, all confirm the dating. This dating is significant to our purposes, for on the other side of the mortar (Fig. 3b) there appears a fragment of a hand in the lower left corner. This hand is also within the C style and is grasping a staff. This association, in turn, lends supporting evidence to the C dating of Figures 4b and c, independent of the obvious similarities in mouth type, etc. They also bear similar elements which, following Rowe, will be designated atlatls and darts. Not only does this association support the occurrence of Feature 43 eye forms in this period, but it dates the first appearance of warriors and the trophy-head cult in Chavín art as well. Needless to say, we must now question whether or not the trophy-head cult was a non-Chavinoid trait as has been claimed by Sawyer (1966:87).

There are "mythical" figures which also share many stylistic traits with normally depicted human beings. One such figure is shown in Figure 5. It has the Feature 43 eye form associated with a conservative mouth form and a hand form which can be directly compared to the figures from the Tello Obelisk (see Fig. 2c).

Period C is also highly significant for the evolution of the snake motif. The later variety of the simple snake appears here for the first time. The mouth becomes an extension of the eyebrow line and the nose is omitted. This is a logical result of the economy of effort any artist adopts when faced with duplicating an element as ubiquitous as the snake head. As an *a priori* experiment before this seriation was started, the following sketch was made of the steps one might have gone through in that context. Perhaps it is relevant to reproduce it here:

Indeed, most of these steps will be found in Chavín art, and in precisely this order of occurrence. The older variety of the simple snake, however, still survived, sometimes even on the other end of a staff from its simplified cousin (see Fig. 4a). Yet another variant of the simple snake appears on the Tello Obelisk (Feature 63). This elaboration did not continue; it probably represents a process of elaboration parallel to what was happening with the collared cat-snakes in this period (see Feature 62). The latter were transformed to the degree that they resemble cats more than snakes.

C-D TRANSITION

THOUGH THIS DISCUSSION is based on the stylistic features of only one piece, the Lintel of the Jaguars (Fig. 9), this point in the continuum will be treated as a sub-unit, to show some important trends connecting Phases C and D. It could just as easily have been considered terminal C or initial D. If the fragment illustrated by Tello (1960: Fig. 68) is not part of the same sculpture pictured by Rowe (1967: Fig. 19)— and one has difficulty in deciding from Tello's illustration—it is a contemporary piece differing from the one Rowe illustrates in about the same degree as the columns of the Black-and-White Portal differ from each other, one being essentially an elaboration of the other within the same stylistic period. At any rate, Figure 9 represents a nearly perfect mid-point in the sequence. There are as many correspondences to the AB end as to the EF extreme in this work. The behind-the-neck profile agnathic mouth is only modified from the very early AB type by the addition of a central fang. The little swirl-faces are replicas of the body swirl-faces on the AB Lintel of the Jaguar from the southwest corner of the temple. In the opposite direction, the eye form is the perfect precursor of the characteristic D eye form (see Chart III) and the mouth is the perfect intermediary between the mouth with points above the base of the canine, occurring in C, and the decorative corner point of D.

PHASE D

PHASE D appears to be very important in the evolution of the Chavín style. Not only does it reach a new level of elaboration with individual components often being more "baroque" than their counterparts in the succeeding EF Phase, which is often considered the height of complexity, but also, to judge from the vast number of works that can be attributed to this phase, it was the most expansive period of the cultural system supporting the art form.

A new formal device, applied to the whole figure, makes its appearance in this phase. For the sake of graphic description, it will be designated here as the "flayed-pelt convention" or, alternatively, as "split representation," following Claude Lévi-Strauss (1967: 245 ff.). The entire animal, in order to be depicted on a flat surface, is divided by an imaginary line down the center and split out so that mirror-images are created by the two sides. By the use of this convention, both sides of the whole figure can be seen at once even though it is depicted on a two-dimensional surface. The effect of this symmetry generated through reflection is much the same as that attained in Shang and Chou art in the T'ao T'ieh mask, and in Northwest Coast art of North America. When coupled with an increasing profusion of detail this procedure tends to fragment the psychological impact of the design. As an illustration of this process, one may compare the classically D, Ica painted textile (Fig. 19) with its AB counterpart (Fig. 1a and b). Both representations belong to the cat-bird guardian-angel type with the characteristic four wing units. In contrast to the "transparency" already alluded to for the AB end of the spectrum, the D example is barely recognizable! The profusion of detail has destroyed the previous clarity of the design so that it is not understandable without recourse to its predecessor. One reason for this visual confusion is that the head has been split in two and laid out so that it shares a common mouth. While the creature represented is the same as in Figure 1a and b, a front-facing cat/bird, the effect is totally different. Quite appropriately, the behind-the-neck profile agnathic face, as it

appeared in the AB examples, also changes according to the same convention so that it now becomes a full-front agnathic face. The wing units on the D specimen are kenned as snakes and are pushed down so that they even sprout from the legs, while the tail-feather assemblage is replaced by a face in precisely the same position. But, even where substitution occurs between different parts, the same structural divisions persist.

The Yauya Stela is a classic example of the "flayed-pelt convention" (Fig. 11). It is a cayman similar to the Tello Obelisk in most respects. Whereas the Tello Obelisk presented two profile views that must be viewed separately and cannot be joined, the Yauya was split open medially and laid out flat so that it, like the guardian figure from Ica, shares a common mouth.

The Yauya Stela is a very interesting monument which has been dated here as early Phase D. It is transitional in much the same sense as the Lintel of the Jaguars is, but demonstrably later. The piece is very complex and mirrors the forces of compression that Chavín art was undergoing in this and the succeeding phases. It carries over such conservative elements as the guilloche and the main-figure eyebrow extension ending in a snake head. It also exhibits, however, a far greater number of Phase D traits. One such trait is the eye to which the conservative eyebrow extension was attached, a perfect Phase D form. The mouth bands that traverse the animal's body at four points are analogous to the "bat-wing" mouth bands held in the hands of the figures on the Black-and-White Portal columns. The only difference between the mouth bands of the specimens just cited and those of the Yauya is that the Black-and-White Portal examples are more extreme in respect to curvature and the presence of definite points. The line of continuous saw-teeth inside the lip line (Feature 92) can be duplicated from some of the Phase D profile birds on the cornice associated with the Black-and-White Portal. In addition, the presence of the little profile subsidiary face, presented here as Feature 89, with the characteristic Phase D L-shaped blunt canines, marks the Yauya Stela as Phase D.

This discussion of the Yauya Stela brings up the problem of the divinity which Carrión Cachot has quite appropriately called the "felinic dragon," here designated, following Rowe, as the cayman figure. The cayman shares traits with the feline and, as far as the Chavín artist was concerned, undoubtedly partook of its essence. The fact that the sculptor went to the trouble to portray it, using canons different from those applied to the feline, and that it appears only in Phases C and D (that is, differentiated not only by convention but by chronology), indicate that on at least one level it was conceptually separate from the feline. No more graphic illustration of this separation can be given than Rojas Ponce's reconstruction (Carrión Cachot 1948: Pl. XVIe and f) of what were actually portrayals of the cayman. By pinning incongruous-looking feline tails to their hind sections, he produced a result so distressing that it discounts the possibility that the original depictions were meant to represent cats.

As mentioned above, the elaborate designs of Chavín art can often be understood best by reference to relatively realistic examples meant to represent the same concept. In this connection the Pallka cayman from the Casma Valley (Fig. 7e) provides the perfect model of which the Tello Obelisk, the Yauya Stela, the Lintel of the Jaguars, and Figure 17 are all elaborations. Among the conventions that differentiate the cayman from the feline, the most obvious is the manner in which the legs are shown. Both front and rear legs are invariably bent on a plane parallel with the body rather than straight down, perpendicular to the body, as in a cat drawing. No doubt, this manner of depiction was meant to reflect both the much lower posture of the reptile and its characteristic mode of progression. Furthermore, there is a stylized spinal column, portrayed X-ray fashion as in Australian aborigine art, running down the middle of the body toward the tail that, when preserved, is straight and not feline-like.

One of the recently discovered painted fabrics from Ica, also attributable to Phase D, shows how far stylization could remove a depiction from its original naturalistic model. If the Yauya Stela (Fig. 11) is a derived Tello Obelisk, then in terms of representation, the Ica piece (Fig. 12) is a derived Yauya Stela/ Lintel of the Jaguars. Following the pattern of omission in these fabrics, which will be discussed more fully later, the cayman's legs are deleted but the result is still split open, pelt-like. All the other requirements for a cayman portrayal, such as the spinal column and back-crests, are present.

But if the cayman was differentiated from the feline, what about the persistent association of a fish element which Tello (1923: Pl. 2) originally recognized in the Yauya Stela? Rowe has, quite rightly, stressed the cayman nature of such works: "There is only one animal figure which is represented in Chavin art in such a way as to suggest that it might be a deity or important mythological figure, and that is the alligator, or more properly cayman, which is represented on the so-called 'Tello Obelisk'" (1967:82). He theorized, however, that the appearance of a fish tail on the Tello Obelisk might have been a mistaken association: "this mythical detail may be no more than a misunderstanding on the part of artists who were not personally familiar with their subjects, caymans occurring only at a much lower altitude" (Rowe 1967:83). While this guess is not incompatible with what we know about the kind of misunderstandings that can arise when artists are unfamiliar with their subject—witness the early attempts of European artists to draw the elephant or rhinoceros—it can now be shown that the appearance of a fish tail on the Tello cayman was not the result of a misunderstanding. This statement is based on the performance of the artist of Pallka who managed to portray a cayman quite accurately with a reptilian tail (Fig. 7e). Since I have heard of no case where the cayman was indigenous to the North Central Coast, this artist was about as familiar with a cayman as an artist of Chavín de Huantar, or even less so, considering the greater distance from the selva. Hence, the fish element was a conceptually significant component of the mythical cayman as represented at Chavín de Huantar since it was deliberately affixed. This mixture of biological traits does not demean the abilities of the native taxonomist. It is not difficult to imagine that, because of its way of life and appearance, the cayman should have been shown with both feline and fish attributes while remaining an entity separate from either.

To follow one of the main themes of this study, the continuing evolution of the human figure, one should turn to the relief of the "Smiling God" (Lumbreras 1967:53). Though certainly executed in D, it shares many affinities with the Lanzón. It even retains the very conservative variant of the simple snake complete with indicated nostril (Feature 33). However, several important things have happened. For one thing, the image has borrowed a filler and/or subsidiary eye form that goes all the way back to Phase AB (Feature 7, consult Chart III). It differs from the earlier ancestor in being more rectangular while it carries on the Phase C tendency for the top line to be concave. Simplification of the hand and foot continues. The number of fingers is reduced to two, as are the toes (or talons in this case). The shape of the head is very important for comparative purposes. By mentally blocking out the features, hair, and ears, one perceives that the head has become a perfect rectangle. This modification is in keeping with the increasing trend toward rectangularity in the style as a whole. This same block-like head shape appears in the obelisk from Gotush (Fig. 23) and in the depictions at Monte Calvario (Figs. 25a and b, 26).

There are two very important pieces showing non-mythical figures that can be assigned to this phase, even though they have strong resemblances to, and are demonstrably derived from, Phase C in such traits as the stockiness of the extremities, the wide-lipped mouth, and the C-derived eye (see Feature 83). In the first example (Fig. 28a; Tello 1960: Fig. 80), the ⊂-shaped foot remains, but the shape of the toes has been further simplified by leaving out the nails. The hands can be enclosed in an imaginary box without violating their contours, so great is the rectangularity. The unfortunately fragmentary remains of a human figure (Fig. 28c) appear in the upper register of one of the textiles from Ica (Fig. 17). When it is compared with the other examples of the

human form belonging to this phase (Fig. 28a), it is clear that the appearance of the figure is compatible with the date assigned to the textile on which it appears. Both show many Phase D characteristics. The feet of Figure 28c are distinctly squared off, nails are not indicated on the toes, and the heel is represented by a swirl. In the other example (Fig. 28b; Tello 1960: Fig. 82), the foot is modified still more to assume this outline, ⊂, an important diagnostic trait for the period. Nails are likewise removed from the hands, and the toes of the feet are squared. The nose, in both cases, has become more rectangular than its antecedents.

While the elaborate collared cat-snake still remains, as in the above-the-nose fold on the south column of the Black-and-White Portal (Rowe 1962: Fig. 9), the central characteristic of Phase D is the overwhelming frequency of the later variant of the simple snake (Feature 64). In examples like one of the birds of the Black-and-White Portal cornice (Rowe 1962: Fig. 1), the simple snake is stacked alternating with recurved rays in a manner that foreshadows Phase EF. In some cases, such as another of the birds on the cornice (Rowe 1967: Fig. 15), this later variant of the simple snake is the only one pictured accompanying the main figure. Thus begins the temporal trend toward increasing domination by the simple snake.

Another variant of the snake, yielding a clue for the dating of the rare iconographic designs associated with the Mosna ceramics, makes its appearance in Phase D stone sculpture. It is a small subsidiary double-curl-headed snake (Feature 116) found on the columns of the Black-and-White Portal. This element (Fig. 38d) can be traced through a design commonly found on Cupisnique ceramics (Fig. 38b) which is nothing more than a simplified version doubled in reflectional symmetry. In turn, the Cupisnique version of the element, sharing the same rectangular teeth, can be directly related to the painted design on the Mosna bottle (Fig. 38a and c). The Mosna design is a visually ambiguous one in that, by mentally "changing gears," one can see figure as ground and ground as figure, alternatively.

It is both positive and negative. If one focuses on the white ground between the painted lines, making it the point of interest, this negative design appears as a variety of the double-curl-headed snake shown in Figure 38d. The isolated "teeth" appear to have climbed up the brow in the form of little white dots. Being painted, it is more cursive than its stone counterpart, but it is D.

PHASE EF

PHASE EF carries with it the paradox of great organizational complexity accompanied by a simplification of the constituent parts used to construct the complicated designs. The impression that EF is more flamboyant, more intricate, than the preceding D Phase, is derived from a seemingly endless replication of like elements, themselves often simplified versions of their corresponding Phase D counterparts. The co-existence of the two trends, one toward complexity, the other toward simplicity, goes a long way toward explaining the stylistic evolution of the human figure and the serpent.

Phase EF sees the culmination of the tendency toward rectangularity in the portrayal of the human body. This is illustrated by the crucial Figure 81 in Tello (1960), reproduced here as Figure 28e. This figure will henceforth be referred to as the "Head-Bearer." Here the mythical human being bears a Raimondi Stela mouth-type seen in profile. The hands are perfectly rectangular; even the fingernails are reduced to squares. The heel, as well as the entire foot, has become squared off rather than rounded as it was earlier. Tello (1960: Fig. 87; Fig. 28d, this paper) illustrates still another fragment which, if it is what it appears to be, carries the stylistic pressures evident in the Head-Bearer to their logical conclusion, the whole foot becoming an internally undifferentiated rectangle. Other parts of the specimen in Figure 28e show how every component was subjected to the same pressures. The nose, derived from representations of Feature 47, has likewise been pushed in and made square.

Significantly, the simple snake is the only kind pictured on the Raimondi Stela, "type specimen"

for the EF Phase. True, there are two variants of the later simple snake on the Raimondi—one with a pointed snout—but both are well within the category as defined. The snake's body becomes longer and longer as it is used in conjunction with simple recurved ray elements, the shanks of which are also appreciably lengthened over their Phase D predecessors. Both elements are stacked as space-fillers in great profusion. The kind of baroque impression this concatenation of intrinsically simple elements can give is well illustrated by another specimen in Tello (1960: Fig. 52). The collared cat-snake is present in Phase EF (*ibid.*: Fig. 69), but it has been simplified to approximate the old variant of the simple snake and appears only very rarely. In summation, the snake is a valuable chronological instrument. If it changes less rapidly than the main figures with which it is associated, nevertheless it reflects the same stylistic trends and occurs more frequently.

A final and, in the comparative context, important figure is the naturalistically rendered feline. The most illuminating piece in this regard is shown in Tello (1960: Fig. 62). It is dated very late in this study, possibly EF. Michael Kan (1972:73–4) has pointed out the possible relationship between this Chavinoid piece and the later sculpture at Aija (see Kauffman Doig 1971: Figs. 545, 546, 548). This Chavín cat manifests the trend toward simplification alluded to above, as well as the curious "double-winged" eye form (Feature 145). This last trait, in addition to the depiction of the ear as projecting forward in a single plane with the profile head (Feature 144), is found on a piece (Tello 1960: Fig. 72) which also has the looped, strand-like hair configuration found on Tello's Figure 81, indicating an EF dating for the appearance of the "double-winged" eye form at Chavín. Associations of this feature elsewhere also tend to support a late date. These include naturalistic felines possessing the characteristic Phase D decorative-point mouth form (Larco Hoyle 1945: Fig. 169), a Tembladera piece illustrated in Kauffman Doig (1971: Fig. 367), and a Tembladera pot, obviously Salinar influenced, illustrated by Kan (1972: Fig. 16A).

Viewed generally, the Phase D–EF continuum is the most difficult to break stylistically. Outside of the Raimondi, individual works are often difficult to place. The wall-plaque bird-guardians illustrated in Tello (1960: Figs. 42, 39, etc.), and correctly reconstructed in Carrión Cachot (1948: Fig. 10) are typical in their intermediate position. Phase EF is marked by an intensification of existing features, rather than by the appearance of many new ones. However, the increasing repetition of simplified detail seems to argue for a kind of "pattern exhaustion" in the Kroeberian sense (1944, 1952), which led, on the one hand, to the simplified depictions of the snake, human figure, and feline, and, on the other, to the visual complexity of the Raimondi Stela. Both extremes show the effects of the same pressures toward rectangularity, simplification, and replication of design-element templates, and indeed were the end products of those same pressures. One gets the impression that the fabric of Chavín art was stretched to the breaking point trying to encompass and realize the contradictions in its canons. It disintegrated, and in the process left its legacy to a host of successor traditions.

Extensions of the System

EXTENDING A SERIATION based on the stone sculpture of Chavín de Huantar entails certain difficulties. There will always be ambiguity in assigning a particular piece from outside the core area of the initial sample. That ambiguity, expressed in a scattered distribution of features, will vary directly with the degree of cultural autonomy shown by the area to be encompassed by the expansion of the seriation. This is obvious, but it should be pointed out that sheer physical distance may not be directly related to such autonomy. For example, the painted Chavín textiles of Ica are so close to Chavín canons that they were certainly either trade pieces or were made by Chavín artists resident in the valley. Ancón also shows Chavín art in a very pure form, while the Casma and Nepeña centers are more divergent. Nevertheless, enough specific parallels remain between the central sequence

and those counted as extensions of the system to make the task of cross-dating productive, though challenging.

PACOPAMPA

ALL OF THE CLASSICAL Chavinoid materials from this site are clearly Phase D in the central sequence (see Fig. 24a–d and Chart II). This determination was first made on the basis of the subsidiary head (Feature 89) found on the illustrated Pacopampa mortars (Larco Hoyle 1946: Pl. 65), with its characteristic L-shaped canine. Since then, the recent work of Rosas at the site has greatly increased the sample of Chavín depictions. A number of modeled clay faces of classic D configuration occur on the necks of large urns. These faces show both the decorative point on the mouth corners and the Feature 76 eye form. A small cylinder seal of carved bone also exhibits these same characteristics (Fig. 24c). The famous "Feline of Pacopampa" (Fig. 24a) also shows the decorative point, the tendency for the teeth to extend up the lip line, and the transparently square head shape, all characteristic of Phase D. However, it also manifests some traits which argue for a dating near the end of that period since they are features of Phase EF. The mouth is a squared approximation of the Raimondi mouth type. But the way that the top lip breaks at a right angle to form the base of a canine-like element is a carry-over from the D convention shown in Feature 87. The treatment of the extremities shows an extreme rectangularization that indicates a very late D or early EF dating for this piece.

The Pacopampa naturalistic felines (Fig. 24b; from a photograph of another similar specimen discovered by Rosas), although very eroded and hence difficult to deal with iconographically, do offer a number of possibilities for relative dating, possibilities not inconsistent with what has been said above. Figure 24b, now outside the Larco Herrera Museum in Lima, stands in contrast to conceptually similar early sculpture in the round, like the AB University of Pennsylvania mortar. The early, fully sculptural treatment of the jaguar is proportionately high and narrow, while the Pacopampa jaguar is wide and low, testifying in its proportions to the same pressures of compression and consequent widening illustrated in the Raimondi Stela. The mouth style of the Pacopampa feline can be interpreted as analogous to the D variety mouth with decorative point. It is, therefore, interesting to note that this same mouth type is shared by the Punkurí naturalistic feline, tending to confirm its late date.

KOTOSH

AT PRESENT, there does not seem to be enough iconographic evidence to date securely the Chavín manifestation at the Kotosh site. All that can be done is to present a tentative argument based on certain elements of ceramic form and their associated designs. Unfortunately, while both lines of evidence are consistent with each other, they do not appear together in the same vessel-shape category. This is, however, not a crucial objection here because the stirrup-spout bottle and the open, flat-based bowl, each of which contains certain elements that will be used in the dating argument, occur together in the same Kotosh Kotosh or Chavín Kotosh component at the Kotosh site.

The face pictured here as Figure 20a is incised on a flat, open bowl of Chavín type. It has an eye form (Feature 76) which is a Phase D characteristic everywhere it occurs. Furthermore, this pot is not an isolated example. One of the most common incised design elements on Kotosh Kotosh ceramics is a shorthand version of this same eye type (Fig. 20b). This particular depiction can be directly compared with the eye on the small, typically Phase D tenoned head from Chavín de Huantar pictured here as Figure 20c. There is, in addition, a provocative sherd which was used to reconstruct the vessel figures in Izumi and Sono 1963 as Plate 126, no. 14. This can best be interpreted as precisely the kind of lip with canines sprouting from the entire lip line shown here as Feature 96, a D trait. The design is very similar to examples also from that phase, which are illustrated here as Figure 39e, i–k.

This evidence for a Phase D dating on the basis of the designs agrees with what evidence is available

from vessel shape. The stirrup-spout vessels associated with the vessels carrying the designs show a beveled rim modification (Izumi and Sono 1963) that is a more delicate version of that found with precise D association in the Ica Valley (Fig. 40a, b, and c) and late contexts in the Chongoyape finds in Lambayeque. One might even present a thumbnail sketch of the evolution this particular stirrup-spout form, beginning with the rim type found on early, presumably AB, vessels from Chavín de Huantar and Cupisnique forms (Fig. 35a), and going on to vessels with Phase D and later affiliations. Incidentally, one could seriate this kind of rim directly into Moche I with very little difficulty.

While these data are insufficient to date the Chavín component at the Kotosh site to Phase D of the central sequence with absolute certainty, they are at least provocative.

KUNTUR WASI OR LA COPA

KUNTUR WASI appears to be within the same general time range as Pacopampa, although perhaps enduring somewhat longer. The regional peculiarities of this site, particularly its emphasis on sculpture in the round, show that local divergence is now an important factor. Rowe has dated the lintel (Carrión Cachot 1948: Fig. 17) to Period EF. In addition to the general flamboyance of this sculpture, which might be used to argue for an EF dating, it shows the pattern of a number of saber-like teeth (Phase D) descending from the upper lip, and is analogous to the typical EF mouth type illustrated in Feature 129. The eye form is the counterpart of the D depictions (compare the La Copa examples particularly with Rowe 1967: Fig. 15). A tendency for the teeth to climb up the lip line (Feature 96) is also a Phase D diagnostic trait. The tendency for the canine to become transformed into serpents, probably a late trait, is evident on Carrión Cachot's Plate XX (1948). The squaring of the extremities on the human figure shown on the reverse side of that figure follows precisely the treatment of the feet on Figure 28e and argues for an EF dating. Even more specific than the square rendition of the Raimondi Stela mouth type on the previous specimen is the almost exact copy shown on Carrión Cachot's Plate XXIb (1948). Here again, the feet are almost perfect rectangles, although the hands are treated in a more naturalistic fashion.

In summary, there is a mixed assortment of Phase D and EF features on the Kuntur Wasi sculpture, but with the definite predominance of EF features. This assemblage can best be explained by assigning an EF dating to the site, but with the assumption of some significant Phase D survivals.

MONTE CALVARIO, CATACHE

THE RECENTLY DISCOVERED rock paintings and petroglyphs of the Monte Calvario district of Catache, near a small tributary of the Río Chancay, Lambayeque (Mejía Xesspe 1968:17), fit well within the above seriation and conform to the pattern of late Chavín influence in this general area. Although Mejía Xesspe limits himself to observing that the generalized characteristics of the paintings are Chavinoid, and does not assign them to a period of the Rowe chronology, it is relatively easy to make the assignation. Mejía's Figures 1, 10, and 22 (see Figs. 25b, 26, this paper) all have the Phase D mouth characterized by the decorative point added to the corners. Furthermore, the heads of Figures 25b and 26 and Mejía's Figure 1 (1968) are of the same rectangular type as the obelisk from Gotush and the Phase D "Smiling God" portrayal. The Monte Calvario paintings are rather late D as the extreme squaring-off of the feet and heels and the presence of the Staff God indicate. Figure 26 shows a Phase D warrior, very closely linked in spirit to similar representations at Cerro Sechín. Figures 25a and 26 may actually belong to Period EF, to judge from the treatment of the extremities.

LAMBAYEQUE

MOST OF THE NUMEROUS examples of metalwork which have been recovered from the Lambayeque Valley appear also to be of late date, Periods D and EF (Lothrop 1951: Pl. 18b; Rowe 1962: Fig. 27). The Hacienda Almendral finds at Chongoyape, 50 kilometers from the sea, offer an interesting case study. Due caution should be observed in assigning a date to this collection because of the material and method of execution, embossing in this case. Nonetheless, certain features do approximate closely those defined from Chavín. The presence of Feature 132, canines represented by snake rays, links the material to Phase EF (Lothrop 1941: Fig. 26c), while the progression of teeth up the lip suggests a date no earlier than D (Lothrop 1941: Fig. 29a). The specific treatment of the ear, the presence of the mirror-face technique of Feature 146 (two faces sharing the same eye, in this case) makes an EF dating likely (Lothrop 1941: Fig. 26b).

The "Reservoir hoard," also from Lambayeque, is more difficult to date, the only exact resemblance being in the treatment of the ear, Feature 126, an EF diagnostic. Lothrop (1941: Pl. XX; 1951), in his early attempt at the seriation of the two finds, placed the Reservoir hoard after the Hacienda Almendral hoard. The above discussion tends to reinforce his judgment. The fact that few traits could be found to date the Reservoir hoard argues for, not against, the later date. Lothrop (1941: Fig. 28a and b) illustrates two unusual specimens from Lambayeque which have the canine-curl substitution of period EF but which are clearly post–Hacienda Almendral, carrying to the logical extreme the stylization characteristic of period EF. Cross-dating of both groups can be achieved thanks to the near-identity of the ear treatment shown by Lothrop (1941: Figs. 26c, 28b) and the EF lintel from La Copa (Carrión Cachot 1948: Fig. 17).

From the airfield at Chiclayo, Lambayeque, comes the Pickman strombus (Rowe 1962: Figs. 40, 40a) which Gordon Willey saw as similar to the Cerro Sechín carvings: "The face, seen in profile, is quite similar to the Sechín human figures. The eye has a curved band extending down onto the cheek which is suggestive of, although it does not duplicate, Sechín portrayals. A flowing headdress, extending over the back of the individual, is also like a similar headdress and sash from a Sechín carving. This specimen, more than any other, offers some sort of stylistic link between Chavín and Cerro Sechín (1951:116)." Although we now have works that are much more closely related to the Sechín figures than this strombus, it is, nevertheless, related. The treatment of the feet, though rectangularized, is naturalistic and is linked with the specimen of C date shown by Rowe (1962: Fig. 17). The agnathic faces in the background date the shell to D, as does the girdle. It could be argued that the eye-form is an adaptation of C-phase Features 43 and 44, and the D-phase 83. Since it is suggested that the D form evolved out of its C analogue, this combination also argues for a D dating. On balance, a date early in Phase D is plausible.

Chavín influence also extended into Phase EF in Lambayeque. Figure 34 illustrates one of the specimens which is more akin to Sechín than to the Pickman strombus. It comes from a turquoise vase and has a typical EF mouth configuration (Feature 128). Indeed, it is a representation in which everything seems to work perfectly in the seriational terms of this paper. All traits present are late and consistent with each other. The "simple snake" appears with a figure whose head is completely square in outline (Feature 103). The late double-lobed eye form is also present on subsidiary figures (Feature 145). Even the trophy head held by streaming hair with stylized blood falling from its severed neck is identical in concept to Sechín portrayals (see Fig. 29d), and cross-dates with the very similar EF sculpture shown here as Figure 28e. In the case of Figure 34, however, an extremely interesting manipulation of the trophy-head motif exists. Note that the hand of the main figure clutches the upright hair elements of a head more feline in character than human. In this case, the blood falling downwards is represented by the hair hanging from an inverted human trophy head smaller than the first. This piece, along with Figure 28e, is one of the key works for understanding later Chavín and Chavinoid art.

ALTO DE LA GUITARRA
THE ALTO DE LA GUITARRA site between the Virú and Moche Valleys has yielded a petroglyph much more similar to the Sechín carvings than is the Pickman strombus (Fig. 27; Disselhoff and Linné 1960: Fig. 58). It shows confronting warriors with shields

comparable to the shield on the already-cited petroglyph at Cataché and to the Sechín depictions. The squareness of the head and modified Feature 83 eye form argue for a Phase D ascription.

CHICAMA AND THE NORTH COAST
THIS IS NOT the place to examine the seriation of Cupisnique vessel shapes in the Chicama Valley. It is sufficient to point out that the evolution of the pottery in the Chicama Valley closely parallels the seriation set up by Lumbreras (1970:138–9) in most essential details. In Chicama the trends evident in the vessel shapes are consistent with the stylistic evolution of the designs represented on the pots, as was the case at Chavín de Huantar. Accordingly, I have illustrated several stages in the evolution of the stirrup spout, together with the designs that appear on them, to make the general point that there is a correspondence (Figs. 35a–f and 36a–d).

While very few designs on the earlier vessels can be related directly to the Rowe seriation, the style of stirrup-spout vessels shown in Rafael Larco Hoyle (1941: Fig. 47) and in Figure 39f have depictions that are amenable to comparison. These vessels, with a triangular void described by the stirrup and with a peculiar rim and lip treatment, are directly comparable to the Mosna group at Chavín de Huantar. On the basis of iconographic elements Mosna can be dated to Phase D, as has already been argued. If, on the basis of vessel shape, certain Cupisnique pots correspond to Mosna, then the Chicama specimens should exhibit figures that also date to Phase D. That is, in fact, the case.

As Figure 39a–h is intended to illustrate, the designs on this type of pot can only be dated to Phase D for they have such D diagnostic traits as the L-shaped canine feature, the rectangular eye form, and teeth continuing up the lip line in the front of the face (Feature 96). This specific feature and the treatment of the extremity on Figure 39d can be compared directly with the Gotush Stela (Fig. 23), a D piece.

It is also possible to confirm the long-standing suspicion that the vessel pictured in Figure 41a–c was an anachronism when it was made. Rowe has also argued for this interpretation (1971:113–16). While in form it appears to correspond to the earlier stirrup-spout Cupisnique bottles (such as Fig. 36a), the face on its surface could have been executed only in Phase D or later. The front face is the same as the small subsidiary head serving as an anklet on the columns of the Black-and-White Portal. The ear indications (Feature 102) are also derived from the same source. The stepped or tiered bridge of the nose treatment (Fig. 41c; Rowe 1971: Figs. 21, 22), also a Phase D characteristic (Feature 85), finds its parallels on pieces of a similar date such as the gold mask illustrated by Lothrop (1941: Pl. 18b). Even the L-shaped canine, common in the profile heads of this period (see Feature 89), is present on this specimen. The snake head with the upturned snout is also a late variant; a nearly identical example can be found in the upper register of the painted fabric from Ica (Fig. 17). Most of the Chicama specimens cluster late in time although the continuity of influences with Chavín de Huantar through earlier times appears more consistent in this area than in many others.

A relatively late date also characterizes many of the regional styles of the general North Coast area like that of the Jequetepeque. Many of these specimens have a kind of stirrup spout like Figure 39f. If cross-dating with the Mosna Phase at Chavín de Huantar (see Fig. 38a) can be relied upon, these pots should be late. This interpretation is reinforced by the occurrence of Salinar influence on many examples.

Salinar influence may be present on more than just ceramics. The two bone spatulas shown here as Figure 22a and b were found, according to Larco Hoyle, in Salinar graves. While vaguely Chavinoid of a late date, as the square-tipped canines and the general rectangularity of the figures indicate, they are clearly more removed from the Chavín tradition than Figure 21a and b. Despite the fact that more work has been done in the North Coast than many other areas of Peru, its culture history is still particularly obscure. More work is needed in unraveling local sequences and determining the roles of such cultures as Salinar and Vicús before much can be done with specimens from this area.

ANCON

PERHAPS Carrión Cachot's designation of Ancón as a "colony" of Chavín de Huantar was not too far from the truth. At any rate, the Chavín material found in the Ancón area (including Willey and Corbett's finds, those of Carrión, and those of Rosas) is stylistically far closer to the material produced at Chavín de Huantar itself than is any of the other material from outside the core area dealt with so far. All of it dates securely within Phase C of the Rowe seriation. The specimen shown by Rosas (n.d.: Pl. XVI) duplicates the mouth band from the Tello Obelisk almost exactly. Plate XVIII of the same study shows the front part of a dragon similar in every way to the Tello Obelisk. The ceramic piece now on exhibition at the Museo Nacional in Lima (Fig. 8) shows the naturalistic and fleshy treatment of the hands characteristic of the famous obelisk. Details of eye type (Feature 41) and of the mouth form with a raised point over the base of stubby canines also confirm the Phase C dating of this piece. Indeed, a small neckless *olla* pictured in Rosas La Noire's chronological chart bears a classic Ofrendas head.

As a glance at the seriation Chart II will demonstrate, the finds of Carrión Cachot correspond in every way to these more recent finds. Of the specimens recovered by Willey and Corbett the easiest to recognize iconographically is a completely normal Phase C textile (1954: Pl. XXIV). Once the constraints of material are taken into account, its conformity to the canons of Chavín de Huantar is obvious. The mouth and canine form correspond to Features 49 and 55. The form of the eye, intended to be a Feature 43, lenticular variant, was forced, through the mechanics of warp and weft, to become a hexagon.

All of the material that has been cited thus far from Rosas' excavations came from what he has designated as "Phase VI, Classical Chavín." The only illustrated specimen that indicates anything later than Phase C is a specimen that may date to his "Phase VII." It is a stirrup-spout vessel (Fig. 39b) with a form and incised design so similar to the material illustrated in Larco Hoyle's *Los Cupisniques* (Fig. 39c–f, h–o) that it could almost be thought to have been made in the Chicama Valley and not Ancón (Fig. 39b, g). Since the Ancón specimen is dated here as D, the correspondence would seem to be exact. In summation, the vast bulk of Chavín material from Ancón dates to Period C and resembles the work at Chavín de Huantar very closely. There is some evidence, on iconographic grounds, that the Chavinoid occupation lasted at least into Period D.

ICA

DUE TO certain ambiguities in the ceramic record, the advent of Chavín influence in the Ica Valley is a moot point. This involves the question, was Chavín art introduced into the Ica Valley during Phase D of the central sequence? In other words, does Phase 1 in the Ica sequence correspond to Phase D of the Chavín sequence? Perhaps Grieder (personal communication) is correct when he maintains that, "I suspect Ocucaje 1 pots are just old-fashioned provincial versions related to middle or later Chavín-heartland style. There is no question in my mind that Menzel *et al.*'s Phase 1 examples are at the beginning of the Ica sequence, but I do not see that the Ica sequence tells us much about the early stages of the style in Ancash."

The chief difficulty that I want to examine briefly here is the seriation of the Ica stirrup-spout vessels. It may be questioned on what basis the Olsen bottle (Fig. 40a), which is essentially the sample for this Phase 1 vessel body form, can be separated by three phases from the Tishman bottle, "the exact homologue of Phase 1 stirrup-spout bottle in shape, as well as in decoration" (Menzel, Rowe, and Dawson 1964:34). These authors (1964:11) describe the Olsen bottle type as forming "a separate, comparatively conservative descent line through succeeding phases to Phase 4." There is no associational data to bolster the relative placement. One trend in the Ica sequence, as those authors present it, is the trend away from two-dimensional modeling, which is always described as a "conservative" trait when it appears in later phases, to one-dimensional treatment (incision).

Judged by this criterion, the Tishman bottle should be seriated before its identical counterpart since it has modeled ears and the Olsen bottle lacks them. A third stirrup-spout bottle from Ica is pictured here as Figure 40b and c. It has the broad, thickened, slightly beveled rim modification characteristic of the other two pots. Unlike them, however, the modeled face which is portrayed shows definite Phase D characteristics which Menzel, Rowe, and Dawson are quick to point out (1964:39). The most obvious of these characteristics is the mouth form with decorative points on the corners. Elsewhere, I have argued that there is some evidence to associate this rim form with the later phases in the evolution of the Chavín stirrup-spout bottle, specifically Phase D and later. The iconographic elements seem to be consistent with this dating.

All of this leads to several alternative possibilities to the one advanced by Menzel, Rowe, and Dawson, which have the merit of greater simplicity while still relating to the broader trends within the Chavín style. One alternative is to place both the Olsen and the Tishman bottles in Phase 1 and keep the Figure 40b bottle in Phase 4. Then the conservatism would be more plausible when argued in terms of vessel shape only rather than both vessel shape and surface decoration. Another possibility, and the one I prefer, is to place all three vessels together in Phase 1 on the specific grounds of form, thus eliminating complicated genealogical lines. According to this scheme, Phase 1 in Ica might be comparable to Phase D at Chavín.

Whether or not the Chavín style first came to the Ica Valley in Phase D, the first massive impingement in the artistic tradition of Ica can be securely dated to that phase, with textiles probably playing a seminal role.

The painted Chavín textiles known for some time from Callango (Figs. 13 and 19) have now been joined by a group of new *huaquero* finds described as coming from seven to eight kilometers to the south of the Paracas Necropolis. All of these fragments are contemporary and all date from Phase D. All are apparently trade pieces, so close is their adherence to the canons of Chavín art as defined at Chavín de Huantar itself. The only other possibility that would explain their close identity is that they were made by locally resident artists who had emigrated from Chavín de Huantar. The suggestion recently made by Alan Sawyer (1972) that Chavín iconography and style may have been brought to Ica via the painted textiles makes immediate sense to anyone who has attempted to transport ceramics any distance, even under relatively ideal conditions. What more compact, non-breakable, and convenient form for the transfer of style could have been chosen?

The sample includes the two specimens that Rowe illustrated (Figs. 13, 19), now in the Dumbarton Oaks Collection; a number of pieces recently in the Textile Museum, Washington; and six fragments in the Amano Museum in Lima, which Yasushi Miyazaki was kind enough to let me examine. Tracings of the Amano group on polyethylene form the basis of the renderings in the illustration section of this paper (Figs. 12, 14–18). Small space-filler geometric appendages that project on small stems from the main figure are a stylistic peculiarity of this whole assemblage. These appendages are either rectangles or doughnut-shaped circles and are not found on any of the stone specimens from Chavín itself. Other than this divergence, there is little that is new in the Ica finds. The tail element of Figure 19, for example, is the same as the front-face visage (Feature 101) used as an anklet on the columns of the Black-and-White Portal. A peculiar subsidiary figure in the form of a bird head with a three-element head projection, probably related to the three-piece serpent tongue, appears on several of the recently discovered textiles (Figs. 12, 17). It will now be designated as the "hammer-headed falcon." An exact parallel appears on the lower right-hand side of the north column of the Black-and-White Portal. A somewhat similar figure occurs on the pyroengraved gourd that Tello (1959: Fig. 33) illustrates for the Ica Valley; a D dating is indicated here by the treatment of the head and the type of snake.

Figure 16 shows a unique circular organization with typical Phase D agnathic mouth masks and a human figure of the mythical variety that has a head very similar to several late coastal depictions of the human head (Fig. 40e). Figure 15 is a miniature of the larger "Staff God" depictions and the central figure is comparable to the gold plaque from Lambayeque illustrated by Rowe (1962: Fig. 27), thus providing some links for cross-dating. Figure 17 represents two bird-guardian figures (always readily distinguishable from the human-felines by the presence of a rear talon instead of a plain human heel). The twined snake belt appendages are analogous to the spiraled serpents in Figure 19, showing a form that will manifest itself later in the lower snake elements of the Raimondi Stela.

The basic impression one brings from studying these textiles is that of the cursive quality which pervades the drawings. The proportions of mirror-image figures are not quite as exact as in the stone sculpture, and "plan ahead" problems begin to crop up. Where, for example, is the left, fourth wing element on the bird-guardian (Fig. 19) to correspond to the element on the right? No room has been left for it. Similarly, on Figure 15 one can catch the Chavín artist in a very rare violation of his own canons. The left hand of the staff figure has been preserved but is misdrawn, judged from the point of view of how taloned hands are invariably drawn in Chavín art. There is one line too many, defining the top line of the finger and the bottom line of the one above it, with the result that one line ends in mid-air without being attached to the fingernail-talon. The right hand has been reconstructed (it is indicated in dotted lines) and shows how the hand should have been depicted. Such little items serve to reinforce the impression of skillful, if somewhat careless, execution. One final detail will serve to end the discussion of these pieces. R. T. Zuidema has pointed out to me (personal communication) that the little front-face, centrally placed head in the bird-guardian's mouth in Figure 19 is exactly analogous to the small head held in the center of the body in the cupped hands of the Kuntur Wasi stela (Carrión Cachot 1948: Pl. XXX). Their close relation in age makes this correspondence significant.

Gradually, the Ica sequence began to diverge from the Chavín sequence at an accelerated pace as Chavín influences became assimilated into the local tradition. Figure 40d illustrates this process. It pertains to a Phase 6 specimen from Callango. Despite its local character, it retains enough of Chavín to demonstrate how general trends in the evolution of the Chavín style were being mirrored in a regional sequence. Compare the execution of the hands and feet of this specimen to those pictured in Chart IV. The same pressures for total rectangularization are evident in both. The head of the Callango piece is perfectly square (Feature 103). While in part this has resulted from the geometrical bias of the Ica style, other features indicate that more than parallel stylistic evolution is at work. The eye form, with its extreme flattening and elongation, is very similar in concept to the eye on the Raimondi Stela (see Feature 125). The canines have flattened tips (Feature 133). As on the Raimondi, only the simple variant of the snake appears in association with the figure. One pair even corresponds to the pointed-snout variety represented on that monument (Feature 142). Thus, there would seem to be reason to place Phase 6 in some kind of relationship with Phase EF in the Chavín heartland. Later Ica phases have broken away completely—except for certain very basic and highly generalized characteristics—from the Chavín tradition. Indeed, they persisted after the demise of Chavín (see Menzel, Rowe, and Dawson 1964: Fig. 49c; Sawyer 1966: Fig. 198).

HUARA

THE ONLY PIECE attributed to the Huara Valley is a carved bone spatula shown here as Figure 6. The mouth configuration with a point above the base of the canine, the wide, saber-like canine itself with a nearly vertical trailing edge, and the eye form all identify it as a very typical Phase C piece. While it is impossible to date the advent of Chavín influence to a valley on the basis of only one specimen, it at least demonstrates that Chavín influence was present in the Huara Valley during Phase C.

CASMA

THE CASMA VALLEY, and its neighbor the Nepeña, are the focal points of this study. The Casma, in particular, forms a natural corridor leading to the Callejón de Huaylas and, in turn, to the Marañon, the Puchka, and the site of Chavín de Huantar. It is no surprise, therefore to note that the earliest Casma Chavinoid centers, Pallka and Moxeke, are relatively far up the Casma and that Chavín influences reached them relatively early, but not in the first phase of its development.

The site of Pallka is located far up the Casma on a tributary of that name. Situated on the natural platform of a rocky promontory, Pallka is surrounded by formidable mountain peaks. From the site came the *representación felínica* which I have identified as a cayman and which is presented here as Figure 7e. The string of interlocked circular elements on its back represents the spinal column which may be noted on all the cayman depictions reproduced here. The specific treatment of the feet and nose, with the characteristic concave upper line, indicate a Phase C date for this piece. As noted earlier, the Pallka specimen may be used as a naturalistic model which makes all of the later and more complex representations of the cayman decipherable.

The next Casma center that can be dated to this period is the famous site of Moxeke, farther down the valley toward the sea. In front of the third platform of the structure, facing front and flanking the stairway to the right, Tello encountered five badly eroded "idols," modeled in clay over a core of conical adobes, each placed within a separate niche (Tello 1956:60–1). The figures had originally been gaudily painted in earthen pigments of white, blue, yellow, red, gray, and green. The main building itself showed traces of having been painted red (Thompson 1962b:207). *Idolo cuarto* (Fig. 7a) has two pairs of snakes hanging over the shoulders (Tello 1956: Figs. 27, 30). Because of damage, it is uncertain where the snakes are coming from. They are, however, an early, elaborate version of the simple snake. The Moxeke snakes are exact copies of the snakes on the

Lanzón and show characteristics which do not survive beyond Phase C at Chavín de Huantar. This is the only type of snake presented here; it indicates a dating to the early half of the sequence. Perhaps the most specific comparison, in terms of method as well as technique of execution, is with the recently discovered specimen from Ancón (Fig. 8). Both specimens show the same double-forked serpent tongue, a naturalistic element that differs from the three-pronged tongue for serpent heads prevailing at Chavín de Huantar.

The way the hands of the Moxeke figures are executed (Fig. 7b) exactly parallels the treatment of hands on the Tello Obelisk, and also closely parallels the hands on the Ancón specimen which also has been dated, on other bases, to Phase C. In addition, Figure 7c displays an eye form characterized by a concave upper line and a semicircular lower outline. This eye form occurs on the Tello Obelisk. Note that Figure 7d is identical to 7c except that the eyes and mouth are closed in the latter case. Perhaps the closed eyes indicate death here, as they do in the later and related Sechín style. If so, its appearance alongside a "live" representation probably carried some structural meaning for the people who made it. This meaning may be related to the appearance in Sechín of more elaborate figures, invariably with eye markings, in association with their unadorned victims with closed eyes.

One specific iconographic element that Moxeke shares with the early end of the Chavín seriation is the presence of the pleated kilt (Feature 39) which is worn by the main figure. A comparison with the Lanzón shows that it too is wearing a pleated kilt. In later periods in Chavín art, this kilt is replaced by a G-string ending in double serpent appendages, a trait that continues right on into Moche iconography. On balance, an early date for Moxeke, probably Phase C, is indicated.

There are a number of specific correspondences between the sculpture at Moxeke and that at Cerro Sechín. These include: eyes in the form of a half-moon, the flat side being pointed up and the round side down; a band descending down the check from the eye (in the case of Moxeke, it starts from the lower edge of the eye, while in the case of Sechín it also extends above the eye); a broad pug nose, depicted most often in Sechín in profile and in Moxeke front-face; a mouth consisting of a thick, continuous lip band extending around a mouth full of exposed teeth, in neither case showing canines, as at Chavín; and a pleated kilt. In the case of Sechín, however, the kilt only appears on the defeated prisoner figures. The victors have a girdle with two groups of feathers or plumes extending from each side, which can best be considered a variant of the double-serpent belt of later Chavín representations. Jiménez Borja (1969:40) has mentioned that Tello originally interpreted the eye line at Sechín as the strap that held on the cap. While the presence of this line appears to be a prestige feature in that it is found exclusively on the warriors (who are the only ones to wear caps), the idea that the markings are straps appears invalidated by the fact that they stop above and below the eye and do not cover it as they should if they were functioning straps. A far more plausible suggestion is Jiménez Borja's hypothesis (1969:40) that they probably represent face painting, a custom, he points out, also present in traditional Moche culture. I suggest that these markings may be connected with the phenomenon that Yacovleff (1932) has labeled "hawk-markings." Henceforward they will be referred to as such.

Tello believed that the carved stone blocks at Sechín belonged to a so-called "megalithic" level of Chavín culture, and that the conical adobe structure, in which the carvings were included, belonged to an entirely different and later level, which he termed "sub-Chavín" (1956:280). Tello's belief in two different periods colored his interpretation of the monoliths and what they represented. He found ninety monoliths more or less *in situ*, along and in front of the wall, and eight more 30 to 40 meters away (1956:278). This wall formed by the monoliths stretched 52 meters in length on either side of the central entrance until it turned at both ends. Since Tello thought that the monoliths were earlier, he postulated that they were reused by the builders of the conical adobe platform:

Even though the lateral walls were well-preserved it is possible to affirm that the work was second hand. Those who constructed it paid no attention to the importance the engraved stones had in the context of a building; they were used like mere construction materials, or, perhaps, ornamentation, without awareness of their significance. The large and small monoliths were placed carelessly, and at different levels inside the wall. Some of the little monoliths with human faces on them were placed upside down; and in one case, in place of a large monolith, there had been placed a large, unengraved stone. (1956:278)

It is possible to affirm, using Tello's own data, that such reuse never occurred. Those who carved the monoliths knew very well their significance and arranged them accordingly. In support of this contention, I suggest that an examination of what was depicted yields a coherent picture. In addition to the complete, or mostly complete human bodies represented at Sechín, there are a number of more abstract elements which can be interpreted as parts of human bodies. The example that Tello astutely identified as a spinal column (Fig. 31d) is an element that is also present in the Yauya Stela (Fig. 11) in nearly identical form, and thus serves to date the Sechín carvings in a manner consistent with the other lines of evidence. Disembodied eyes (Fig. 31a) and severed pairs of arms (Fig. 31b) are readily identifiable. Recently, Mendoza and Román (1969:32) have pointed out that Figure 31c probably represents a skeletal human pelvis, an interpretation that is certainly consistent with the other elements.

The trophy-head cult, first evident in Phase C at Chavín de Huantar, has now reached its height. There are stacked trophy heads shown full face with closed eyes indicating death (Fig. 31e). Individual severed human heads are common, either with the neck intact or with three scalloped cuts at the base of the neck to indicate decapitation. All of these decapitated heads have flowing hair coming out of a squarish head in three simple strands (Fig. 29d). There is one specimen, however (Tello 1956: Fig. 98), which has complexly looped hair, just as on the trophy head of Figure 28e from Gotush. Apparently hair with recurved tips was a prestige item reserved for the depictions of warriors. Some of the trophy heads have stylized blood and gore gushing out of cuts in their necks, heads, and eyes (Fig. 29d; Tello 1956: Figs. 86, 89, 92, etc.).

In addition to the dismembered parts of bodies, there are bodies cut into various sections, the cuts again represented by scalloped lines (Fig. 29c). Invariably such bodies are naked or clad only in the pleated skirt or kilt (Fig. 29e). Sometimes the bodies are sprawled, with eyes closed and arms akimbo. Often the body consists of just the torso (Fig. 29e). The only complete figures in the frieze—and it is a real frieze that tells a definite story—are costumed warriors each holding a club with a unique L-shaped head. Each is decked out in elaborate regalia that can include a truncated conical hat, out of which descends one or two sets of feathers, and a girdle with several hanging plumes. This latter element probably derives from the late serpent belt (Feature 123) with plumes replacing serpents. In the details of hands and feet the conquerors are identical to their victims (Fig. 29e).

On either side of the doorway there were two major monoliths which Tello (1956: Fig. 53) described as knives. It is interesting that there are two of them which start a symmetrical organization continued by the distribution of the warriors and their trophies. Clearly the builders were striving for symmetry, a trait which Rowe lists as one of the characteristics of Chavín art, and a pattern unlikely to occur in the casual reuse of older building material.

The monoliths of Cerro Sechín depict much the same story that Gerdt Kutscher has seen in Moche painted ceramics. The same warriors are depicted in all their finery in contrast to their naked prisoners and victims. The images are essentially the same, although, of course, the styles are different. Kutscher describes "a naked man, lying flat on his back, his extremities extended. This was the characteristic position, in the battle scenes, for indicating a corpse. In the same row, lies a severed human head" (1950: 120).

It is a proposition of this paper that a re-examination of Rowe's Chavín seriation coupled with a new seriation of the human figure in Chavín art supports the position that the sculpture of Cerro Sechín is late rather than early.

The crucial piece for the placing of Cerro Sechín in relative time is Figure 28e, the EF carved plaque from Chavín de Huantar designated here as the Head-Bearer. If Sechín is accepted as early, it would be impossible to account for this specimen, which holds a trophy head in his hand; the result would be a bi-model distribution of the trophy-head cult. One would have to explain why it was present in the earliest times, absent in Phase AB, and then present again in Phase C. With Cerro Sechín dated late, there is no such difficulty. The extreme preoccupation of Sechín art with the trophy-head cult and warfare would merely form an intensification of what happened earlier at Chavín, and would fit in with what was going on in the other regional centers.

The treatment of the trophy head itself in Figure 28e shows several specific resemblances to details of the Sechín rendering of this theme. In Cerro Sechín convention, the blood that gushes from the severed neck of the trophy head was represented by blunt strands, with a line separating the tips from the main portions of the strands. Apparently this device was used to differentiate the stylized blood from hair, which was portrayed in a similar fashion only without the separating line or the blunted tips. Exactly the same convention appears in Figure 28e, of EF dating. In this case, the blunt tips appear as small squares at the ends of the strands (also three in number) coming down out of the neck just as they do at Cerro Sechín. Moreover, the hair of the trophy head is depicted in exactly the same manner as the hair of the Sechín carvings, as pointed strands looped together in a manner identical to that illustrated in Tello (1956: Fig. 98). To expand the list of similarities, the eye form of the trophy head on Figure 28e is the same as that found on the Sechín works. The fact that it lacks a pupil suggests that the artist was trying to depict a closed eye, indicating death by the same convention current at Sechín. The treatment of the hands and feet in Figure 28e and in the Cerro Sechín carvings converge, both approximating rectangles but with the heel showing a stronger tendency

toward rectangularization than the hands (Tello 1956: Figs. 77, 63).

The presence of a conservative trait in Cerro Sechín art, like the pleated kilt, can be explained as a continuation of the earlier Moxeke convention, which was derived from Chavín, rather than as a result of direct contacts between early Chavín and Cerro Sechín. The closer similarities between Moxeke and Chavín than between Sechín and Chavín (outside of the chronologically specific cluster of traits relating to the trophy head) would tend to support such a position. In short, these detailed comparisons justify an earlier statement by Lathrap (1971:74), "I am completely unconvinced by the argument that Chavín originated in the north-central coast valleys such as Casma or Nepeña. I think that Lanning's (1967:93, 101) identification of the Cerro Sechín carvings as pre-Chavín is extremely dubious. In a number of specific details the Cerro Sechín carvings suggest a rustic rendering of the EF segment of Rowe's (1962) chronology for Chavín rather than a precursor of Chavín AB."

HUAYLAS

THOMPSON (1962c) discovered two works in the town of Huaylas in the Callejón de Huaylas which display the closest affinities to the monoliths of Cerro Sechín of any sculpture found outside the Casma Valley. "Resemblances to the sculpture at Cerro Sechín Temple appear to be greater than to that of the Chavín style. . . . The scalloped neckline, generally believed to indicate a severed trophy head, occurs frequently at Cerro Sechín, but such heads usually have closed eyes there. The ear and mouth treatment, except for the possible pointed tooth, can be roughly duplicated at Cerro Sechín as can the headdress or hair lock of one figure" (Thompson 1962c:246). As a glance at Figure 30a and b shows, the resemblances are more than a rough duplication. Figure 30a is very similar to 30c, a specimen from the most recent excavations at Cerro Sechín. The eye form is in both cases identical. The bulbous nose on the Huaylas piece is in line with the lip line to a degree that few Sechín works can match, but the close similarity of the two groups of works shows that this cannot be used as a chronological argument with respect to Cerro Sechín.

Another peculiarity retained by Figure 30a and b is the above-the-nose fold, a feature absent in Sechín art. However, the line behind the mouth on Figure 30a probably represents the above-the-mouth crease descending from the nose, as shown in Figure 30c. Unfortunately, in the case of Figure 30a, this crease has eroded away from the vicinity of the nose. Before weathering, Figure 30a probably also possessed teeth executed in the same pattern as on Figure 30c. The mouth in both instances pinches out in the middle in hourglass configuration. To expand the points of similarity of the Huaylas pieces with those of Cerro Sechín mentioned by Thompson, the heads in Figure 30b and d show the same looped depiction of hair. The ear type of the Huaylas pieces is a classical Sechín ear. In conclusion, to quote from Thompson: "The dating of Cerro Sechín Temple remains uncertain, but all presently available information tends to favor a date shortly following the Chavín horizon. . . . Although the Huaylas pieces are out of context, a similar date might be suggested for them on the basis of the resemblances to Cerro Sechín Temple and the features reminiscent of the Chavín style" (1962c:246). The "unique" site of Cerro Sechín is no longer unique.

NEPENA

Judging from the stylistic evidence, the site of Cerro Blanco flourished a little later than Pallka and Moxeke in the Casma. Rowe (1967:76) dates Cerro Blanco to his Phase C. Certainly, the presence of the mouth form with a mid-rib, a Phase C diagnostic trait (Feature 54, and Kubler 1962: Pl. 124), argues for a C dating, as does the point above the base of the canines in the painted mouth bands surrounding the modeled relief. However, in this case the continuance of the point to the exterior lip-line does not occur; the line is straight, and the canines are flat at the end, a late trait. The extreme rectangularization of the opposed mirror-image faces, as well as the extreme flattening of the eye, when coupled with the presence

of the Phase D, L-shaped canine, tend to argue for a slightly later date. Though some traits indicate Cerro Blanco is Phase C, others make it most plausible to place the monument at the very end of C, or perhaps early D.

The other major Nepeña center is Punkurí. One of the two pieces usable for dating is the modeled upper portion of a realistic cat that occupied the center of the main stairway (Soriano Infante 1941: Fig. 22; Larco Hoyle 1941: Fig. 7; Kubler 1962: Pl. 123b). Immediately notable is the fact that the mouth type of this cat corresponds exactly to that of the Pacopampa cat (Fig. 24b). This correspondence suggests a late dating for Punkurí which is strengthened by the fact that the cat from Pukurí bears the "double-winged eye" (Feature 145), also a late trait at Chavín. Yet another corroborating detail linking Punkurí to Cerro Sechín is a red-painted feline (Tello 1956: Fig. 109), found in the temple of Cerro Sechín. Although incomplete, it is related both to the Punkurí feline and to two specimens from Chavín (Tello 1960: Figs. 62, 72) dated in this study as later (see Feature 144).

The painted bas-relief of Punkurí (Carrión Cachot 1948: Pl. XIX-4) reinforces a late dating for the cat since it is clearly a transitional piece that bridges the gap between the Chavín and Moche traditions. This figure displays very few specific Chavín elements and yet succeeds in looking perfectly Chavinoid. Perhaps it is a cayman like those already investigated, but one in which the fish element has begun to assume primary importance. The treatment of the small figures within the divisions of the main figure, particularly the monkey and the seal, appear very Moche-like. This curious figure is related to Cerro Sechín sculpture through its rectangular girdle consisting of an inner and outer rectangle, the same as that worn by the warriors at Cerro Sechín (Fig. 29a). A late date for Punkurí is consistent with its similarities to Cerro Sechín and the Nepeña centers of Cuchipampa and Siete Huacas with their Sechín-style depictions.

As intimated above, the stone lintels from Cuchipampa (Cusi-pampa?) and Siete Huacas, found by

Proulx (1968), show that Cerro Sechín is no longer unique, as was once imagined (Fig. 32a and b). Figure 32b in particular can be considered a crude rendering of its Sechín counterpart, Figure 29a, a standing warrior in full regalia brandishing a club in one hand. The girdle is of the same form as that in the Punkurí mural and even closer to the Sechín examples (cf. Fig. 32c and d) and is characterized by a single series of plumes extending from the back.

For yet another close parallel to Cerro Sechín, one must go to the stone mortar (or mortars) pictured in Larco Hoyle (1963: Fig. 32; Carrión Cachot 1948: Pl. XI-5; Fig. 33a and b, this paper). These drawings show figures comparable to the Sechín figures in both general appearance and specific portrayal of the characteristic Sechín girdle already discussed. They seem to represent the end of the trend toward rectilinear treatment which Sechín shared with Late Chavín. The hair strands on the Lambayeque mortar are the same as at Sechín. The earplug of the right-hand figure has the design from the ball-butt of the club used by the warriors at Sechín (Fig. 29b), while the design of the headdress is that of the head of that club. It will be noticed that the outlines of the hair on the left half of the figure are softer, and that the head lacks the club attributes. Perhaps we are dealing here with the concept of duality so often encountered in Cupisnique ceramics, and the right-hand figure is a symbolized weapon, while the left is life, the unhappy victim. Such an interpretation is suggested by scenes in Moche art in which weapons are personified and on occasion give battle to humans.

In brief, what then are the implications of this seriation for Chavín chronology and cultural history? It would seem that this study can shed little light on the first appearance of a full-fledged and mature Chavín art style at Chavín de Huantar since it cannot furnish plausible antecedents. It does, however, provide a coherent picture of the later history of the Chavín style (see Chart VI). In the earliest Phase, AB, the influence of the art of Chavín was relatively narrow, not extending much beyond the Puchka River Basin. In Phase C, Chavín art spread to the Huara and Casma Valleys, and to Ancón. The purity of these distant manifestations and the cultural homogeneity which it implies argue for communication and some degree of political control uniting the various Chavín centers. This spread of Chavín influence is not inconsistent with the fact that the trophy-head cult and an emphasis on warriors appear in this phase. The presence of war clubs (Rowe 1962: Figs. 35–38) on the North Coast, where the only suitable big game is other men, and the actual presence and implied use of such clubs at Supe, also in a Phase C context where "the skulls from Supe show four cases of fracture or inflammatory lesions, probably of traumatic origin [and] the male skull and skeleton from Grave 10 at the Lighthouse site showed five extensive healed fractures" (Willey and Corbett 1954:144), seems to indicate that the spread of the Chavín cult was not always so peaceful as was once assumed.

The extension of Chavín artistic influence reached its maximum in the following phase, D, as the large number of examples attributable to this stage indicates. Finally, this uniformity broke down as regional differences began to assert themselves. There is evidence of an increasing preoccupation with warriors and head-taking in these regional cultures. One gets the impression of small and warring political communities whose autonomy was reflected in the divergence among their artistic traditions and the details of their martial regalia. Specific Chavín elements declined as the local art became more and more the product of the local situation. It is in this milieu that one must place Alto de la Guitarra, Monte Calvario, Cusi-pampa, and Cerro Sechín.

Explanation of the Illustrations

SINCE THERE IS an unfortunate but understandable tendency for the more renowned pieces of Chavín art to be reillustrated in every new work in this field, they need not be repeated here. One thing the literature does not need is yet another set of illustrations of the Lanzón, the Raimondi Stela, the "Smiling God," the Tello Obelisk, and the Black-and-White

Portal. Thus, while these specimens are discussed at length in this work, they are not illustrated in it. Instead, the opportunity has been taken to show more obscure specimens, new views of familiar specimens, and those not pictured in an adequate way before. At least in part, this approach is intended to remedy the difficulty of attempting to study Chavín art when many interesting and some crucial pieces are not generally current in the literature. Therefore, this work is meant to be read in conjunction with a small number of standard works in the field of Chavín art, most notably Rowe 1962 and/or 1967 and Tello 1956 and 1960, rather after the fashion of a gloss. Many excellent illustrations of the most famous pieces can be found in these sources.

Chavín pottery and the iconographic evidence derived from it were treated here as unavoidably relevant, but not as the main subject of inquiry. Hence, ceramics are illustrated after depictions derived from stone sculpture, wood and bone carving, and textiles. More attention was focused on the designs incised and modeled on the ceramics than on associated forms. This does not mean that the author feels an analysis of form cannot be worked out, only that a full treatment is not possible here. As a partial compromise, pottery designs are illustrated along with the vessel shapes on which they commonly occur.

Chronological arguments and their relation to spacial distribution having been presented in the text, the illustrations are ordered by time rather than space. However, where possible, specimens from the same area pertaining to the same relative time period are grouped together. Works pictured come from all over Peru.

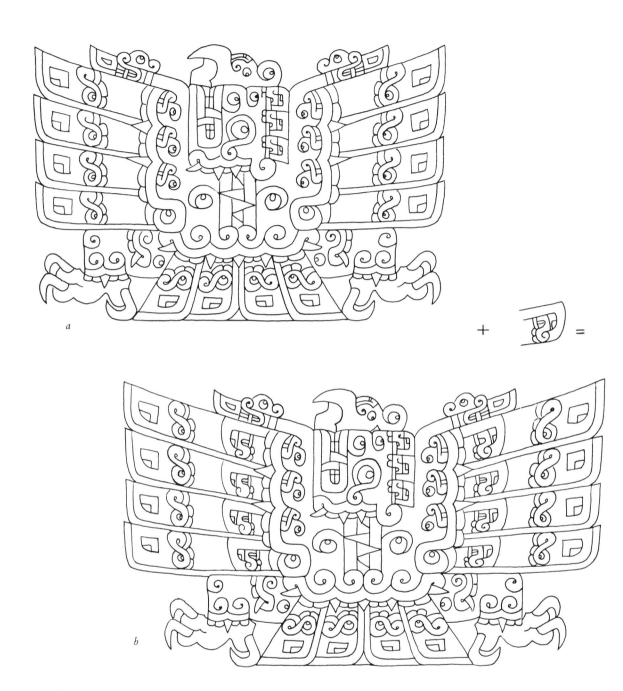

Fig. 1 Cornices found off the northeast corner of the old
south wing of the temple, Chavín de Huantar. (Adapted
from Rowe 1967: Figs. 13 and 12.)

40

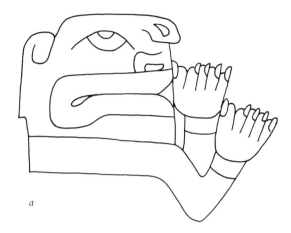

a

Fig. 2 Tello Obelisk, presumably found in the Epoch III sunken courtyard, Chavín de Huantar. (Adapted from Tello 1960: Fig. 31.) *a.* (Corresponds to Rowe 1967: Fig. 7, A-15.) *b.* (Corresponds to Rowe 1967: Fig. 7, B-17.) *c.* (Corresponds to Rowe 1967: Fig. 7, A-25, A-26, A-27, A-29.)

b

c

a

b

a

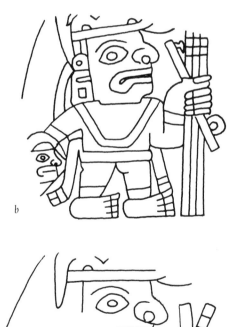

b

c

42

Fig. 3 (opposite, above) Stone mortar, Chavín de Huantar. (Adapted from Tello 1960: Figs. 126b and 126a.)

Fig. 4 (opposite, below) Chavín de Huantar. *a*. Square framed relief. (Adapted from Ayers 1961: Fig. 14.) *b*. Relief fragment. (Adapted from Rowe 1962: Fig. 17.) *c*. Relief fragment, part of the same wall frieze as *b*. (Adapted from Tello 1960: Fig. 85.)

Fig. 5 (above) Relief, Chavín de Huantar. (Adapted from Kauffmann Doig 1971: Fig. 268.)

Fig. 6 (below) Carved bone spatula, Huara Valley. (Adapted from Tello 1960: Pl. XLIXc.)

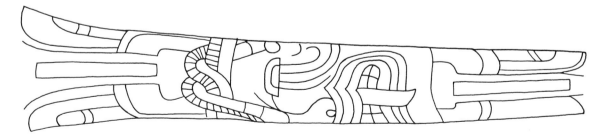

43

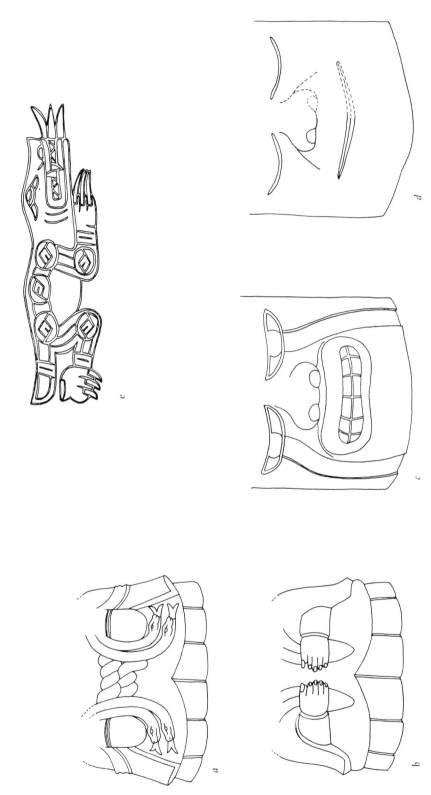

Fig. 7 Casma Valley. *a–d.* Idols on the temple platform, painted mud sculpture, Moxeke: IV, III, V, and VI. (Adapted from Tello 1956: Figs. 30, 29, 31, and 27-VI.) *e.* Carved bone, Pallka. (Adapted from Tello 1956: Fig. 22.)

44

Fig. 8 Modeled ceramic vase, Ancón. (Adapted from Rosas n.d.:Pl. XIII.)

45

Fig. 9 (opposite, above) "Lintel of the Jaguars," Monumental Stairway, Chavín de Huantar. (Adapted from Rowe 1967: Fig. 19.)

Fig. 10 (opposite, below) Design element modules of the "Lintel of the Jaguars," Chavín de Huantar. (Adapted from Rowe 1967: Fig. 19.)

Fig. 11 (above) Yauya Stela, Yauya. (Adapted from Rowe 1962: Fig. 31 and from a drawing by Pablo Carrera M. distributed by the National Museum [Espejo 1964].)

Fig. 12 (below) Painted textile, recent find in the Ica Valley, 7-8 km. south of Necropolis, now on loan to the Museo Amano, Lima. (Adapted from a tracing of the original specimen.)

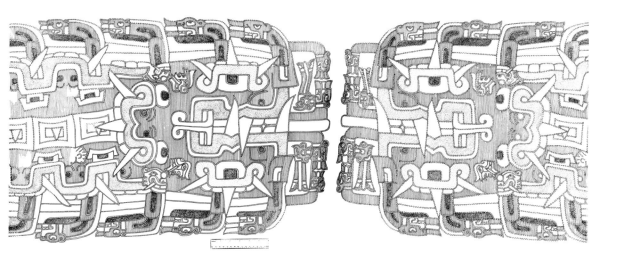

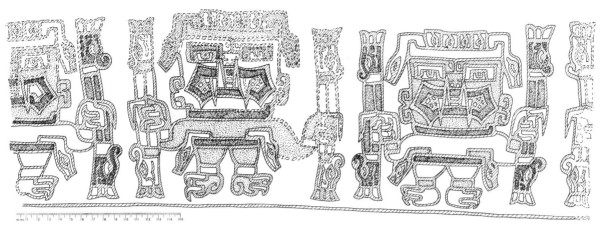

Fig. 13 (opposite, above) Painted textile, Callango, Ica Valley. (Adapted from Rowe 1962: Fig. 29.)

Fig. 14 (opposite, below) Painted textile of the same type as Fig. 13, recent find in the Ica Valley, 7–8 km. south of Necropolis, now on loan to the Museo Amano, Lima. The original border had tassles fringing the right and bottom edges. (Adapted from a tracing of the original specimen.)

Fig. 15 (above) Painted textile, recent find in the Ica Valley, 7–8 km. south of Necropolis, now on loan to the Museo Amano, Lima. (Adapted from a tracing of the original specimen.)

Fig. 16 (below) Painted textile, recent find in the Ica Valley, 7–8 km. south of Necropolis, now on loan to the Museo Amano, Lima. (Adapted from a tracing of the original specimen.)

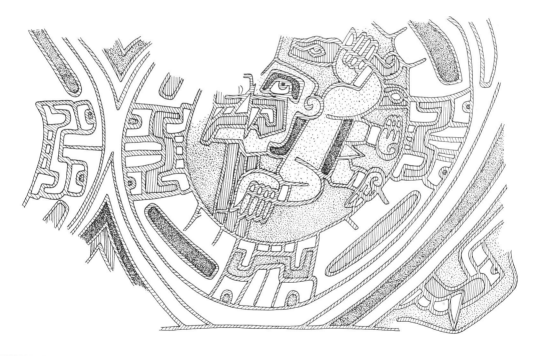

Fig. 17 (above) Painted textile, recent find in the Ica Valley, 7-8 km. south of Necropolis, now on loan to the Museo Amano, Lima. (Adapted from a tracing of the original specimen.)

Fig. 18 (below) Painted textile, recent find in the Ica Valley, 7-8 km. south of Necropolis, now on loan to the Museo Amano, Lima. The circles were tie-dyed before the textile was painted. (Adapted from a tracing of the original specimen.)

Fig. 19 (opposite) Painted textile, Callango, Ica Valley. (Adapted from Rowe 1962: Fig. 30.)

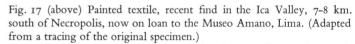

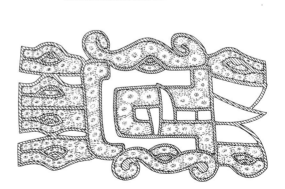

a

b

c

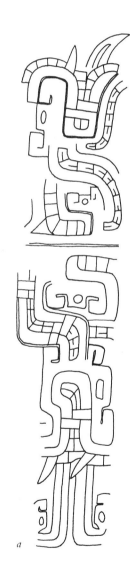

a

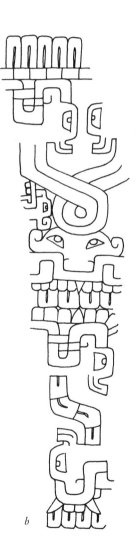

b

c

d

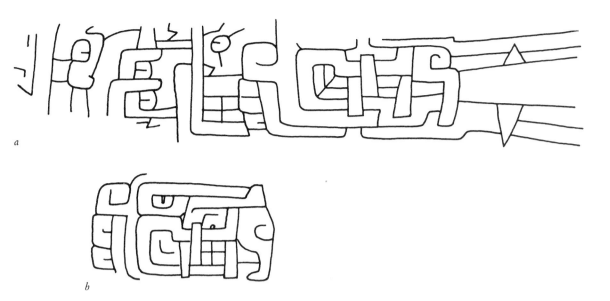

a

b

Fig. 20 (opposite, above) *a,b*. Kotosh Well-Polished ceramic vessels, Kotosh. (Adapted from Izumi and Sono 1963: Pls. 127-1 and 127-2.) *c*. Small tenoned stone head, Chavín de Huantar. (Adapted from Tello 1960: Fig. 96.)
Fig. 21 (opposite, below) Larco Herrera Museum, Lima. (Drawings from the original specimens.) *a,b*. Carved bone. *c*. Small double-chambered stone bowl. *d*. Spindle whorl.
Fig. 22 (above) Carved bone spatulas, found in Salinar culture graves, Chicama Valley, now in the Larco Herrera Museum, Lima. (Drawings from the original specimens.)
Fig. 23 (below) Gotush Obelisk, Gotush. (Adapted from Tello 1960: Pl. XLIII.)

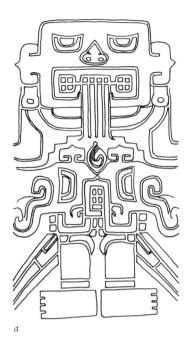

Fig. 24 Pacopampa. *a.* "Feline of Pacopampa" Stela. (Adapted from Larco Hoyle 1945:3.) *b.* Jaguar sculpture. This specimen is too eroded to seriate according to features. (Adapted from Sawyer 1968: No. 19.) *c.* Carved bone. (Rubbing of the original specimen collected by Rosas.) *d.* Modeled ceramic vessel, now in the National Museum, Lima. (Adapted from a photograph of the original specimen.)

a

b

c

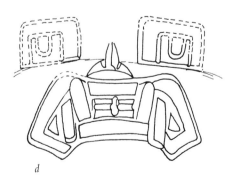

d

54

a

Fig. 25 Polychrome wall paintings, Monte Calvario, Catache. (Adapted from Mejía Xesspe 1968: Figs. 5 and 2.)

b

55

Fig. 26 (right) Petroglyph from the *meseta*, Monte Calvario, Catache. (Adapted from Mejía Xesspe 1968: Fig. 10.)

Fig. 27 (below) Petroglyph, Alto de la Guitarra, between the Virú and Moche Valleys. (Adapted from Kauffmann Doig 1971: Fig. 313 and Disselhoff and Linné 1960: Fig. 58.)

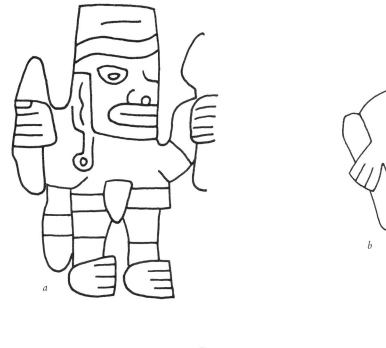

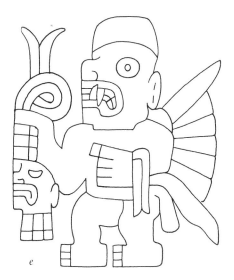

Fig. 28 *a*. Rectangular framed relief, Yura-yako, Chavín de Huantar. (Adapted from Tello 1960: Fig. 80.) *b,d*. Rectangular framed reliefs, temple, Chavín de Huantar. (Adapted from Tello 1960: Figs. 82 and 87.) *c*. Detail of the partially preserved human figure in the upper register of Fig. 17, Ica Valley. *e*. Rectangular framed relief, "Head-Bearer," Yura-yako, Chavín de Huantar. (Adapted from Tello 1960: Fig. 81.)

Fig. 29 Stone monoliths from the north facade of the temple, Cerro Sechín, Casma Valley, *a,e*. East side. (Adapted from Tello 1956: Figs. 57 and 59.) *b,c,d*. West side. (Adapted from Tello 1956: Figs. 72, 82, and 84.)

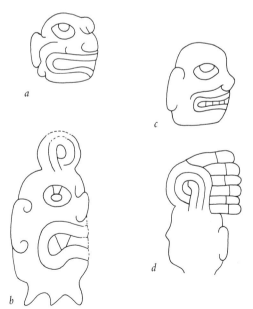

Fig. 30 Stone monoliths. *a,b*. Huaylas. These specimens can be seriated only in relation to Sechín and therefore cannot be listed in the seriation charts. (Adapted from Thompson 1962c: Figs. 1 and 2.) *c*. Cerro Sechín, Casma Valley. (Adapted from Mendoza and Román 1969: Fig. 13.) *d*. Lower part of temple. Cerro Sechín, Casma Valley. (Adapted from Tello 1956: Fig. 98.)

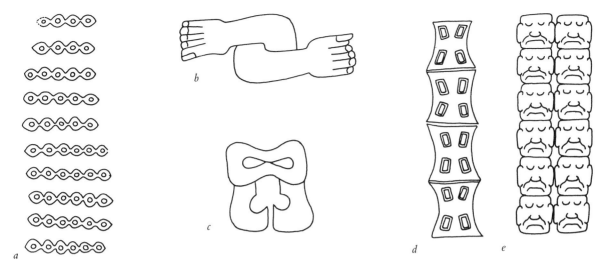

Fig. 31 Stone monoliths from the temple, Cerro Sechín, Casma Valley. *a,d,e*. East side of north facade. (Adapted from Tello 1956: Figs. 58, 55, and 56.) *b*. West side of north facade. (Adapted from Tello 1956: Fig 88.) *c*. Lower part of temple. (Adapted from Tello 1956: Fig. 103.)

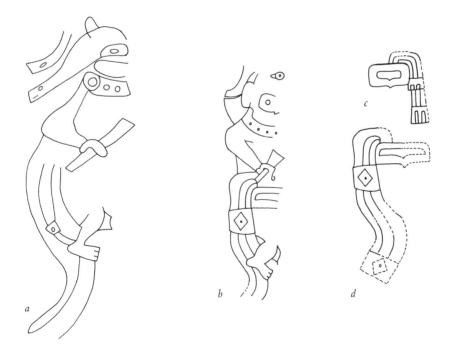

Fig. 32 *a*. Stone lintel, Siete Huacas, Nepeña Valley. This specimen can be seriated only in relation to Sechín and therefore cannot be listed in the seriation charts. (Adapted from Proulx 1968: Plan 11.) *b,d*. Stone carving. Cuchipampa (Cusipampa?), Nepeña Valley. This specimen can be seriated only in relation to Sechín and therefore cannot be listed in the seriation charts. (Adapted from Kauffmann Doig 1971: Fig. 303.) *c*. Stone monolith, west side of the north facade of the temple, Cerro Sechín, Casma Valley. (Adapted from Tello 1956: Fig. 77.)

59

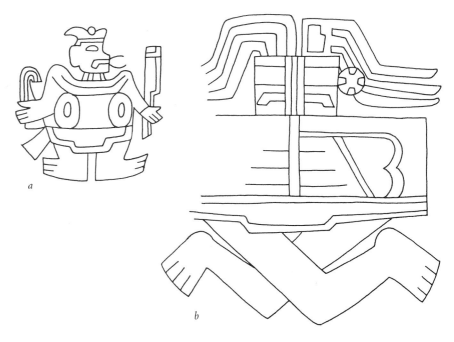

a

b

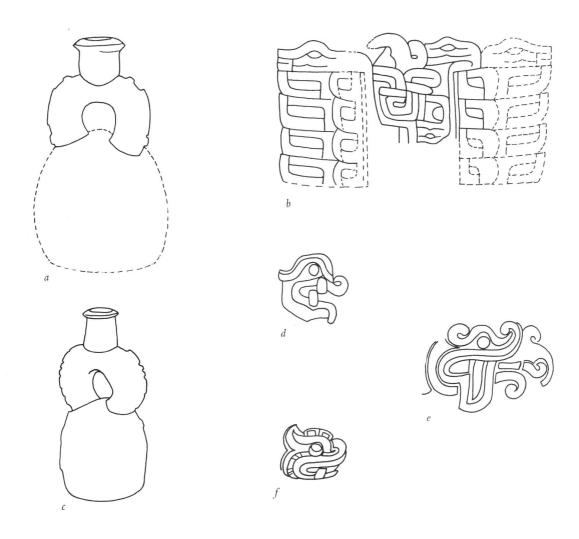

Fig. 33 (opposite, above) Stone mortars, Lambayeque Valley. Both of these specimens can be seriated only in relation to Sechín and therefore cannot be listed in the seriation charts. *a*. (Adapted from Carrión Cachot 1948: Pl. XI-5.) *b*. Perhaps the other side of *a*. (Adapted from Larco Hoyle 1963: Fig. 32.)

Fig. 34 (opposite, below) Turquoise vase, Lambayeque Valley. (Adapted from Carrión Cachot 1948: Pl. XVIII-3).

Fig. 35 (above) Ceramic vessels. *a,b,f*. Rocas, Chavín de Huantar. (Adapted from Lumbreras 1970: 138, 138, and 142.) *c,e*. Early Cupisnique, Chicama Valley. (Adapted from Sawyer 1968: No. 29.) *d*. Early Cupisnique, Chicama Valley. (Adapted from Larco Hoyle 1938: Pl. III.)

Fig. 36 Chicama Valley. *a*. Transitional Cupisnique ceramic vessel. (Adapted from Larco Hoyle 1966: Fig. 9.) *b*. Cupisnique ceramic vessel. (Adapted from Larco Hoyle 1966: Fig. 9 and 1963: Frontispiece.) *c,d*. Cupisnique ceramic vessels. (Adapted from Larco Hoyle 1941: Figs. 23 and 210.)

Fig. 37 Ofrendas vessels, Chavín de Huantar. *a.* (Adapted from Lumbreras 1970: 138.) *b–h.* (Adapted from Lumbreras and Amat 1966: Figs. 4, 3e, 3a, 7e, 5, 3b, 3c.)

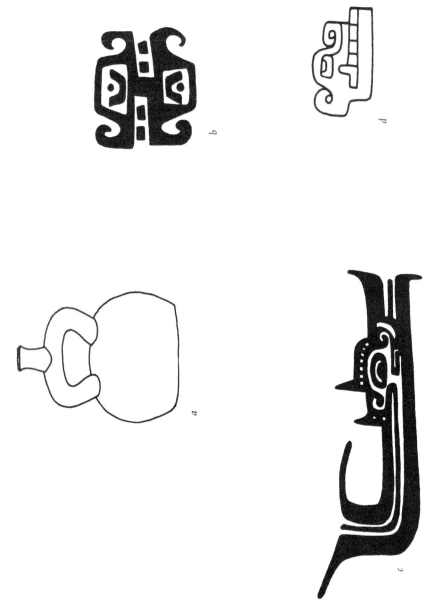

Fig. 38 (above) *a.* Mosna ceramic vessel, Chavín de Huantar. (Adapted from Lumbreras 1970: 138.) *b.* Stirrup spout vessel (?), Chicana Valley (?). (Adapted from Larco Hoyle 1941:83.) *c.* Mosna ceramic vessel, Chavín de Huantar. (Adapted from Lumbreras and Amat 1966: Fig. 13b.) *d.* Black-and-White Portal column, Chavín de Huantar. (Adapted from Lumbreras 1970:96.)

Fig. 39 (below) By my placing all of these specimens together I am not necessarily assuming that they occur stylistically at the same time. In fact, Figs. *c–e* and *n–o* have been arranged into what might be a seriational sequence from more controlled to more cursive variants. *a,b,g.* Ceramic vessels, Ancón. (Adapted from Rosas n.d.: Pls. XIV 4, XIV 6, and XIV 6.) *c–f, h–o.* Ceramic vessels, Chicama Valley. (Adapted from Larco Hoyle 1941: Fig. 110, frontispieces to Capítulos VI and V, Fig. 54, frontispieces t · Capítulos I, VII, and IV, p. 219, Fig. 212, and frontispieces to Capítulos IV, VII, and II.)

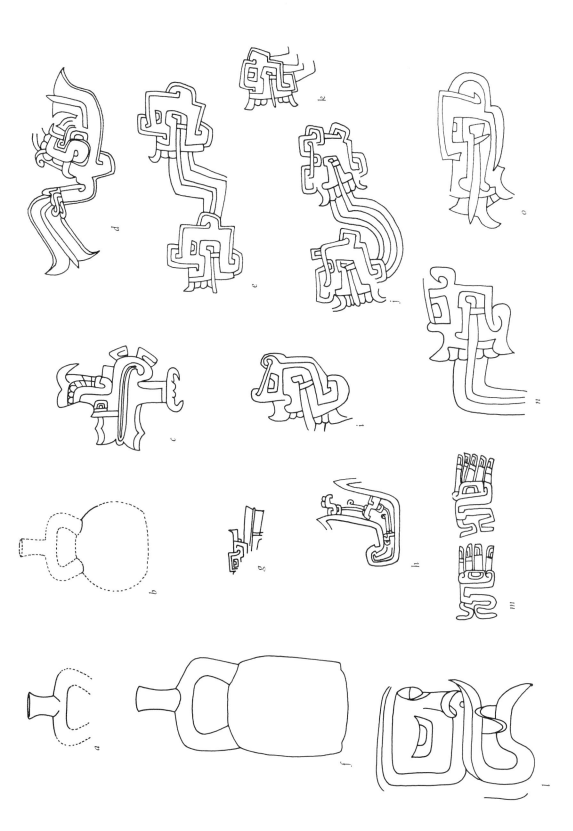

Fig. 40 Ceramic vessels, Ica Valley. *a*. Phase 1, Callango. (Adapted from Menzel, Rowe, and Dawson 1964: Fig. 1a.)
b,c. (Adapted from Ubbelohde-Doering 1952: Pl. 235.) *d*. Phase 6, Callango. (Adapted from Rowe 1962: Fig. 52.)

Fig. 41 Ceramic vessel, Chicama Valley (?). (Adapted from Larco Hoyle 1941: Fig. 211.)

67

PRIMARY-FIGURE EYES   SECONDARY-FIGURE EYES

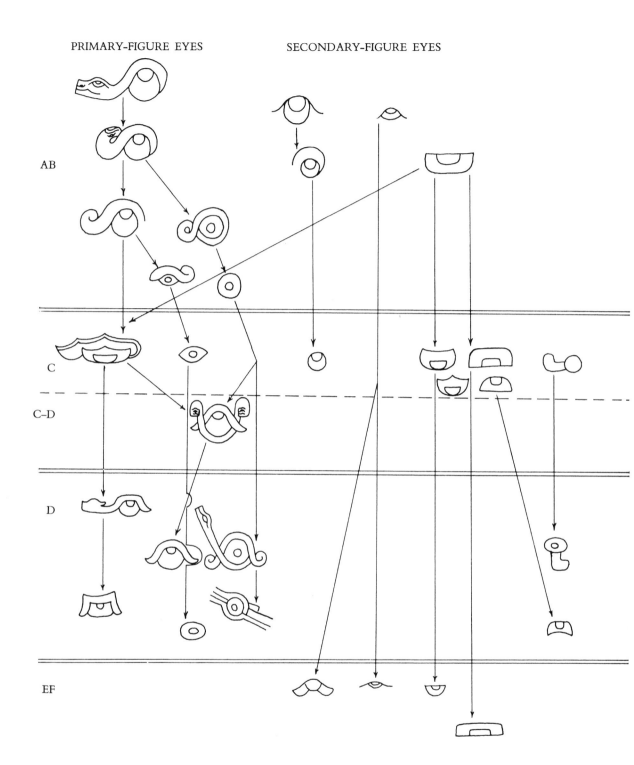

AB

C

C–D

D

EF

CHART III

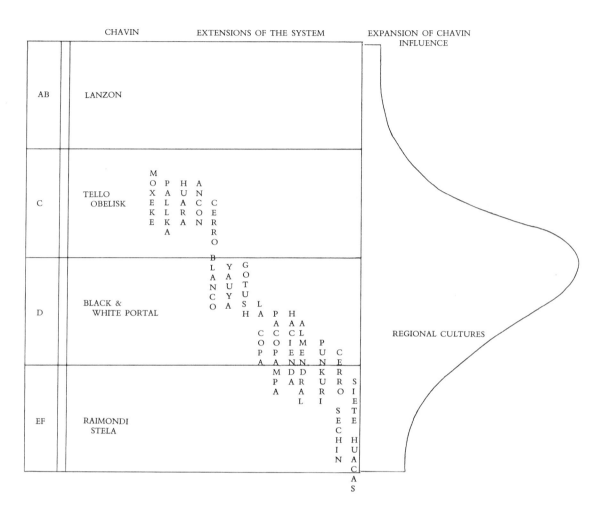

CHART VI

Bibliography

AYERS, FRED D.
1961 Rubbings from Chavín de Huántar, Peru. *American Antiquity*, vol. 27, no. 2, pp. 239–245. Salt Lake City.

BENNETT, WENDELL C.
1942 Chavín Stone Carving. *Yale Anthropological Studies*, vol. III. New Haven.
1943 The Position of Chavín in Andean Sequences. *Proceedings of the American Philosophical Society*, vol. 86, no. 2, pp. 323–337. Philadelphia.
1944 The North Highlands of Peru: An Account of Exploration and Excavation in Viru and Lambayeque Valleys. *Anthropological Papers of the American Museum of Natural History*, vol. XXXIX, part 1. New York.
1946 The Archaeology of the Central Andes. *In* Handbook of South American Indians (Julian H. Steward, ed.), *Bureau of American Ethnology Bulletin 143*, vol. 2, pp. 61–147. Washington.
1954 Ancient Arts of the Andes. The Museum of Modern Art, New York.

BENNETT, WENDELL C., and JUNIUS BIRD
1960 Andean Culture History. (Second and revised edition.) American Museum of Natural History, Handbook Series, no. 15. New York.

BUSE, HERMANN
1957 Huarás-Chavín. Juan Mejía Baca and P. L. Villanueva, Lima.

BUSHNELL, G. H. S.
1957 Peru. Ancient Peoples and Places Series. Frederick A. Praeger, New York.
1965 Ancient Arts of the Americas. Frederick A. Praeger, New York.

CARRIÓN CACHOT, REBECA
1948 La Cultura Chavín. Dos nuevos colonias: Kuntur Wasi y Ancón. *Revista del Museo Nacional de Antropología y Arqueología*, vol. II, no. 1, pp. 99–172. Lima. (Reprint.)
1955 El culto al agua en el antiguo Perú. La Paccha elemento cultural Pan-andino. Separata de la *Revista del Museo Nacional de Antropología y Arqueología*, vol. II, no. 2. Lima.
1959 Ultimos descubrimientos en Chavín—La serpiente simbolo de las lluvias y de la fecundidad. *In* Actas del XXXIII Congreso Internacional de Americanistas, vol. II, pp. 403–415. San José.

CASAFRANCA, JOSÉ
1960 Los nuevos sitios arqueológicos chavinoides en el Departamento de Ayacucho. *In* Antiguo Perú, Espacio y Tiempo, pp. 325–333. Librería-Editorial Juan Mejía Baca, Lima.

COLLIER, DONALD
1962 Archaeological Investigations in the Casma Valley, Peru. Akten des 34 Internationalen Amerikanistenkongresses, pp. 411–417. Vienna.

COSSIO DE POMAR, F.
1966 La Cultura Chavín. *Cuadernos Americanos*, Año XXV, vol. CXLVI, no. 3, pp. 159–172. Mexico.

DISSELHOFF, HANS-DIETRICH, and SIGVALD LINNÉ
1960 America Precolombina. El Arte de los Pueblos Series, Editorial Seix Barral S.A., Barcelona.

ENGEL, FRÉDÉRIC
1956 Curayacu—A Chavinoid Site. *Archaeology*, vol. 9, no. 2, pp. 98–103. Brattleboro.

ESPEJO NUÑEZ, JULIO
1964 Sobre un nuevo fragmento de la Estela de Yauya. *Boletín del Museo Nacional de Antropología y Arqueología*, año 1, no. 1. Lima.

HEINE-GELDERN, ROBERT
1959 Representations of the Asiatic Tiger in the Art of the Chavín Culture: A Proof of Early Contacts Between China and Peru. *In* Actas del XXXIII Congreso Internacional de Americanistas, vol. 1, pp. 321–326. San José.

IZUMI, SEIICHI, and TOSHIHIKO SONO
1963 Andes 2: Excavations at Kotosh, Peru 1960. Kadokawa, Tokyo.

JIMÉNEZ BORJA, ARTURO
1969 El Estilo Sechín. *Amaru, Revista de Artes y Ciencias de la Universidad Nacional de Ingeniería*, no. 11, pp. 39–41. Lima.

KAN, MICHAEL
1972 The Feline Motif in Northern Peru. *In* The Cult of the Feline: A Conference on Pre-Columbian Iconography (Elizabeth P. Benson, ed.), pp. 69–90. Dumbarton Oaks Research Library and Collection, Washington.

KAUFFMANN DOIG, FEDERICO
1963 La Cultura Chavín. Los Grandes Civilizaciones del Antiguo Perú, tomo III. Peruano Suiza, S.A., Lima.
1971 Arqueología Peruana: Visión Integral. Iberia S.A., Lima.

KELEMEN, PAL
1943 Medieval American Art: A Survey in Two Volumes. The Macmillan Co., New York.

KOSOK, PAUL
  1965 Life, Land and Water in Ancient Peru. Long
        Island University Press, New York.

KROEBER, ALFRED L.
  1926 Archaeological Explorations in Peru. Part I: An-
        cient Pottery from Trujillo. *Anthropology Memoirs*,
        vol. II, no. 1. Field Museum of Natural History,
        Chicago.
  1944 Peruvian Archaeology in 1942. *Viking Fund Publi-
        cations in Anthropology*, no. 4. New York.
  1952 The Nature of Culture. The University of Chi-
        cago Press, Chicago.
  1953 Paracas Cavernas and Chavín. *University of Cali-
        fornia Publications in American Archaeology and
        Ethnology*, vol. 40, no. 8, pp. 313-348. Berkeley.
  1957 Style and Civilizations. Cornell University Press,
        Ithaca.

KUBLER, GEORGE
  1962 The Art and Architecture of Ancient America:
        The Mexican, Maya, and Andean Peoples. Pen-
        guin Books, Baltimore and London.

KUTSCHER, GERDT
  1950 Iconographic Studies as an Aid in the Reconstruc-
        tion of Early Chimu Civilization. *In* Peruvian
        Archaeology: Selected Readings (John H. Rowe
        and Dorothy Menzel, eds.), pp. 115-124. Palo
        Alto.

LANNING, EDWARD P.
  1963 Olmec and Chavín: A Reply to Michael D. Coe.
        American Antiquity, vol. 29, no. 1, pp. 99-101.
        Salt Lake City.
  1967 Peru Before the Incas. Prentice-Hall, Englewood
        Cliffs.

LARCO HOYLE, RAFAEL
  1941 Los Cupisniques. Trabajo presentado al Congreso
        Internacional de Americanistas de Lima, Lima.
  1945 Los Cupisniques. Buenos Aires.
  1946 A Cultural Sequence for the North Coast of Peru.
        In Handbook of South American Indians (Julian
        H. Steward, ed.), *Bureau of American Ethnology
        Bulletin 143*, vol. 2, pp. 149-175. Washington.
  1948 Cronología Arqueológica del Norte del Perú.
        Sociedad Geográfica Americana, Buenos Aires.
  1963 Las Epocas Peruanas. Lima.
  1966 Peru. Archaeologia Mundi Series. World Publish-
        ing Co., Cleveland and New York.

LATHRAP, DONALD W.
  1971 The Tropical Forest and the Cultural Context of
        Chavín. *In* Dumbarton Oaks Conference on
        Chavín (Elizabeth P. Benson, ed.), pp. 73-100.

Dumbarton Oaks Research Library and Collection, Washington.

LÉVI-STRAUSS, CLAUDE
  1967 Structural Anthropology. Anchor Books, Double-
        day & Co., Garden City.

LOTHROP, S. K.
  1941 Gold Ornaments of Chavín Style from Chongo-
        yape. *American Antiquity*, vol. VI, no. 3, pp. 250-
        262. Menasha.
  1951 Gold Artifacts of Chavín Style. *American Anti-
        quity*, vol. XVI, no. 3, pp. 226-240. Menasha.

LUMBRERAS, LUIS GUILLERMO
  1967 Para una Revaluación de Chavín. *Amaru, Revista
        de Artes y Ciencias de la Universidad Nacional de
        Ingeniería*, no. 2. Lima.
  1969 De los pueblos, las culturas y las artes del Antiguo
        Perú. Moncloa-Campodonico, Editores Asoci-
        ados, Lima.
  1970 Los Templos de Chavín: Guía para el Visitante.
        Publicación del Proyecto Chavín de Investiga-
        ciónes Arqueológicas, Corporación Peruana del
        Santa, Lima.

LUMBRERAS, LUIS GUILLERMO, and HERNÁN AMAT
OLAZÁBAL
  1966 Informe Preliminar Sobre Las Galerias Interiores
        de Chavín: Primera Temporada de Trabajos.
        Revista del Museo Nacional, vol. 34, pp. 143-197.
        Lima.

MASON, J. ALDEN
  1957 The Ancient Civilizations of Peru. Penguin Books,
        Harmondsworth and Baltimore.

MAZESS, RICHARD B., and D. W. ZIMMERMAN
  1966 Pottery Dating from Thermoluminescence. *Sci-
        ence*, vol. 152, no. 3720, pp. 347-348. Washington.

MEJÍA XESSPE, TORIBIO
  1968 Pintura chavinoide en los lindes del arte rupestre.
        La Revista San Marcos, Numero Noveno-Segunda
        Epoca, Lima.

MENDOZA, ALBERTO BUENO, and LORENZO
SAMANIEGO ROMÁN
  1969 Sechín: Una Nueva Perspectiva. *Amaru, Revista
        de Artes y Ciencias de la Universidad Nacional de
        Ingeniería*, no. 11, pp. 31-38. Lima.

MENZEL, DOROTHY, JOHN H. ROWE, and LAWRENCE
E. DAWSON
  1964 The Paracas Pottery of Ica: A Study in Style and
        Time. *University of California Publications in Ameri-
        can Archaeology and Ethnology*, vol. 50. Berkeley
        and Los Angeles.

78

MUELLE, JORGE
 1937 Filogenia de la Estela de Raimondi. *Revista del Museo Nacional*, vol. 6, no. 1, pp. 135–150. Lima.
 1955 Del Estilo Chavín. *Baessler-Archiv*, Neue Folge, Band III, pp. 89–96. Berlin.

PATTERSON, THOMAS C.
 1971 Chavín: An Interpretation of Its Spread and Influence. *In* Dumbarton Oaks Conference on Chavín (Elizabeth P. Benson, ed.), pp. 29–48. Dumbarton Oaks Research Library and Collection, Washington.

PICKERSGILL, BARBARA
 1969 The Archaeological Record of Chili Peppers (Capisicum Sp.) and the Sequence of Plant Domestication in Peru. *American Antiquity*, vol. 34, no. 1, pp. 54–61. Salt Lake City.

POLO, JOSÉ TORIBIO
 1899 La piedra de Chavín. *Boletín de la Sociedad Geográfica de Lima*, año IX, tomo IX, nos. 4–6, 7–9, pp. 192–231, 262–290. Lima.

PROULX, DONALD A.
 1968 An Archaeological Survey of the Nepeña Valley, Peru. *Research Reports*, no. 2. Department of Anthropology, University of Massachusetts, Amherst.

REICHLEN, HENRY
 1965 Dos telas pintadas del norte del Perú. *Revista Peruana de Cultura*, no. 5, pp. 5–15. Lima.

ROMERO, EMILIA
 1951 Existe alguna relación entre "Los Danzantes" de Monte Albán en México y los monolitos de Cerro Sechín en el Perú? *In* The Civilizations of Ancient America: Selected Papers of the 29th International Congress of Americanists (Sol Tax, ed.), pp. 285–290. University of Chicago Press, Chicago.

ROSAS LA NOIRE, HERMILIO
 n.d. La secuencia cultural de período formativo en Ancón. Thesis for the degree of Bachelor in Archaeology, 1970. Universidad Nacional Mayor de San Marcos, Lima.

ROSSELLÓ TRUEL, LORENZO
 1959 Exposición de nuevos elementos de serie para la cerámica Paracas. *Actas y Trabajos del II Congreso Nacional de Historia del Perú, 1958, Epoca Prehispánica*, tomo I. Lima.
 1960 Sobre el estilo de Nasca. *In* Antiguo Peru, Espacio y Tiempo. Trabajos presentados a la Semana de Arqueología Peruana (9–14 de Noviembre de 1959), pp. 29–45. Librería-Editorial Juan Mejía Baca, Lima.

ROWE, JOHN H.
 1958 La seriación cronológica de la cerámica de Paracas elaborada por Lawrence E. Dawson. *Revista del Museo Regional de Ica*, año IX, no. 10, pp. 9–21. Ica.
 1960 The Origins of Creator Worship Among the Incas. *In* Culture in History: Essays in Honor of Paul Radin (Stanley Diamond, ed.), pp. 408–429. Columbia University Press, New York.
 1962 Chavín Art: An Inquiry into its Form and Meaning. The Museum of Primitive Art, New York.
 1967 Form and Meaning in Chavín Art. *In* Peruvian Archaeology, Selected Readings (John Howland Rowe and Dorothy Menzel, eds.), pp. 72–103. Palo Alto.
 1971 The Influence of Chavín Art on Later Styles. *In* Dumbarton Oaks Conference on Chavín (Elizabeth Benson, ed.), pp. 101–124. Dumbarton Oaks Research Library and Collection, Washington.

SAWYER, ALAN R.
 1966 Ancient Peruvian Ceramics: The Nathan Cummings Collection. The Metropolitan Museum of Art, New York Graphic Society, Greenwich.
 1968 Mastercraftsmen of Ancient Peru. The Solomon R. Guggenheim Foundation, New York.
 1972 The Feline Motif in Paracas Art. *In* The Cult of the Feline: A Conference on Pre-Columbian Iconography (Elizabeth Benson, ed.), pp. 91–115. Dumbarton Oaks Research Library and Collection, Washington.

SOLDI, PABLO
 1956 Chavín en Ica. Imprimería "La Voz de Ica," Ica.

SORIANO INFANTE, AUGUSTO
 1941 Monografía de Ancash: Nepeña (Provincia de Santa). *Revista del Museo Nacional*, vol. 10, no. 2, pp. 263–277. Lima.

TELLO, JULIO C.
 1923 Wira Kocha. *Inca*, vol. 1, no. 1, pp. 93–320, vol. 1, no. 2, pp. 583–606. Lima.
 1943 Discovery of the Chavín Culture in Peru. *American Antiquity*, vol. 9, no. 1, pp. 135–160. Menasha.
 1956 Arqueología del Valle de Casma. Culturas: Chavín, Santa o Huaylas Yunga y Sub-Chimú. Publicación Antropológica del Archivo "Julio C. Tello" de la Universidad Nacional Mayor de San Marcos, vol. 1. Lima.
 1959 Paracas, Primera Parte. Publicación del Proyecto 81 del Programa 1941–42 de The Institute of Andean Research de New York. Lima.
 1960 Chavín, Cultura Matriz de la Civilización Andina, Primera Parte. Publicación Antropológica

del Archivo "Julio C. Tello" de la Universidad Nacional Mayor de San Marcos, vol. 2. Lima.

THOMPSON, DONALD

1962a The Problem of Dating Certain Stone-faced, Stepped Pyramids on the North Coast of Peru. *Southwestern Journal of Anthropology*, vol. 18, no. 4, pp. 291–301. Albuquerque.

1962b Formative Period Architecture in the Casma Valley, Peru. *In* XXXV Congress Internacional de Americanistas, Actas y Memorias, vol. 1, pp. 205–212. Mexico City.

1962c Additional Stone Carving From the North Highlands of Peru. *American Antiquity*, vol. 28, no. 2, pp. 245–246. Salt Lake City.

TOKYO, UNIVERSITY OF

1960 Andes, The Report of the University of Tokyo Scientific Expedition to the Andes in 1958. Tokyo.

UBBELOHDE-DOERING, HEINRICH

1952 The Art of Ancient Peru. Frederick A. Praeger, New York.

VALCÁRCEL, LUIS E.

1957 Nuevos descubrimientos arqueológicos en el Perú: Chavín. *Cuadernos Americanos*, año XVI, vol. XCIII, no. 3, pp. 180–184. Mexico.

WALLACE, DWIGHT T.

1962 Cerrillos, An Early Paracas Site in Ica, Peru. *American Antiquity*, vol. 27, no. 3, pp. 303–314. Salt Lake City.

WILLEY, GORDON R.

1945 Horizon Styles and Pottery Traditions in Peruvian Archaeology. *American Antiquity*, vol. 11, no. 1, pp. 49–56. Menasha.

1951 The Chavín Problem: A Review and Critique. *Southwestern Journal of Anthropology*, vol. 7, no. 2, pp. 103–144. Albuquerque.

WILLEY, GORDON R., and JOHN M. CORBETT

1954 Early Ancón and Early Supe Culture: Chavín Horizon Sites of the Central Peruvian Coast. *Columbia Studies in Archaeology and Ethnology*, vol. III. New York.

YACOVLEFF, EUGENIO

1932 Las Falcónidas en el Arte y las Creencias de los Antiguos Peruanos. *Revista del Museo Nacional*, vol. 1, no. 1, pp. 35–111. Lima.

STUDIES IN PRE-COLUMBIAN ART AND ARCHAEOLOGY NUMBER FOURTEEN

A MAN AND A FELINE
IN MOCHICA ART

ELIZABETH P. BENSON

Dumbarton Oaks   Trustees for Harvard University   Washington, D.C. 1974

ACKNOWLEDGMENTS

I am grateful for the interest and cooperation of G. H. S. Bushnell, Nathan Cummings, Dieter Eisleb, Peter T. Furst, Julie Jones, Otto Klein S., Alan Sawyer, Anne-Louise Schaffer, Allen Wardwell, S. Henry Wassén, and Raymond Wielgus.

EPB
Dumbarton Oaks

Fig. 1 Mochica turquoise carving with pyrite inlay. Dumbarton Oaks Collections, Washington.

Fig. 2 Other side of the turquoise carving. Dumbarton Oaks Collections, Washington.

4

A Man and a Feline in Mochica Art

I

THIS PAPER had its genesis in the attempt to make a brief catalog description of a Mochica piece (Figs. 1, 2, and 3) in the Dumbarton Oaks Pre-Columbian Collection. The object is a small turquoise carving, 4 centimeters high by 3.4 centimeters wide by 5.9 centimeters in depth, with pyrite inlay. The carving represents an animal, most certainly a feline, crouching behind a disproportionately small human being. The animal's mouth is open, and its muzzle rests on the man's head, with the forepaws flanking the head. The animal is more realistically rendered than the man, whose head is approximately of equal length with the rest of his body. He wears a hat—a sort of toque with side flaps—but the rest of his clothing, if any, is unclear. There is a rope around his shoulders which appears to tie a bundle on his back. His hands are together in front.

The problem, of course, lies not in the physical description of this piece, but in its meaning or meanings. The Mochica have left, on painted and modeled pots, more vivid pictures of their world than any other Pre-Columbian people, perhaps more various and telling pictures than any other ancient people. There are representations of their flora and fauna and portraits of their chieftains and warriors, their diseased and disfigured. These are often rendered with such extraordinary realism that one knows exactly what sort of bird or squash or deer or disease is represented. Equally often, however, the motifs are blended in what is to us fantasy: beans have human faces and legs, weapons are anthropomorphized, and warriors have wings and hawk beaks. In the attempt to sort out the realities and relationships of the Mochica world, one can neither take the literal for granted, nor dismiss as fantasy the extraordinary combinations of motifs, for the Mochica view of reality was not that of modern man, and, because they were preliterate people, a high degree of symbolism was involved in their representations.

Who is the man in this turquoise piece, and what is the significance of the feline? What is the relationship between feline and man? Is the feline a predator attacking the man; is it a protector standing behind him; or is there another explanation along the continuum between these two extremes? Does the object represent a real event, a ceremony, a drug-induced hallucination, or a mythical or supernatural situation? Or is it a combination of motifs "readable" only to the initiated?

Fig. 3 Front of the turquoise carving. Dumbarton Oaks Collections, Washington.

5

Figs. 4 and 5 Gallinazo pot. Virú Valley. Formerly in the collection of James A. Ford. Photos courtesy of the American Museum of Natural History, New York.

In Pre-Columbian art and in contemporary native Latin-American myth, various large felines are common, the most important of which is the jaguar. The jaguar is the largest cat in the New World; it can stand at least as tall as a large man and may weigh up to 300 pounds. It is a powerful predator, carnivorous, nocturnal, and associated with waterways in the rain forest. A vast ethnographic lore concerns the jaguar in direct relationship with a human being. There is the concept of the "alter ego," a human being's double in the animal world, this animal double being most commonly a jaguar. There is the belief that a shaman or priest can change himself into a jaguar, or the idea that a shaman who has been wounded by a jaguar and recovers acquires special powers. The ethnographic literature also describes circumstances in which jaguars of awe-inspiring size appear in narcotic-induced dreams; the jaguar may be seen as a dead ancestor or as a shaman who has assumed the form of a jaguar. All these beliefs probably center around the notion of groups of people—clans, tribes, nations—who identify with the jaguar's prowess as a hunter and power as a spirit, and consider themselves "the jaguar's people." The best summary of this subject has been made by Peter Furst (1968).[1]

[1] This motif also appears elsewhere around the Pacific Basin. See *Early Chinese Art and the Pacific Basin* 1968: 65–81.

6

Fig. 6 Recuay pot. Photo by J. Oster, courtesy of the Musée de l'Homme, Paris.

The theme of a feline (often of disproportionately large size) and a human figure occurs with some frequency on a number of artifacts from various periods and regions in Peru,[2] but principally in pottery from the Mochica civilization. As far as I know, the motif does not exist in Chavín art. An early representation is seen on a Gallinazo pot (Figs. 4 and 5), found in the Virú Valley, which shows a very large feline with a very small man. The feline canines —interlocked, very stylized and prominent—identify the animal as a feline, as does the heavy, curled tail.

[2] The motif also exists at San Agustín, Colombia, but that facet of the problem will not be considered here. See Reichel-Dolmatoff 1972.

The stance of both figures is more hieratic and symmetrical than that seen in the turquoise piece, but the basic ingredients of the posture are essentially the same: the feline is seated, has its head above that of the man, and its paws at the man's shoulders; the man's hands are in front of him, and both figures face straight ahead. The man in the Virú piece wears only a loincloth on his body, but, in contrast, wears on his head a curious, crownlike headdress and one of a pair of earspools (the other has been broken off). The earspool appears to be of the standard Peruvian type with a shaft that went through a hole in the earlobe. The open mouth of the man, showing prominent teeth, and the closed, slit eyes suggest that he

Fig. 7 Recuay pot. Photo courtesy of the Museum für Völkerkunde, Berlin.

Fig. 8 Vicús stone finial. Formerly, collection of Domingo Seminario, Piura. Photo courtesy of Alan Sawyer.

8

may be blind or grimacing in agony or moribund or even dead (this is a common way of representing the dead in Mexican art, but it is not common in Peru), or it may be that he is in some trancelike state. The enormous size of the feline suggests something supernatural, and the very formal composition perhaps indicates a symbolic meaning. Nonetheless, there are no clear answers here to the meaning of the turquoise piece.

In the Recuay culture we find versions of the same theme. One pot (Fig. 6) depicts a large, patterned animal, whose upholstery-material spots suggest a very stylized jaguar, holding at each shoulder an elaborately dressed man, again shown wearing a headdress and prominent circular ear ornaments. The relative size of the two figures is fairly normal. They stand at right angles to each other, but the frontal character of each figure is maintained. Another, cruder Recuay piece, a double vessel (Fig. 7), has an animal—with similar stylized patterning, but no other particular signs of being a feline—on top of one section, holding by the shoulders a very small human figure. The animal's open mouth rests on the man's doughnut-shaped headdress. Again, the man is wearing earspools and has his hands placed at waist height in front of him. Again, both figures are frontal and the composition symmetrical. Both of the Recuay human beings have wide-open eyes and appear to be alive. The Recuay style, however, is not realistic enough to yield any great insights.

A Vicús stone finial, formerly in the collection of Domingo Seminario (Fig. 8),[3] shows a colossal feline behind a seated man, the feline's chin resting on the man's head. The forepaw visible in the photograph rests at the side of the man's head and the hind foot on the man's shoulder. (I assume that this position is repeated on the other side.) The man appears to have hands clasped in front of him and ears covered with flaps.

The earliest Mochica pottery version of this motif

[3] I am grateful to Alan Sawyer for bringing this piece to my attention.

I have found is a Mochica I pot in the Museum of the American Indian (Figs. 9 and 10), in which the stance of both figures is again frontal and symmetrical. A standing, snarling, polka-dotted feline has a paw on either side of a human head which rests on two ankles and feet. The human head has closed eyes and appears to be dead. This may be a trophy head (a head ritually severed as an offering, most likely to a deity). I had at first thought that the feet were added simply as a device to hold the head up, but there are pots in the shape of head effigies which rest on feet like this when it would have been much easier for the potter to have put the head on a simple base. This may be a trophy head on trophy feet! The idea of the head as a seat of human power is behind the Peruvian decapitation and trophy-head cult, but feet also seem to have had some special significance for the Mochica. There are effigy pots representing feet; a foot and a leg were often added to painted representations of the fish or shark monster; and feet and lower legs are also shown in scenes which relate to human sacrifice by beheading and amputation (Kutscher 1954: Pl. 25B).

Later Mochica trophy heads tend to have eyes open rather than closed, so the head and feet here might possibly be read, not as a form of trophy head, but as an abridged version of a human body. They might also represent a shaman in a closed-eyed trance, in which perhaps only his head and feet feel real to him. In any case, the piece serves to point up something that is generally indicated in all the other versions of this motif: it is the head that the feline always focuses on —his paws and head are always somewhere near the man's head. This may well relate to the fact that the jaguar attacks the head of his prey and apparently will attack only if it can see the head. Both jaguars and pumas generally kill large game by breaking the neck (Perry 1970: 29). This hunting habit may reinforce the significance of the Mochica head cult. Jaguars and pumas rear up on their hind legs before pouncing on their prey. Thus the pose of the feline in all these representations approximates the attack position. (In some of the representations, the cat is sitting rather than crouching or rearing, but this is possibly

Figs. 9 and 10 Mochica pot. Photos courtesy of the Museum of the American Indian, Heye Foundation, New York.

an artistic convention to render the pose compact enough for the sculptural quality of the material.) Not only does the feline focus on the human head in these examples, but the human head tends to be large in proportion to its body. In the Museum of the American Indian piece, the proportion of the head to the "body" recalls the relative size of the head and

body of the human figure in the turquoise piece, where the head is emphasized and the body almost dismissed. The head of the jaguar and the head of the man are approximately the same size, but the total effect is that of a very large feline and a very small human being. The face painting of the man is unusual (early Mochica face painting, however, is gen-

Fig. 11 Mochica pot. Photo courtesy of the Cambridge University Museum of Archaeology and Ethnology, Cambridge.

erally more various and less conventionalized than that of later Mochica art). The man wears no ear ornaments—in fact, his ears do not show—and no headdress, and, of course, no clothing. The feline here has been somewhat anthropomorphized. It stands in a manner suggestive of human stance; its forepaws seem handlike; and its hind paws are represented in a fashion very like the human feet.

In all of the examples so far, the poses of both human and feline are symmetrical, formal, and heraldic, with the disproportionately large cat looking out over the man's head, and its paws evenly placed at the man's shoulders or head, which is large in comparison with his body.

A group of later Mochica pots has closely related but somewhat differing arrangements. A pot in the Cambridge University Museum (Fig. 11) shows a seated human figure with a feline at his right side. The symmetry of the earlier pots has been relaxed, and the piece is much more realistically rendered. The man sits cross-legged with his head to one side as he looks slightly upward, while the cat looks out over the man's shoulder, snarling at the world. Even here, though, some elements of the earlier formula remain: the man's hands are clasped at waist height in front of him, the feline has a paw symmetrically placed on each of the man's shoulders, and the cat is behind the man. The feline is painted with a pattern of short, straight lines—probably a shorthand statement for hair—and is most likely a puma. The head of the feline is slightly larger than that of the man, and their heights are comparable when both are seated; there is thus a realistic size relationship. The man's head is slightly oversized in relation to his body, but it still maintains fairly naturalistic proportions.

The man wears neither ear ornaments nor headdress. He has the hairdress associated with prisoners of war, a sort of soup-bowl haircut with a tuft over the center brow. The garment he wears seems to be a simple sleeved shirt or shift with painted designs. The cuffs have a variation of the swirl, a common and important Mochica motif associated with the sea, and perhaps having other meanings as well. This swirl pattern appears again at the neck. The stepped design —another important motif—is barely visible at the bottom of the garment. There is also a diagonal band across the chest, with a motif that may indicate rattles, snails, or possibly jugs. It is possible that these designs may not be on a garment, but may indicate body painting or ceremonial binding instead. Such designs are sometimes seen as face painting or tattooing on objects of pottery and metal. In fact, there is a painted design on this man's chin.

The man appears to be blind in one eye—one eye is closed while the other is wide open. The closed eye is rather like the slit eye of the Gallinazo and Mochica I pieces (Figs. 4, 5, 9, and 10). There are a number of depictions of blind people in Mochica art; blindness seems to have had mystical significance. Even the deity is depicted at times as blind in one eye (Wassermann–San Blas 1938: Fig. 534). The eyes and mouth on the Cambridge pot may indicate facial paralysis (see Matos Moctezuma 1970), another ailment that was represented with respect in Mochica art, although the mouth is probably not sufficiently distorted to support this interpretation. The grimace, with teeth prominently displayed, suggests the possibility that this is the human emulation of the feline's snarl. On the Cambridge pot the painting of the eyebrows is particularly interesting. The open eye has a brow like that painted on a doll—it looks more like lashes than a brow. The brow over the closed eye is drawn in a plain arc. Also notable are the man's cauliflower ears. They are quite large and stand away from the head.

Although the feline is menacing, it is not clear whether it is threatening the man or someone facing it and the man. The cat here may very well be a protective figure. It looks as if it might be saying, "Don't touch this man—he's mine!" But for what purpose? The man's face indicates some state of anguish or supplication. His hands are clasped in a sort of prayer pose.

A figure similar to this was published in the Wassermann–San Blas Collection and is now in the private collection of Nathan Cummings (Fig. 12). The human figure has the same tufted hairdress, is blind in one eye, and has a curious jack-o'-lantern mouth with teeth showing. The right ear, standing somewhat away from the head, has a hole in it, as if an ornament were intended to be attached; the left ear is only roughly rendered and does not appear to have this hole. The figure has hands clasped in front of his chest, and his head leans slightly to the left, away from the feline that leans over his right shoulder, placing a paw on each of his shoulders. The feline here is much smaller in relation to the man than the Cambridge feline, its head being only about half the

Fig. 12 Mochica pot. Collection of Nathan Cummings, New York. After Wassermann–San Blas 1938: Fig. 463.

size of the man's. The decoration of the human figure suggests body painting rather than a garment, although the checkerboard bib may be of cloth. Certainly the lower part of the body is unclothed; the phallus and pubic hair are plainly visible. (This was probably also true of the Cambridge pot, but the condition in this area is poor, making definite determination impossible.) There are curious stripes on the legs of the

Figs. 13 and 14 Mochica pot. Photos courtesy of the Museum für Völkerkunde, Berlin.

man, and various geometric motifs and animal figures on his arm and body.[4]

[4] Mr. Cummings tells me that this vase has been repainted,
which may account for certain eccentricities in the designs.
Parts of it appear to have been restored.

The Museo Larco Herrera in Lima has another
version of this theme. The feline looks out over the
shoulder of the man, who is seated crosslegged with
hands in prayer pose and head to one side. He is blind
in one eye and has "Maltese-cross" face painting. The

surface of the figure is eroded, but there are traces of paint around the neck, indicating a design similar to that on the neck of the Cambridge figure, with traces of a checkerboard design below it. Again, the phallus is prominent.

A Mochica IV pot in the Museum für Völkerkunde, Berlin (Figs. 13 and 14; Schmidt 1929: Pl. 152, left), represents a man, apparently kneeling. Again, his hands are clasped in front and his head, having the same sort of soup-bowl haircut with a tuft above the brow, is slightly upturned. As on the Cambridge and Cummings pots, the man is blind in one eye. His face is painted with a circle on each cheek and one on the chin. He wears an unusual type of ear ornament and a garment with a checkerboard pattern which covers his arms to the wrists—it does not seem to have sleeves but only slits for the hands to come through. (Mochica artists were quite capable

Fig. 15 Mochia pot. Photo courtesy of the Peabody Museum, Harvard University, Cambridge.

of depicting sleeves when they wanted to.) The garment is tight around the man's neck. Again, this man has prominent teeth and no headdress. Again, he seems to be unhappy about his situation; he does not project a sense of security about the protectiveness of the feline who crouches to his right. Again, there is a possessive paw placed on each of the man's shoulders, but the feline appears to be gnawing on one of the shoulders. The feline here is small and is possibly an ocelot or a very young jaguar.

An effigy pot in the Peabody Museum at Harvard (Fig. 15) shows a feline seated behind and to the right of a man. The man is also seated and has a tilted, up-turned head with the same sort of hairdress and prominent ears and teeth as on the two previous illustrated pots. Both creatures are approximately the same size. The feline, who is nibbling on the man's shoulder, is apparently a puma. It has a solid dark coat with a white-freckled muzzle and underbelly. The man is completely nude except for a rope around his neck. He has Maltese-cross face painting, and both eyes are open and tilted to the heavens. Unlike the previous figures, though, his hands are tied behind his back.

All five of these later Mochica modeled pots suggest some extraordinary state of being. It can be read most simply as the agony, pain, and fear of being attacked by a fierce feline. It might also indicate, however, a shaman's state of exhilaration or intoxication while hallucinating the feline or undergoing initiatory wounding.

In the Art Institute of Chicago, there is a variation of this theme on a Mochica IV painted pot (Figs. 16 and 17), the variation perhaps being to some extent dictated by the technique. There is a similar scene on either side of the pot. In both scenes the jaguar and the man sit facing each other instead of the jaguar's being behind the man. The jaguar's outstretched claws reach toward the man's neck. The man sits with head tilted back, teeth prominent, eye closed. (This may well be intended as another figure blind in one eye; it was a convention of Mochica pot painters to show figures in profile.) Here the hairdress con-

sists of a pony-tail in back rather than the frontal tuft seen on the modeled figures. This is probably a normal hairdress, but would rarely be seen because most figures wear some sort of headgear.

The painted figures are seated in a landscape with cacti and clouds of sand around them. On one side of the pot, the man, seated crosslegged, has his arms extended in front (Fig. 16). They may be bound together in a sort of handcuff, or the dark bands at the wrists may be bracelets or wrist-guards (such do exist). In any case, he is again in prayer pose. He wears what looks like a primitive straitjacket, the designs of which are also worn by Mochica warriors. The panel to the left probably has small disks attached; what may be metal plaques around the waist are common on warriors' garments. This uncommon side view of a warrior's "armor" shows the back ties of the garment. This is the first example seen in this paper of a figure dressed in at least the partial garb of a warrior. He does not wear the warrior's helmet, however.

The ear of this figure is particularly notable. Three of the four modeled Mochica IV pieces have distended ears with no ear ornaments. The ear here—which is drawn in a rather stylized way—is also without an ornament. The Cummings piece has a hole in the lobe which might be construed as a hole for an ear ornament to be attached to the pot. The indication on the painted pot, however, is that this is a representation of a man who would normally be wearing ear ornaments, but who is not wearing them on this occasion. I think that this is also the explanation for the prominent ears on the modeled pots: they were enlarged and pulled forward by the habitual use of ear ornaments which the figures are no longer wearing. All of these men were important enough to have worn large and impressive ear ornaments.

A scene similar to the one just discussed is painted on the other side of the pot (Fig. 17). Here the jaguar's forelegs go straight out so that only the claws of the uppermost paw threaten the neck of the man, who again sits with head tilted, eye closed, teeth

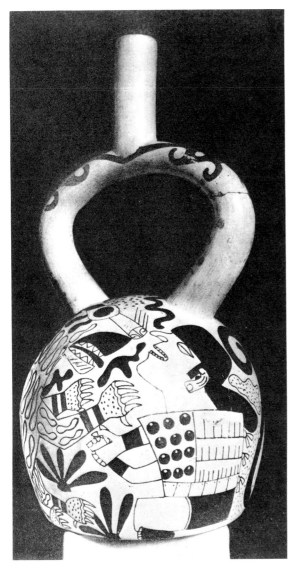

Fig. 17 Mochica pot. Photo courtesy of the Art Institute of Chicago.

Fig. 16 Mochica pot. Art Institute of Chicago. After Lehmann and Doering 1924: Pl. 85.

Fig. 18 Mochica wooden ceremonial staff or digging stick. Collection of Mr. and Mrs. Raymond Wielgus. Photo courtesy of the Metropolitan Museum of Art, New York.

Fig. 19 Mochica pot. Museo Nacional de Antropología y Arqueología, Lima.
Photo by the author.

bared, and ear unornamented. The man has a rope around his neck; his hands seem to be tied behind his back; and, again, his shirt is that of a warrior, suggesting that perhaps he is a prisoner-of-war stripped of his headdress and weapons. His teeth are clenched, and blood seems to be issuing from his mouth. This man is actually being attacked by the jaguar and suffering wounds.

Although in the modeled pots the human beings look pained or moribund and the felines aggressive,

it is still possible that some extraordinary experience is being represented. This painted pot, however, suggests more strongly an attack by the large cat and the wounding of the man.

A Mochica wooden ceremonial staff or digging stick (Fig. 18) shows a different formal arrangement of this motif. A very large jaguar, with an open mouth and holes for inlay, grabs with both forepaws the chest of a man who lies in an agonized supine position. The rear feet of the jaguar rest on the man's knees. Certainly nothing here indicates the protective quality of the feline. We are reminded that a jaguar, after sucking blood from its victim, will eat its flesh from the neck and breast. The wooden piece seems to express this interest of the feline in the man's chest. (It may also express sacrifice by ripping the heart from the chest.) We have now gone beyond the concepts of the alter ego or hallucination, and, I believe, even beyond the idea of a man's being wounded by a jaguar and acquiring

special powers upon recovery. It is hard to believe that this man will recover from the feline attack. The man's mouth is open; the eyes are empty sockets. He appears to be not only already dead, but already skeletal. He seems to be undeniably the victim of the jaguar.

A pot in the Museo Nacional de Antropología, Lima (Fig. 19), rendered in a crude and decadent Mochica style, shows a version of the theme similar to the Cambridge and Cummings pots. A man kneels

Fig. 20 Pot from Cajamarquilla. After d'Harcourt 1924: Pl. 31.

in prayer pose, leaning away from a feline who rests on his right shoulder. The man is dressed in a garment similar to that of the Cambridge pot, with step-scroll designs around the bottom of the kilt and a diagonal pattern across the chest. But the spirit of the motif as seen in the Mochica IV pots has already changed. The man has both eyes open; his mouth appears to be open, but the teeth are not shown. The hairdress is different, although his visible ear is prominent and unornamented. His sexual organs are covered. The feline no longer grasps the man, nor seems to threaten him. Rather, it holds its right paw rather pensively at its own mouth, looking out with an almost benign expression. The motif shows a weakening that led Valcarcel (1937: 3) to describe the pot as follows [author's translation]:

... in this vase the *tigrillo* is raised on the shoulders by a man, like something without much importance. The feline lacks dreadfulness, is inoffensive and almost friendly. . . . This treats of a scene from ordinary life, purely anecdotal, without transcendence or special significance.

One would not have written this description for the wooden representation. This pot seems to have been copied from an earlier pot by someone who did not understand its significance.

A curious Mochica pot, published by Klein (1967: Cover and Fig. 21), shows a man with closed eyes and lopsided face, wearing the kind of ear ornaments that are often shown on ceremonial coca-chewers. A small feline behind him at his right side stretches a paw across to the man's neck, touching his chin. Although the position of the man and the feline is reminiscent of the theme treated in this paper and may well be related to it, I believe that this pot belongs essentially to another complex that shows a feline and a tuber with a human face, a snake, a skull, etc. (Tello 1938: Pls. 210–12).

The theme dealt with in this paper appears occasionally in other times and places in the Andes. A pot from Cajamarquilla (Fig. 20), published by d'Harcourt (1924: Pl. 31) as being in his collection, shows an enormous seated feline with stylized square spots holding the body of a small, nude, sexless figure

Fig. 21 Huari–Tiahuanaco double vessel. Museo Nacional de Antropología y Arqueología, Lima. Photo by the author.

with a large hole in its chest. The figure is lying at the feline's feet, and the feline is not in an attacking position, but has one forepaw on the human's head and the other on the wound. The motif here seems very closely related to that of the wooden Mochica piece.

There is also a South Coast Huari–Tiahuanaco double vessel in the Museo Nacional de Antropología (Fig. 21), one part of which is a painted kero and the other an effigy seated jaguar. The latter is painted with trefoil pelage markings and holds in its forepaws the head of a man. This head has open, white-painted eyes and wears a close-fitting dark cap (this kind of cap appears also on certain Mochica figures). There is no indication of a body; this appears to be a trophy head. This piece seems to relate to the North Coast tradition and to the Museum of the American Indian pot in particular: again, there is an oversized jaguar in a very symmetrical pose, fangs bared, its paws on the man's head.

Fig. 22 Bone Huari-Tiahuanaco spear-thrower. After Nordenskiöld 1931: Fig. 8.

Another Huari-Tiahuanaco vessel was illustrated in a recent sales catalog of Sotheby Parke Bernet (1972: No. 123). It consists of a large feline and a small human being combined into a single pot form. The open-mouthed feline has a paw—as on some of the earlier pieces, it resembles a hand—which seems to tickle the chin of the human, which here has no apparent body, only an extended arm.

Part of a bone spearthrower from Tiahuanaco (Fig. 22), published by Nordenskiöld (1931: Fig. 8), shows a large feline grasping a masklike human head.

What is curious about this version of the motif is the head and paws of a feline cub visible in the side view of the object.

An Inca wooden *paccha* in the British Museum (Fig. 23) was used for the ceremonial drinking of chicha, which was first poured into the bowl and then allowed to trickle through the feline body and out through the mouth of the man. The large snarling feline stands on four feet behind the rather small man who sits with legs extended. The man is nude and unornamented—at least his dress is not indicated.

Fig. 23 Inca wooden *paccha*. Photo courtesy of Trustees of the British Museum, London.

22

Although it is outside the limits of the region chosen for this paper, I would like to mention a stone piece from the Río Trombetas, Amazon Basin, Brazil (Fig. 24), now in the Göteborg Ethnographic Museum, because it is remarkably like the Gallinazo piece (Figs. 4 and 5). The oversized feline is rampant behind the man, its head on the man's head and its paws at either side of the man's head. The man is grimacing. There is a cavity in the back of the feline, which Wassén (1967: 114) suggests might have been intended as the storage place for some form of psychotomimetic powder used in ceremonial snuffing.

Fig. 24 Stone snuff container from Sucurujú, Río Trombetas, Brazil. Göteborg Ethnographic Museum, Göteborg. Photo courtesy of S. Henry Wassén.

AN ANTHROPOMORPHIC DEITY with feline canines and snakes emerging from its belt appears in Chavín art, and some descendent of this deity (if it was not assumed to be the same deity who had earlier been worshiped in the mountains) was taken over or inherited by other Peruvian peoples, including the Mochica on the North Coast. The Mochica deity had—in addition to the feline canines and the snake belt—round, wide-open eyes, snakehead earrings, and, most commonly, a headdress with a jaguar head at the front. I am assuming a single deity, although this was undoubtedly a dual, if not a tripartite, deity —that is, there was god-the-father and god-the-son, if not god-the-father and twin sons. God-the-father was probably a creator god, the god of the sky, the sun, and the mountains. The Mochica presumably went into the mountains, where this deity dwelt, to make sacrifices. A number of pots show two victims who were apparently pushed—or made to jump— from a mountain peak (e.g., see Kutscher 1954: Pl. 78). These sacrifices undoubtedly propitiated the mountain deity, who must also have been the deity of fresh water, of the rivers that come down from the mountains to make agriculture possible in the coastal desert. God-the-son was an active god, most frequently depicted fighting the battles of the coastal people; he was the super-Mochica who fished or fought a shark-monster or a crab-monster. He probably came down from the mountains and was another aspect of the supreme creator god. God-the-son is shown in another type of sacrifice scene in which two victims appear to be drowning in the sea, one on the top of a breaking wave and the other sprawled on the lowest of three steps below the wave (Benson 1972: Pls. 2-11, 2-12).

There is usually a pair of victims in the sacrifice scenes. The Mochica tended to think in terms of pairs or twins. Sometimes there is a scene painted all around a pot, but more commonly there is a pair of scenes, one on either side. The Chicago pot (Figs. 16 and 17), with its two painted scenes, is an example of

this. Notable here is the fact that one of the victims on the Chicago pot is in prayer pose, while the other has his hands tied behind his back. In most of the examples of this theme in modeled Mochica pottery, the hands are in prayer pose; the Peabody pot (Fig. 15), is unusual in depicting the hands tied behind. Mochica pots were sometimes—if not always—made in pairs, and it may well be that for each pot with hands in prayer pose there was a pot with hands tied behind.

Since the majority of figures in this study are depicted in the prayer pose, it seems worthwhile to note where and when this gesture occurs. The hands are usually shown clasped or overlapping, held away from the body, and at a height from just above the waist to face level. In our culture this would most commonly indicate either prayer or applause. The Mochica figure making this gesture usually has an upturned head. The deity himself is thus depicted on several pots where the scenes have to do with ritual coca-taking (Kutscher 1950a: Fig. 26 and Pl. 69, left). An anthropomorphic lizard, who frequently appears with the deity, is often pictured facing the deity and making this gesture, as if it were applauding him (ibid.: Fig. 64). Several anthropomorphic owls, or men with owl masks, are shown in prayer pose (Wassermann–San Blas 1938: Fig. 259). (Owl demons, like the lizard, are associated with the deity.) An anthropomorphic deer, seated and with a rope around its neck, is also depicted in this pose (Larco Hoyle 1966: Pl. 43). Again the gesture is found on modeled pots which represent an anthropomorphized phallus (Larco Hoyle 1965: 54). It is also a common pose of "death-priests" (Benson n.d.a; e.g., see Rautenstrauch-Joest-Museum, Köln, 1959: Pl. 25). The gesture always appears to be one of veneration or respectful greeting, and is often directed toward—or has some relationship to—the deity. For the most part, it is made by creatures who themselves have some supernatural power.

Four of the late Mochica examples of the man-feline theme seem to have mostly body painting in varied designs rather than garments (Figs. 11, 12, 19, and the unillustrated Larco pot). Of the remaining modeled pots, the Peabody one (Fig. 15) has no clothing at all, and the Berlin one (Figs. 13 and 14) has a garment with a checkerboard design, a motif that also appears, along with other patterns, on the Cummings and Larco pots. A checkerboard garment is frequently shown on people involved in a ritual in which coca leaves are chewed with lime (Kutscher 1950a: Fig. 26). The pattern also sometimes appears on shirts held by people wearing disk ear ornaments and caps like that depicted on the trophy head in Figure 21. The cap and disk ear ornament are commonly worn by people holding coca-taking equipment (Sawyer 1966: Fig. 69), and most of the people holding shirts have a coca pouch at the shoulder. Coca bags, or *chuspas*, frequently have a checkerboard design also (Kutscher 1950a: Pl. 34). Certain other seated or kneeling figures wear a checkerboard garment similar to that on the Berlin pot (Sawyer 1966: Fig. 23). Sometimes the feet protrude below it, but more often it seems to be a sort of bag enclosing the feet. The garment rarely has sleeves, and sometimes hands and arms do not show at all. In some cases the wearer looks like a bundle. One wonders if it is possible that the wearer of the checkerboard garment was intended to look like a *chuspa*, or if he was at least intended to be dressed in the same kind of "garment" that the coca leaves are kept in. The effigy figures shown wearing this garment are occasionally depicted in prayer pose (Kroeber 1925: Pl. 54g), and wearing circular face painting (Sawyer 1966: Fig. 23), like the Berlin figure. Maltese-cross facial designs, like that on the Peabody pot, are sometimes associated with the checkerboard garment (Kutscher 1950a: Fig. 26) and frequently with coca-chewing (Larco Hoyle 1966: Pl. 22).

A rectangle quartered to form a slightly lopsided pinwheel or Maltese cross appears frequently on warriors' gear, especially on shirts, but also on helmets and shields. It is often associated with an angular S. In one instance it is shown on the shirt of a conquered warrior being held by the hair by another warrior with a shirt and helmet of swirl design (Ubbelohde-Doering 1954: Pl. 175). The man in the Peabody pot, with his Maltese-cross face painting and his resemblance to captured warriors in various painted scenes (see Kutscher 1954: Pl. 23), may represent a prisoner-of-war. Similarly, body painting, which has some relationship to that on the four man-feline pots mentioned above, appears on a defeated warrior in another painted scene (Kutscher 1950a: Fig. 23), suggesting that the Cambridge, Cummings, Museo Nacional, and Larco pots may also have been prisoners-of-war.

The Chicago figures are clearly warriors, without the symbolic dress or paint shown on other figures mentioned here. A pot in the Museo Larco Herrera (Larco Hoyle 1938–39, II: Fig. 199) shows two warriors fully clad, facing two large jaguars. This is the only composition of this kind that I know of, and at first I rejected it as not being part of this sequence. But now I believe that it is closely related and reinforces the notion that some, if not all, of the jaguar's victims were warriors.

The Mochica were a warlike people who extended their territory by conquest, seeking new valleys to irrigate and plant. They captured prisoners-of-war, stripped them of clothing and paraphernalia, and led them triumphantly back by ropes around the neck, like that on the man in Figure 15. A *florero* in the Berlin Museum shows just such a scene (Schmidt 1929: Pl. 201). Prisoners were then presented by the commanding general to the chieftain and/or chief priest, who wore, in part, the costume of the feline god (see Kutscher 1954: Pl. 23). The prisoners sat crosslegged, with ropes around their necks, hands in front (but not clasped), and faces painted. Behind them their captured clothing and weapons indicated their previous occupation. In addition to painted pots, there are also a number of modeled effigy pots representing captured warriors or victims with a rope around the neck, a soup-bowl haircut with a frontal tuft, and ears without ornaments.[5] This latter feature does not necessarily mean that the victorious Mochica deprived their captives of ear ornaments,

[5] There are a number of unpublished examples in the Museo Larco Herrera, Lima.

25

but that ornaments were probably not worn into battle; there was instead a protective ear disk attached to the Mochica warrior's helmet. Nevertheless, ear ornaments were symbolically important, and their presence or absence in Mochica art is significant. Battle scenes often show the victorious warrior grasping the hair of his defeated, helmetless enemy. Headgear clearly had ritual meaning, and its absence, like that of ear ornaments, is significant. Hair seems to have had both practical importance (i.e., as a handle) and symbolic importance (i.e., the cutting of the hair of prisoners—except for the forelock—had a Samsonian mystique). Trophy heads were often held by the hair; the tufted haircut may have been part of the trophy-head ritual.

Mochica potters must have seen actual large felines, for there are a number of realistic representations. Some are effigy jaguars in the same rampant pose in which such cats are shown with human beings (Larco Hoyle 1965: 77). There are also recumbent jaguars (Tello 1938: Pls. 178–80) and felines standing on four legs. Many of the Mochica effigy cats are depicted with a rope around their necks, which may mean that they were tied to a stake (although a rope around the neck clearly had symbolic connotations as well as practical ones). A painted pot in the Museum für Völkerkunde, Berlin (Kutscher 1954: Pl. 75), depicting a mythical or hallucinated scene—or possibly an earthquake—shows a jaguar held by an anthropomorphized stake in a temple. A large number of effigy pots show a seated man holding a small jaguar; sometimes the man has the prisoner's haircut (Sawyer 1966: Fig. 80) or Maltese-cross face painting.

The Mochica must have made regular trips to and beyond the mountains for trade and ritual purposes. The finest coca, for example, comes from the eastern slopes of the Andes. It is likely that the Mochica, at some special time in the sacred calendar, brought feline cubs down to the coast, where they were kept by the priest for use at other moments in the ritual calendar. Jaguars can survive in a wide range of climate, and do so if there is a need to follow game into, say, higher altitudes or drier regions than their preferred rain-forest habitat. They would probably have survived a certain length of captivity on the coast. It is therefore possible that the representations of the feline and man may have represented an actual event in Mochica life. The feline would have been identified not only with the fanged deity but with what must have been the sacred land on the far side of the mountains.

There is no clear-cut evidence that prisoners-of-war were sacrificed to a feline. The standard mountain and wave sacrifice scenes do not depict felines. There is, however, a painted pot in the Museum für Völkerkunde, Munich (Kutscher 1950a: Fig. 62), that suggests this possibility. The scene takes place on two tiers, the upper one of which is probably the sky, inhabited by two deities (what seems to have been a militaristic moon deity had by this time become important in Mochica iconography) and many lesser demons. A two-headed sky monster divides this register from the lower one, where there are two nude figures with hands tied, each faced by an anthropomorphic creature who has one hand on the victim's neck and the other on what is apparently a knife. It would seem clear that the fate of these men is decapitation. One of the executioners is an anthropomorphic jaguar-warrior—a warrior with a jaguar face and tail, and bird feet—and the other a curious hawk-faced figure with a poncho that seems to be made of jaguar skins. Watching the scene, while sitting in a litter, is a naturalistic jaguar which belongs to the moon god in the sky level above.

Several scenes on pots seem to represent the presentation and sacrifice of captured warriors. Kutscher (1950b: Fig. 4) reproduces a painted scene with a priest or chieftain seated in a building on a pyramid with three pumas on the roof. Two nude figures are running up the steps of the pyramid, and approaching it at the base is a procession of three litters, borne by nude men and carrying figures who must be prisoners-of-war despoiled of their helmets and garments and probably of all their clothing. The first litter has on it a step motif, symbol of power or rank; the man in the last litter has a rope around his neck. On the lowest level of the pot probably representing a later moment in time, are three nude men, possibly those who are shown above in the litters. At each end of the register is a trophy head, perhaps indicating their fate. On the uppermost level is another scene, probably again intended as a different moment in time. Here there are two seated nude prisoners, one of whom is about to be beheaded by two anthropomorphic monsters.

Another painted pot in the Museo Larco Herrera[6] shows a continuous scene which is probably two related scenes. There are two houses with two figures in each house, one of whom wears a jaguar headdress. A procession of nude figures goes past one house toward the other. One man runs before and one behind, and between them are two men carrying a basket litter in which another man rides. Behind the last man is a decapitated head with a rope through the mouth. This scene merges into one with two mountain peaks, on top of one of which is a monster holding weapons. A nude figure has fallen between the two peaks. Another nude figure stands in prayer pose on the other side of the mountain, with an amputated arm above him and an amputated leg behind him. Farther down the hill two other nude figures approach. A similar theme is more simply expressed on a pot in the Museum für Völkerkunde, Berlin (Kutscher 1954: Pl. 23), where prisoners are seated on the ground facing a chieftain.

In the first of these three presentation and sacrifice scenes felines were depicted on the temple roof (various symbols are often shown on rooftops), but there were no felines in the other scenes. However, two realistic jaguars and what must be the tail of a a third appear between the parts of a related scene or scenes shown on two fragments from a painted pot published by Larco Hoyle (1938–39, II: Lám. xxx). There are no warriors in this scene, but a house with warclubs on the roof is shown on a platform, with

three lizardlike anthropomorphs seated facing it in somewhat the same manner as the prisoners sit on the Berlin pot published by Kutscher (1954: Pl. 23).

The two dominant themes to which the man-feline motif seems to relate in Mochica art are the representations of prisoners-of-war and the depictions of the coca ritual. These two themes are themselves related. A painted scene that shows some relationships to the man-feline subject, as well as to war, is the two-part mountain scene depicting the coca ritual on a pot in the Linden-Museum, Stuttgart (Kutscher 1950a: Fig. 26). In one part, the deity stands under a sky monster and black spots that undoubtedly indicate a night sky. He raises his head and hands (in prayer pose) toward the sky, has a coca bag over his arm, and a lime gourd in front of him. The second half of the scene shows three individuals taking coca, also under a night sky. All three have Maltese-cross face painting, and the central and largest figure wears a loose checkerboard garment; in front of him is a club and shield. This pot and a companion pot (Larco Hoyle 1938–39, II: Lám. xxix) suggest that weapons are part of the coca-chewing ceremony. There is no explicit indication of sacrifice here. This may be some sort of consecration of weapons before battle. On the other hand, these may have been the weapons of a conquered enemy being presented to the god before the sacrifice of their owner.

Another pot relating to the coca ceremony is a modeled one in the Museum of the American Indian (Dockstader 1967: Pl. 118). It represents the deity in prayer pose in the mountains. The deity stands in the center looking upward; there are two secondary figures at the sides. No coca paraphernalia is shown, but the deity wears the sort of ear ornament that is generally associated with coca-chewing, and the scene is very much like a modeled pot in the Museo Nacional, Lima (Tello 1938: Pl. 278), where the deity stands alone in prayer pose with a lime case and a conch shell at his feet. (The conch shell is also associated with the coca ritual.) The two subsidiary figures on the Museum of the American Indian pot

---

[6] There is no good published reproduction of this piece. Larco Hoyle has published a photograph of a partial view (1966: Pl. 48) and a rather unsatisfactory roll-out drawing (1946: Fig. 20c).

are smaller than the deity—and one is considerably smaller than the other. The larger one wears a checkerboard garment, has Maltese-cross face painting, and the tufted hairdress. He grasps a lime gourd in his left hand; one might guess that there is coca in the pack tied on his back. He is somewhat reminiscent of the checkerboard figure on the painted pot in Stuttgart, except that he has no headdress (the one in Stuttgart is elaborate) and his eyes are closed. He is, however, wearing ear ornaments. If the checkerboard garment signifies the carrier of coca or the celebrant in a coca rite, then what is the association with the feline? For one, the figure on the Berlin pot (Figs. 13 and 14) wears this garment with a feline in association; and, for another, the Dumbarton Oaks turquoise figure (Figs. 1–3) has a pack strapped on his back, which might contain coca. Moreover, on the Museum of the American Indian pot, although the man in the checkerboard shift does not appear to be in any imminent danger, he is paired with a small, nude prisoner figure with a rope around his neck, a figure that has open eyes and looks shrunken and, if not skeletal, virtually dead; it is reminiscent of the figure lying under the attacking jaguar in the wooden piece (Fig. 18).

It is possible that the Mochica IV man-feline pots may represent young men undergoing initiation rites for warriors. In Inca times young nobles preparing to be warriors were put through severe tests. If they came through the ordeal successfully, their ears were pierced by the Inca with a gold pin as "the first and principal token of knighthood. . . ." This was a mark of royal and supreme distinction (Garcilaso de la Vega 1966, I: 372). Molina (1873: 38) adds that they were also given *chuspas*, or coca bags. It is possible that these practices are remnants of an ancient ritual. But there are several arguments against this interpretation for the Mochica scenes. The Inca ears were pierced and the *chuspas* given at a time when the young warriors were also presented with rich garments—which is not true in the Mochica scenes. In addition, the men represented on the Mochica pots have ears that are already distended; in other words,

they have already been wearing ear ornaments. (It is true that one must not read too much realism into Mochica representations. The pierced ear may be read simply as a symbol, not just as the representation of a moment in time or the history of a man.) And finally, there is no reference to a feline or feline symbolism in the Inca accounts.

With regard to these effigies of men and felines, it seems more likely that a prisoner-of-war, a foreign chieftain or general, a man who habitually wore elaborate garments and ear ornaments, was captured by "the jaguar's children," in this case the Mochica. The feline represents the spirit or totem of the Mochica, to whom the prisoner is subjected. The prisoner may well have been quite literally presented to a local captive feline, representing not only the power of the Mochica but also the power of their god. Although the modeled pots might still be interpreted figuratively in terms of an initiation, the wooden digging stick seems to make another point. The Mochica would hardly have made an elaborate symbolic object to represent a young man who had failed his initiation; this would seem to be a shameful event to record. The representation of a captured enemy, however, overcome by the power and spirit of the Mochica, *would* be important.

Although the man-feline motif remained visually fairly static throughout a long period of time, its meaning probably did not. As a constantly important motif, it signified a vital relationship between man and feline, which existed throughout indigenous thought in Latin America. But its immediate significance must have been modified by the general beliefs of the times. In the two late pieces, the Inca *paccha* (Fig. 23) and the Río Trombetas snuff container (Fig. 24), this motif is associated with the rituals of chicha and snuff; no concept of human sacrifice seems implied here. In the *paccha* the feline is the medium through which the man receives the ritual chicha. In the Río Trombetas piece the feline is the keeper of the ritual snuff. The Recuay and Virú pots may illustrate a simple alter ego concept: the twin souls of man and animal, or the feline as the protector of the man. In many examples, particularly the earlier and later ones, the feline tends to be oversized, suggesting a mythical or hallucinated creature. The wide distribution of the theme certainly argues for a mythic basis.

In the Mochica IV pottery, however, the felines tend to be of realistic size and are generally more realistically represented. (It is interesting to note that the turquoise and wooden pieces depict instead a gigantic feline.) The references on these pots to the ritual chewing of coca may relate to the mountain deity. Mortimer, in his study of coca at the beginning of this century (1901: 203), reports that it was customary for Indians leaving the coast for a trip to the mountains to throw coca into the air to propitiate the mountain god. He also relates a then-current belief that, if a dying man can taste coca leaves pressed to his lips, he will go to paradise (*ibid.*: 73); here then is a lingering association of coca with death. Amongst the Mochica there probably existed the belief that

someone who had been wounded by a jaguar and survived the attack could become a priest or warrior with special powers. But that belief does not seem to be the only explanation for what is illustrated in these pots. I think that the feline was indeed the protector of the Mochica, but not of the man represented with the animal—unless, of course, the man survived.

The meaning of these pieces probably varied at different times with different emphases, different rituals, and different versions of the basic myth. No one of these meanings precludes the possibility of others. But I think that part of the meaning during the Mochica IV period may have been related to an actual event in which a prisoner-of-war was presented to a feline acting as a proxy of the god, an event closely tied in with ritual, religion, warfare, and the conquest of new lands—new lands dedicated both to the glory of the god with the feline teeth and to the practical need of irrigable land for a growing population.

BIBLIOGRAPHY

BENNETT, WENDELL C.
1954 Ancient Arts of the Andes. The Museum of Modern Art, New York.

BENSON, ELIZABETH P.
1972 The Mochica: A Culture of Peru. Praeger Publishers, New York and Washington.
n.d.a Death-Associated Figures on Mochica Pottery. *In* Death and the Afterlife in Pre-Columbian America (Elizabeth P. Benson, ed.). Dumbarton Oaks Research Library and Collection, Washington. In press.
n.d.b Some Meanings for a Peruvian Turquoise Carving. Lecture presented at Dumbarton Oaks, January 9, 1970. Washington.

BURLAND, C. A.
1967 Peru under the Incas. Evans Brothers Limited, London.

BUSHNELL, G. H. S.
1957 Peru. Frederick A. Praeger, New York.

DISSELHOFF, HANS DIETRICH
1966 Alltag im alten Peru. Verlag Georg D. W. Callwey, München.

DOCKSTADER, FREDERICK J.
1967 Indian Art in South America: Pre-Columbian and Contemporary Arts and Crafts. New York Graphic Society Publishers Ltd., Greenwich.

EARLY CHINESE ART AND THE PACIFIC BASIN
1968 Early Chinese Art and the Pacific Basin: A Photographic Exhibition. Intercultural Arts Press, New York.

FURST, PETER T.
1968 The Olmec Were-Jaguar Motif in the Light of Ethnographic Reality. *In* Dumbarton Oaks Conference on the Olmec (Elizabeth P. Benson, ed.), pp. 143–174. Dumbarton Oaks Research Library and Collection, Washington.

GARCILASO DE LA VEGA
1966 Royal Commentaries of the Incas and General History of Peru. 2 vols. (Trans. with an Introduction by Harold V. Livermore.) University of Texas Press, Austin and London.

D'HARCOURT, R. and M.
1924 La céramique ancienne du Pérou. Éditions Albert Morancé, Paris.

KLEIN, OTTO
1967 La Cerámica Mochica: Caracteres estilísticos y conceptos. *Scientia*, año XXXIII, no. 130. Universidad Técnica "Federico Santa Maria," Valparaiso.

KROEBER, A.L.
1925 The Uhle Pottery Collections from Moche. *University of California Publications in American Archaeology and Ethnology*, vol. 21, no. 5, pp. 191–234. University of California Press, Berkeley.

KUTSCHER, GERDT
1950a Chimu: Eine altindianische Hochkultur. Verlag Gebr. Mann, Berlin.
1950b Iconographic Studies as an Aid in the Reconstruction of Early Chimu Civilization. *Transactions of the New York Academy of Sciences*, Series II, vol. 12, no. 6, pp. 194–203. New York.
1954 Nordperuanische Keramik: Figürlich verzierte Gefässe der Früh-Chimu. *Monumenta Americana, Herausgegeben von der Ibero-Amerikanischen Bibliothek zu Berlin*, I. Verlag Gebr. Mann, Berlin.

LARCO HOYLE, RAFAEL
1938–39 Los Mochicas. 2 vols. Casa Editora "La Crónica" y "Variedades" and Empresa Editorial "Rimac," Lima.
1945 Los Mochicas (Pre-Chimu, de Uhle y Early Chimu, de Kroeber). Sociedad Geográfica Americana, Buenos Aires.
1946 A Culture Sequence for the North Coast of Perú. *In* Handbook of South American Indians (Julian H. Steward, ed.), vol. 2, pp. 149–175. *Smithsonian Institution, Bureau of American Ethnology Bulletin 143.* U.S. Government Printing Office, Washington.
1965 Checan: Essay on Erotic Elements in Peruvian Art. Nagel Publishers, Geneva/Paris/Munich.
1966 Peru. (Trans. by James Hogarth.) The World Publishing Company, Cleveland and New York.

LEHMANN, WALTER, and HEINRICH DOERING
1924 The Art of Old Peru. Ernest Benn, Ltd., London.

MATOS MOCTEZUMA, EDUARDO
1970 Parálisis facial prehispánica. *Publicaciones 25*. Departamento de Investigaciones Antropológicas, Instituto Nacional de Antropología e História, México.

MOLINA, CHRISTOVAL DE
1873 The Fables and Rites of the Yncas. *In* Narratives of the Rites and Laws of the Yncas (Clements R. Markham, ed. and trans.), pp. 1–64. The Hakluyt Society, London.

MORTIMER, W. GOLDEN
1901 Peru: History of Coca, "The Divine Plant" of the Incas. J. H. Vail & Company, New York.

NORDENSKIÖLD, ERLAND
1931 Origin of the Indian Civilizations in South America. Elanders Boktryckeri Aktiebolag, Göteborg.

PERRY, RICHARD
1970 The World of the Jaguar. Taplinger Publishing Co., New York.

RAUTENSTRAUCH-JOEST-MUSEUM, KÖLN
1959 Schätze aus Peru von Chavin bis zu den Inka. Verlag Aurel Bongers, Recklinghausen.

REICHEL-DOLMATOFF, GERARDO
1972 The Feline Motif in Prehistoric San Agustín Sculpture. *In* The Cult of the Feline: A Conference in Pre-Columbian Iconography (Elizabeth P. Benson, ed.), pp. 50–90. Dumbarton Oaks Research Library and Collections, Washington.

SAWYER, ALAN R.
1966 Ancient Peruvian Ceramics: The Nathan Cummings Collection. The Metropolitan Museum of Art, New York.
1968 Mastercraftsmen of Ancient Peru. The Solomon R. Guggenheim Foundation, New York.

SCHMIDT, MAX
1929 Kunst und Kultur von Peru. Propyläen-Verlag, Berlin.

SOTHEBY PARKE BERNET INC.
1972 Pre-Columbian Art, Including Mexico, Costa Rica, Colombia, Ecuador and Peru, from Arts of the Four Quarters, Ltd. Part II. Sotheby Parke Bernet Inc., New York.

TELLO, JULIO C.
1938 Arte Antiguo Peruano: Album fotográfico de las principales especies arqueológicas de cerámica existentes en los Museos de Lima; Primera Parte: Tecnología y morfología. *Inca*, vol. II. Museo de Arqueología, Universidad Mayor de San Marcos, Lima.

UBBELOHDE-DOERING, HEINRICH
1954 The Art of Ancient Peru. Frederick A. Praeger, New York.

VALCÁRCEL, LUIS E.
1937 Dioses, hombres y bestias. *Cuadernos de Arte Antiguo del Perú*, no. 5. Museo Nacional, Lima.

WASSÉN, S. HENRY
1967 Om några indianska droger och speciellt om snus samt tillbehör. *In* Årstryck för 1963, 1964, 1965 och 1966 (S. Henry Wassén, ed.), pp. 97–140. Etnografiska Museet, Göteborg.

WASSERMANN–SAN BLAS, B.J.
1938 Cerámicas del antiguo Perú de la colección Wassermann–San Blas. Buenos Aires.